13th
BLUE BOOK
Dolls & Values®

by Jan Foulke
photographs by Howard Foulke

ANTIQUE SECTION — Pages 17 to 206.
MODERN SECTION — Pages 207 to 309.

Published by Hobby House Press, Inc.
Grantsville, Maryland 21536

2

Other Titles by Author:

Blue Book of Dolls & Values®
2nd Blue Book of Dolls & Values®
3rd Blue Book of Dolls & Values®
4th Blue Book of Dolls & Values®
5th Blue Book of Dolls & Values®
6th Blue Book of Dolls & Values®
7th Blue Book of Dolls & Values®
8th Blue Book of Dolls & Values®
9th Blue Book of Dolls & Values®
10th Blue Book of Dolls & Values®
11th Blue Book of Dolls & Values®
12th Blue Book of Dolls & Values®

Focusing on Effanbee Composition Dolls
Focusing on Treasury of
Mme. Alexander Dolls
Focusing on Gebrüder Heubach Dolls
Kestner: King of Dollmakers
Simon & Halbig Dolls: The Artful Aspect
Doll Classics
Focusing on Dolls
China Doll Collecting
Doll Buying & Selling
German 'Dolly' Collecting

COVER (top to bottom): An almond-eyed *Portrait Jumeau* (For further information see page 106.) 18in (46cm) *Shirley Temple* in a sailor outfit. *H & J Foulke, Inc.* (For further information see page 299.) *American Girl Barbie®* in Saturday Matinee. *Sidney Jeffrey Collection.* (For further Barbie® doll information see pages 237.)
TITLE PAGE: 14-1/2in (37cm) Alexander *Karen Ballerina.* *H & J Foulke, Inc.* (For further information see page 213.)
BACK COVER (top to bottom): *#3 Ponytail BARBIE®.* *Courtesy of McMasters Doll Auctions.* (For further information see page 235.) 12in (31cm) 1948 *Campbell Kid,* all original. *H & J Foulke, Inc.* (For further information see page 247.)

ADDITIONAL COPIES AVAILABLE @ $17.95 plus postage
FROM
HOBBY HOUSE PRESS, INC.
1 CORPORATE DRIVE
GRANTSVILLE, MD 21536
1-800-554-1447

© 1997 by Jan and Howard Foulke

Blue Book Dolls & Values is a federally registered trademark.

ISBN: 0-87588-503-9

USING THIS BOOK

Doll collecting continues to increase in popularity every year. The great number of collectors entering the field has given rise to larger and more frequent doll shows, more dealers in dolls, more books on dolls, thicker doll magazines and more doll conventions and seminars, as well as an overwhelming offering of new dolls by mass-production companies and individual artists. This explosion has also increased the demand for old dolls and discontinued collectors' dolls, causing prices to rise as more collectors vie for the same dolls.

With the average antique or collectible doll representing a purchase of at least several hundred dollars, today's collectors must be as well informed as possible about the dolls they are considering as additions to their collections. Since the first *Blue Book of Dolls & Values* was published in 1974, our objectives have remained the same:

- To present a book that will help collectors to identify and learn more about dolls.
- To provide retail prices as a guide for buyers and sellers of dolls.

Since every edition of the *Blue Book* has sold more copies than the previous one, we can only conclude that these objectives are in line with the needs of the doll lovers, collectors, dealers and appraisers who keep buying the latest editions of our book.

For convenience in locating a doll more quickly, this book has been divided into two sections: *Antique* and *Modern*. Where certain dolls, such as *Raggedy Ann* and *Kewpie*, were made over very long periods, the modern examples are included with the main entry in the *Antique* Section in order

to keep the whole production history of a doll in one place.

The dolls presented in this book are listed alphabetically by maker, material or the trade name of the individual doll. An extensive index has been provided to help in locating a specific doll. For the most part, dolls are listed in chronological order within a main entry.

For the listed dolls we have included historical information, physical description, marks and labels, and the retail selling price. Photographs are also included for many dolls; however, since every doll cannot be pictured in each edition, previous *Blue Books* should be consulted for additional photographs.

In some cases the doll sizes given are the only ones known to have been made, but in the cases of most of the French and German bisque, china, papier-mâché and wood dolls, sizes priced are chosen at random and listed sizes must not be interpreted as definitive. It is impossible to list every doll in every possible size, especially for dolls that range from 6 to 42 inches (15 to 106cm). The user will need to call a little common sense into play to interpolate a price for an unlisted size.

The historical information given for some of the dolls would have been much more difficult to compile were it not for the original research already published by Dorothy S., Elizabeth A. and Evelyn J. Coleman; Johana G. Anderton; and Jürgen and Marianne Cieslik.

The data for retail prices was gathered during 1996 and 1997 from antique shops and shows, auctions, doll shops and shows, advertisements in collectors' periodicals, lists from doll dealers, and purchases and sales reported by both collectors and deal-

4

ers. This information, along with our own valuations and judgments, was computed into the range of prices shown in this book. When we could not find a sufficient number of dolls to be sure of giving a reliable range, we marked those prices with two asterisks ("**").

The price for a doll listed in this guide is the retail value of a doll if purchased from a dealer. In setting a price for each doll, we use a range to allow for the variables of originality, quality and condition that must be reflected in the price. As collectors become more sophisticated in their purchases, fine examples of a doll, especially those which are all original or boxed with original tags or never played with, can bring a premium of at least 50% more than prices quoted for ordinary examples. Sometimes a doll will bring a premium price because it is particularly cute, sweet, pretty or visually appealing, making an outstanding presentation. There is no way to factor this appeal into a price guide.

The international market has been an important factor in the change of domestic doll prices during the past few years. International interest has added a whole new dimension to the American doll market as increasing awareness of antique dolls in Germany, France, Switzerland, Holland, Denmark and other countries is causing a great exodus and a depletion of our supply of antique dolls.

Of particular interest in the international arena are German bisque character children, German bisque babies by Kestner, Kämmer & Reinhardt, and Hertel, Schwab & Co., German bisque "dolly" faces (particularly small sizes) by Kestner, Kämmer & Reinhardt, and Handwerck, Käthe Kruse dolls and German celluloid dolls. This interest has caused continued price increases in these categories.

All prices given for antique dolls are for those of good quality and condition, but showing normal wear, and appropriately dressed in new or old clothing, unless other specifications are given in the description accompanying that particular doll. Bisque or china heads should not be cracked, broken or repaired, but may have slight making imperfections such as speckling, surface lines, darkened

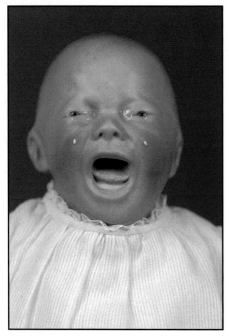

13in (33cm) *OIC #225* screaming baby. *Richard Wright Antiques.* (For additional information see page 126.)

Dressel #1349 Jutta, all original. H & J Foulke, Inc. (For additional information see page 82.)

mold lines and uneven coloring. Bodies may have repairs or be nicely repainted but should be old and appropriate to the head. A doll with old dress, shoes and wig will generally be valued at higher than quoted prices because these items are in scarce supply and can easily cost more than $65 each if purchased separately.

Prices given for modern dolls are for those in overall good to excellent condition with original hair and clothing, except as noted. Composition may be lightly crazed, but should be colorful. Hard plastic and vinyl must be perfect, with hair in original set and crisp, original clothes. A never-played-with doll in original box with labels would bring a premium price.

The users of this book must keep in mind that no price guide is the final word. It cannot provide an absolute answer as to what to pay. This book should be used only as an aid in purchasing a doll. The final decision must be yours, for only you are on the scene, actually examining the specific doll in question. No book can take the place of actual field experience. Doll popularity can cycle; prices can fluctuate; regional variations can occur. Before you buy, do a lot of looking. Ask questions. Most dealers and collectors are glad to talk about their dolls and pleased to share their information with you.

22in (56cm) 1880s china head. *H & J Foulke, Inc.* (For additional information see page 74.)

6

ACKNOWLEDGEMENTS

For their encouragement and support, we again wish to thank our friends, customers, fellow dealers and fans, as well as doll collectors around the world.

Special thanks to:

Those who allowed us to use photographs of their dolls or who provided special information for use in this edition. Their help is greatly appreciated. Rhoda Shoemaker, Rosemary Kanizer, Terri & Cathy's Dolls, Peggy Bealefield of Doodlebug Dolls, Kay & Wayne Jensen, Jim Fernando, Sidney Jeffrey, Nancy A. Smith, Margaret Fay, Tore Scelso, Anna May Case, Cathy Kiefer, Geri and Ralph Gentile, Mary Barnes Kelley, Jennifer Raybarn DeHay, Ruth Covington West, Carole Jean Stoessel Zvonar, Esther Schwartz, Betty Lunz, Barbara Crescenze, Lesley Hurford, Gracia Caiani, Joanna Ott, Miriam Blankman, Becky Lowe, George Humphrey, Susan Babkowski, Victoria's Dolls, Mary Elizabeth Poole, Eleanor Guderian, Rae-Ellen Koenig of The Doll Express, Shari McMasters and Joyce Watson of McMasters Doll Auctions, Richard W. Withington, Inc., Richard Wright Antiques, and H & J Foulke, Inc.

Those who shared their doll collections but wished to remain anonymous are greatly appreciated.

The Colemans, who allowed some marks to be reproduced from their book, *The Collector's Encyclopedia of Dolls.*

Gary and Mary Ruddell of Hobby House Press, Inc., with whom we have worked for more than 20 years; Mary Beth Ruddell, coordinator, and Janet Smith, editor.

Howard, for his beautiful photographs.

All of these people helped make this book possible.

Jan Foulke
June 1997

Out-of-print editions of the *Blue Book® of Dolls & Values* have become collectors' items. Out-of-print books can be found at doll shows or auctions. The following prices are for clean books with light wear on covers and corners.

Blue Book® of Dolls & Values	**$135**
2nd Blue Book® of Dolls & Values	**110**
3rd Blue Book® of Dolls & Values	**75**
4th Blue Book® of Dolls & Values	**75**
5th Blue Book® of Dolls & Values	**50**
6th Blue Book® of Dolls & Values	**40**
7th Blue Book® of Dolls & Values	**35**
8th Blue Book® of Dolls & Values	**35**
9th Blue Book® of Dolls & Values	**25**
10th Blue Book® of Dolls & Values	**25**

INVESTING IN DOLLS

With the price of the average antique or collectible doll representing a purchase of at least several hundred dollars in today's doll market, the assembling of a doll collection becomes rather costly. Actually, very few people buy dolls strictly as an investment; most collectors buy a doll because they like it. It has appeal to them for some reason: perhaps as an object of artistic beauty, perhaps because it evokes some kind of sentiment, perhaps because it fills some need that they feel or speaks to something inside them. It is this personal feeling toward the doll which makes it of value to the collector.

However, most collectors expect to at least break even when they eventually sell their dolls. Unfortunately, there is no guarantee that any particular doll will appreciate consistently year after year; however, the track record for old or antique dolls is fairly good. If you are thinking of the future sale of your collec-

tion, be wary of buying expensive new or reproduction dolls. They have no track record, and most have little resale value. Collectible dolls of the last 30 years are a risky market. Alexander dolls are a case in point. After many years of doubling their value the minute they were carried from the toy store shelves, dolls of the 1960s to 1990s have slid in price so that many are now bringing only 25 - 50% of their cost to collectors.

Because most collectors have only limited funds for purchasing dolls, they must be sure they are spending their dollars to the best advantage. There are many factors to consider when buying a doll, and this chapter will provide some suggestions about what to look for and what to consider. Probably the primary tenet is that a collector who is not particularly well-informed about a doll should not consider purchasing it unless he or she has confidence in the person selling the doll.

MARKS

Fortunately for collectors, most of the antique bisque, some of the papier-mâché, cloth and other types of antique dolls are marked or labeled. Marks and labels give the buyer confidence because they identify the trade name, the maker, the country of origin, the style or mold number, or perhaps even the patent date.

Most composition and modern dolls are marked with the maker's name and sometimes also the trade name of the doll and the date. Some dolls have tags sewn on or into their clothing to identify them; many still retain original hang tags.

Of course, many dolls are unmarked,

but after you have seen quite a few dolls, you begin to notice their individual characteristics and can often determine what a doll possibly is. When you have had some experience buying dolls, you begin to recognize an unusual face or an especially fine quality doll. Then there should be no hesitation about buying a doll marked only with a mold number or no mark at all. The doll has to speak for itself, and the price must be based upon the collector's frame of doll reference. That is, one must relate the face and quality to those of a known doll maker and make price judgments from that point.

QUALITY

The mark does not tell everything about a doll. Two examples from the same mold could look entirely different and carry vastly different prices because of the quality of the work done on the doll, which can vary from head to head, even with dolls made from the same mold by one firm. To command top price, a

bisque doll should have lovely bisque, decoration, eyes and hair. Before purchasing a doll, the collector should determine whether the example is the best available of that type. Even the molding of one head can be much sharper with more delineation of such details as dimples or locks of hair. The molding detail

22in (56cm) *Poupée Peau*, French Fashion. *H & J Foulke, Inc.* (For additional information see page 85.)

Bottom: Left: 18in (46cm) G. Heubach #7850 *Coquette* character girl. *H & J Foulke, Inc.* (For additional information see page 102.)
Right: 8-1/2" (21cm) Recknagel 43 googly. *H & J Foulke, Inc.* (For additional information see page 92.)

24in (61cm) *Pansy II*. *H & J Foulke, Inc.* (For additional information see page 50.)

21in (53cm) *Shirley Temple* baby, all original. *H & J Foulke, Inc.* (For additional information see page 300.)

20in (51cm) *Mollye's Raggedy Ann & Andy,* all original. *H & J Foulke, Inc.* (For additional information see page 170.)

is especially important to notice when purchasing dolls with character faces or molded hair.

The quality of the bisque should be smooth; dolls with bisque which is pimply, peppered with tiny black specks or unevenly colored, or which has noticeable firing lines on the face, would be second choices at a lower price. However, collectors must keep in mind that porcelain factories sold many heads with small manufacturing defects because companies were in business for profit and were producing expendable play items, not works of art. Small manufacturing defects do not devalue a doll. It is perfectly acceptable to have light speckling, light surface lines, firing lines in inconspicuous places, darkened mold lines, a few black specks, or cheek rubs. The absolutely perfect bisque head is a rarity.

Since doll heads are hand-painted, the artistry of the decoration should be examined. The tinting of the complexion should be subdued and even, not harsh and splotchy. Artistic skill should be evident in the portrayal of the expression on the face and in details such as the lips, eyebrows and eyelashes, and particularly in the eyes, which should show highlights and shading when they are painted. On a doll with molded hair, individual brush marks to give the hair a more realistic look would be a desirable detail.

If a doll has a wig, the hair should be appropriate if not old. Dynel or synthetic wigs are not appropriate for antique dolls; a human hair or good quality mohair wig should be used. If a doll has glass eyes, they should be old with natural color and threading in the irises to give a lifelike appearance.

If a doll does not meet all of these standards, it should be priced lower than one that does. Furthermore, an especially fine example will bring a premium over an ordinary but nice model.

CONDITION

Another important factor when pricing a doll is the condition. A bisque doll with a crack on the face or extensive professional repair involving the face would sell for one-quarter or less than a doll with only normal wear. An inconspicuous hairline would decrease the value somewhat, but in a rare doll it would not be as great a detriment as in a common doll. As the so-called better dolls are becoming more difficult to find, a hairline is more acceptable to collectors if there is a price adjustment. The same is true for a doll which has a spectacular face — a hairline would be less important to price in that doll than in one with an ordinary face.

Sometimes a head will have a factory flaw which occurred in the making, such as a firing crack, scratch, piece of kiln debris, dark specks, small bubbles, a ridge not smoothed out or light surface lines. Since the factory was producing toys for a profit and not creating works of art, heads with slight flaws were not all discarded, especially if flaws were inconspicuous or could be covered. If factory defects are not detracting, they have little or no effect on the value of a doll.

It is to be expected that an old doll will show some wear. Perhaps there is a rub on the nose or cheek, a few small "wig pulls" or maybe a chipped earring hole; a Schoenhut doll or a Käthe Kruse may have some scuffs; an old papier-mâché may have a few age cracks; a china head may show wear on the hair; an old composition body may have scuffed toes or missing fingers. This wear is to be expected and does not necessarily affect the value of a doll. However, a doll in exceptional condition will bring more than "book" price.

Unless an antique doll is rare or you particularly want that specific doll, do not pay top price for a doll that needs extensive work: restringing, setting eyes, repairing fingers, replacing body parts, new wig or dressing. All of these repairs add up to a considerable sum at the doll hospital, possibly making the total cost of the doll more than it is really worth.

Composition dolls in perfect condition are becoming harder to find. Because their material is so susceptible to the atmosphere, their condition can deteriorate literally overnight. Even in excellent condition, a composition doll nearly always has some fine crazing or slight fading. It is very difficult to find a composition doll in mint condition and even harder to be sure that it will stay that way. However, in order for a composition doll to bring "book" price, there should be a minimum of crazing, very good coloring, original uncombed hair and original clothes in very good condition. Pay less for a doll that does not have original clothes and hair or that is all original but shows extensive play wear. Pay even less for one with heavy crazing and cracking

BODY

In order to command top price, an old doll must have the original or an appropriate old body in good condition. If a doll does not have the correct type of body, the buyer ends up not with a complete doll but with parts that may not be worth as much as one whole doll. As dolls are becoming more difficult to find, more are turning up with "put together" bodies. Many dolls are now entering the market from old collections assembled years ago. Some of these contain dolls which were "put together" before there was much information available about correct heads and bodies. Therefore, the body should be checked to make sure it is appropriate to the head, and all parts of the body should be checked to make sure that they are appropriate to each other. A body with mixed parts from several makers or types of bodies is not worth as much as one with correct parts.

Minor damage or repair to an old body does not affect the value of an antique doll. An original body carefully repaired, recovered or even, if necessary, completely repainted is preferable to a new one. An antique head on a new body would be worth only the value of its parts, whatever the price of the head and new body, not the the full price of an an-

or other damages. For composition dolls that are all original, unplayed with, in original boxes and with little or no crazing, allow a premium of about 50% over "book" price.

Hard plastic and vinyl dolls must be in excellent condition if they are at "book" price. The hair should be perfect in the original set: clothes should be completely original, fresh and unfaded. Skin tones should be natural with good cheek color. Add a premium of 25-50% for mint dolls never removed from their original boxes.

tique doll. A rule of thumb is that an antique head is generally worth about 40-50% of the price of the complete doll. A very rare head could be worth up to 80%.

If there is a choice of body types for the same bisque head, a good quality ball-jointed composition body is more desirable than a crudely made five-piece body or stick-type body with only pieces of turned wood for upper arms and legs. Collectors prefer jointed composition bodies over kid ones for dolly-faced dolls, and pay more for the same face on a composition body.

Occasionally the body adds value to the doll. In the case of bisque heads, a small doll with a completely jointed body, a French fashion-type with a wood-jointed body, a *Tête Jumeau* head on an adult body or a character baby head on a jointed toddler-type body would all be higher in price because of their special bodies.

As for the later modern dolls, a composition doll on the wrong body or with a body that is cracked, peeling and in poor condition would have a greatly reduced value. The same is true of a vinyl doll with replaced parts, body stains or chewed-off fingers.

CLOTHING

It is becoming increasingly difficult to find dolls in old clothing because, as the years go by, fabrics continue to deteriorate. Consequently, collectors are paying more than "book" price for an antique

doll if it has appropriate old clothes, shoes and hair. Even faded, somewhat worn, or carefully mended original or appropriate old clothes are preferable to new ones. As collectors become more

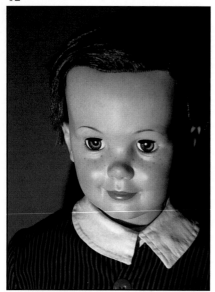

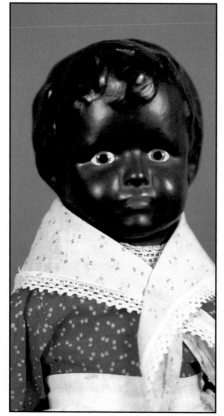

Previous Page: Top: Left: 35in
(89cm) Ideal *Peter Playpal,* all original. *Doodlebug Dolls.* (For additional
information see page 285.) *Right:* 12-
1/2in (32cm) boy with molded hat by
artist Kathy Redmond. (For additional information see page 230.) *Bottom
Left:* 16in (41cm) *Deco Aunt Dinah,*
all original. *H & J Foulke, Inc.* (For
additional information see page 257.)
Right: 14in (36cm) *Jackie Coogan,*
all original. *H & J Foulke, Inc.* (For
additional information see page 276.)

Above: Left: 18in (46cm) *General
Douglas MacArthur,* all original.
H & J Foulke, Inc. (For additional
information see page 269.) *Right:*
18in (46cm) American Character
Sweet Sue, all original. *H & J
Foulke, Inc.* (For additional informa-
tion see page 227.)
Right: 21in (53cm) Alexander *Cissy,*
#2114, 1957, all original except hat.
H & J Foulke, Inc. (For additional
information see page 217.)

14

sophisticated and selective, they realize the value of old doll clothing and accessories. Some dealers are now specializing in these areas. Good old leather doll shoes will bring more than $75 per pair; a lovely Victorian white-work doll dress can easily cost $75; an old dress for a French fashion lady, $300 and more. Good old doll wigs can bring from $25 to $250.

However, when clothing must be replaced and appropriate old clothing cannot be obtained, new clothes should be authentically styled for the age of the doll and constructed of fabrics that would have been available when the doll was produced. There are many reference books and catalog reprints showing dolls in original clothing, and doll supply companies offer patterns for dressing old dolls.

To bring top price, a modern doll must have original clothes. It is usually fairly simple to determine whether or not the clothing is original and factory made. Some makers even placed tags in the doll's clothing. Replaced clothing greatly reduces the price of modern dolls. Without the original clothing, it is often impossible to identify a modern doll because so many were made using the same face mold.

TOTAL ORIGINALITY

Today totally original dolls are becoming rare. It is often difficult to determine whether the head and body and all other parts of a doll, including wig, eyes and clothes, have always been together. Many parts of a doll may have been changed and clothing and accessories could have been added over the years. Many dolls labeled "all original" are simply wearing contemporary clothing and wigs. Some collectors and dealers are "embellishing" more expensive dolls by taking original clothing and wigs from cheaper dolls to further enhance the value of the more costly ones. Dolls with trunks of clothing and in boxed sets are particularly vulnerable to this type of raiding.

Collectors should examine clothes and accessories carefully before they pay ultra-high prices for such ensembles. Of course, when these ensembles are genuine, they are the ultimate in doll collecting.

AGE

The oldest dolls do not necessarily command the highest prices. A lovely old china head with exquisite decoration and very unusual hairdo would bring a price of several thousand dollars but not as much as a 20th century German bisque character child. Many desirable composition dolls of the 1930s and BARBIE® dolls of the 1960s are selling at prices higher than older bisque dolls of 1890 to 1920. So, in determining price, the age of the doll may or may not be significant.

SIZE

The size of a doll is usually taken into account when determining a price. Generally, the size and price for a certain doll are related: a smaller size is lower, a larger size is higher. However, there are a few exceptions. The 11in (28cm) Shirley Temple and tiny German dolly-faced dolls on fully-jointed bodies are examples of small dolls that bring higher prices than their larger counterparts.

AVAILABILITY

The price of a doll is directly related to its availability in most cases. The harder a doll is to find, the higher will be its price. Each year brings more new doll collectors than newly discovered, desirable old dolls; hence, the supply of old dolls is diminished. As long as the demand for certain antique and collectible dolls is greater than the supply, prices will rise. This explains the great increase in prices of less common dolls, such as the K & R and other German character children, early china heads and papier-mâchés, composition personality dolls, Sasha dolls and some Alexander dolls that were made for only a limited period of time. Dolls that are fairly common, primarily the German dolly faces and the later china head dolls made over a long period of production, show a more gentle increase in price

POPULARITY

There are fads in dolls just as in clothes, food and other aspects of life. Dolls that have recently risen in price because of their popularity include the early Jumeaus, all-bisques, German character children, *Patsy* family dolls, *Shirley Temples*, large composition babies, early *BARBIE®* dolls, composition personality dolls and hard plastic dolls. Some dolls are popular enough to tempt collectors to pay prices higher than the availability factor warrants. Although *Shirley Temples*, *Tête Jumeaus*, *Bye-Los*, *Hildas*, K & R 117, and some plastic Alexander dolls are not rare, the high prices they bring are due to their popularity. American cloth dolls, Schoenhuts, Heubachs and Greiners are in a soft period, so many bargains can be found in this category.

DESIRABILITY

Some very rare dolls do not bring a high price because they are not particularly desirable. There are not many collectors looking for them. Falling into this category are the dolls with shoulder heads made of rubber or rawhide. While an especially outstanding example will bring a high price, most examples bring very low prices in relationship to their rarity.

UNIQUENESS

Sometimes the uniqueness of a doll makes price determination very difficult. If a collector has never seen a doll exactly like it before, and it is not cited in a price guide or even shown in any books, deciding what to pay can be a problem. In this case, the buyer has to use all available knowledge as a frame of reference for the unknown doll. Perhaps a doll marked "A.M. 2000" or "S & H 1289" has been found, and the asking price is 25% higher than for the more commonly found numbers by that maker. Or perhaps a black *Kamkins* is offered for twice the price of a white one, or a French fashion lady with original wardrobe is offered at 60% more than a redressed one. In cases such as these, a collector must use his or her own judgment to determine what the doll is worth.

VISUAL APPEAL

Perhaps the most elusive aspect in pricing a doll is its visual appeal. Sometimes, particularly at auction, we have seen dolls bring well over their "book" value simply because of their look. Often this is nothing more than the handiwork of someone who had the ability to choose just the right wig, clothing and accessories to enhance the doll's visual appeal and make it look particularly cute, stunning, beautiful or otherwise especially outstanding.

Sometimes, though, the visual appeal comes from the face of the doll itself. It may be the way the teeth are put in, the placement of the eyes, the tinting on the face or the sharpness of the molding. Or it may not be any of these specific things; it may just be what some collectors refer to as the "presence" of the doll, an elusive indefinable quality which makes it the best example known!

SELLING A DOLL

So many times we are asked, "How do I go about selling a doll?," that it seems a few paragraphs on the topic are in order. The first logical step is to look through the **Blue Book** to identify the doll and to ascertain a retail price. Work from there to decide what you might ask for your doll. It is very difficult for a private person to get a retail price for a doll.

Be realistic about the condition. If you have a marked 18in (46cm) *Shirley Temple* doll with combed hair, no clothing, faded face with crazing and a piece off of her nose, do not expect to get the "book" price of $1,000 for her because that would be a retail price for an excellent doll, all original, in pristine unplayed-with condition if purchased from a dealer. Your very used doll is probably worth only $50 to $75 because it will have to be purchased by someone who wants to restore it.

If you have an antique doll with a perfect bisque head but no wig, no clothes and unstrung, but with all of its body parts, you can probably expect to get about half of its retail value depending upon how desirable the particular doll is. If your doll has a perfect bisque head with original wig, clothing and shoes, you can probably get up to 75% of its retail value.

As to actually selling the doll, there are several possibilities. Possibly the easiest is to advertise in your local paper. You may not think there are any doll collectors in your area, but there probably are. You might also check your local paper to see if anyone is advertising to purchase dolls; many dealers and collectors do so. Check the paper to find out about antique shows in your area. If anyone has dolls, ask if they would be interested in buying your doll. Also, you could inquire at antique shops in your area for dealers who specialize in dolls. You will probably get a higher price from a specialist than a general antique dealer because the former are more familiar with the market for specific dolls. A roster of doll specialists is available from The National Antique Doll Dealers Association, Inc., P.O. Box 81143, Wellesley Hills, MA 02181-0001.

You could consign your doll to an auction. If it is a common doll, it will probably do quite well at a local sale. If it is a more rare doll, consider sending it to one of the auction houses that specializes in selling dolls; most of them will accept one doll if it is a good one, and they will probably get the best price for you. It would probably be worth your while to purchase a doll magazine from your local book store, doll shop or newsstand; most doll magazines include ads from auction houses, doll shows and leading dealers. You could advertise in doll magazines, but you might have to ship the doll and guarantee return privileges if the buyer does not like it.

If you cannot find your doll in the **Blue Book**, it might be a good idea to have it professionally appraised. This will involve your paying a fee to have the doll evaluated. We provide this service and can be contacted through the publisher. Many museums and auction houses also appraise dolls.

For more detailed information about collecting and selling dolls, consult my book *Doll Buying and Selling*, available from Hobby House Press.

ANTIQUE & VINTAGE DOLLS

Values given in this section are retail prices for clean dolls in very good overall condition with no cracks, chips or repairs in porcelain heads and with proper bodies and appropriate wigs and clothes. Naked, wigless, dirty, unstrung "attic dolls" are worth 40-65%, depending upon the rarity of the doll.

15in (38cm) 115 toddler. *H & J Foulke, Inc.*
(For information see page 115.)

ALABAMA INDESTRUCTIBLE DOLL

Early Alabama Baby: All-cloth painted with oils, tab-jointed shoulders and hips, flat derriere for sitting; painted hair with circular seam on head, molded face with painted facial features; applied ears; painted stockings and shoes (a few with bare feet); appropriate clothes; all in good condition, some wear acceptable, no repaint or touch up.

11-15in (28-38cm)	**$ 1400 - 1600**
21-24in (53-61cm)	**2500 - 3000**
Black, 14-19in (36-48cm)	**6600****
Wigged, 24in (61cm)	**3000-3500****

Later doll, molded ears, bobbed hairdo:

14-15in (36-38cm)	**$ 800 - 1000**
21-24in (53-61cm)	**2000 - 2500**
Black, 14-19in (36-48cm)	**3000**

**Not enough price samples to compute a reliable average.

FACTS

Ella Smith Doll Co., Roanoke, Ala., 1899-1925.

Mark: Various stamps, including:

PAT. NOV. 9, 1912

NO. 2

ELLA SMITH DOLL CO.

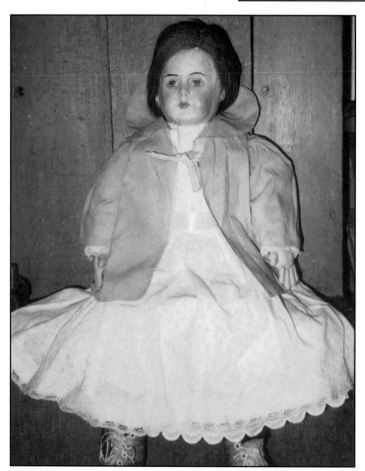

26in (66cm) wigged *Alabama Baby* with jointed knees and elbows with gussets. *Courtesy of Margaret Fay.*

HENRI ALEXANDRE

H.A. Bébé: 1889-1891. Perfect bisque socket head, closed mouth, paperweight eyes; jointed composition and wood body; lovely clothes; all in good condition.

Mark:

17-19in (43-48cm)   **$ 5500 - 6500****

Bébé Phénix: 1889-1900. Perfect bisque head, closed mouth, paperweight eyes, pierced ears, good wig; composition body sometimes with one-piece arms and legs; well dressed; all in good condition.

Mark: Red Stamp Incised

PHÉNIX
★95

Approximate Size Chart:
*81 = 10in (25cm)
*84 = 12in (31cm)
*85 = 14in (36cm)
*88 = 17in (43cm)
*90 = 18in (46cm)
*92 = 19-21in (48-53cm)
*93 = 22in (56cm)
*94 = 23-24in (58-61cm)
*95 = 23-25in (58-64cm)

17-18in (43-46cm)   **$ 3600 - 4000**
22-23in (56-58cm)   **4500 - 5000**

Open mouth,
17-19in (43-48cm)   **$ 2000 - 2200**

**Not enough price samples to compute a reliable range.

FACTS
Henri Alexandre,
Paris, France,
1888-1892;
Tourrel 1892-1895;
Jules Steiner
and successors
1895-1901.
Designer:
Henri Alexandre.
Trademark:
Bébé Phénix.

18-1/2in (47cm)
Phénix Bébé ★90.
Tore Scelso.

ALL-BISQUE DOLLS (So-Called French)

All-Bisque French Doll: Jointed at shoulders and hips, swivel neck, slender arms and legs; solid dome head, good wig, glass eyes, closed mouth; molded shoes or boots and stockings; appropriately dressed; all in good condition, with proper parts.

3-3/4in (10cm)	$	950*
5in (13cm)		1150 - 1250*
6in (15cm)		1900 - 2200*
With bare feet:		
5in (13cm)		1350 - 1450*
6in (15cm)		2000 - 2300*
8in (20cm)		4500**
With jointed elbows and knees,		
5-1/2in (14cm)		4250**
With jointed elbows,		
5-1/2in (14cm)		4000**

Painted eyes,
4–4-1/2in (10-12cm),		
all original	$	750 - 850
2-1/2in (6cm), blue boots,		
all original		225 - 250

*Allow extra for original clothes.
**Not enough price samples to compute a reliable average.

┌─────────── FACTS ───────────┐
Various French and/or German firms.
Ca. 1880-on. Smiling-faced dolls made
by Simon & Halbig for the French trade.
Mark: None, sometimes numbers.
└──────────────────────────────┘

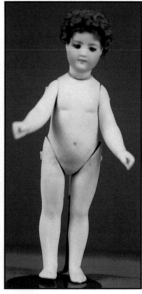

8-1/4in (21cm) French all-bisque by Simon & Halbig with bare feet.
H & J Foulke, Inc.

ALL-BISQUE DOLLS (GERMAN)

All-Bisque with molded clothes: Ca. 1890-on. Good quality work; all in good condition, with proper parts.

Children:

3-1/2-4in (9-10cm)	$ 115- 150
5-6in (13-15cm)	175 - 225
7in (18cm)	250 - 275

FACTS

Various firms including Hertwig; Alt, Beck & Gottschalck; Kestner; Kling; Simon & Halbig; Hertel, Schwab & Co.; Bähr & Pröschild; Limbach; Ca. 1880-on.
Mark: Some with "Germany" and/or numbers; some with paper labels on stomachs.

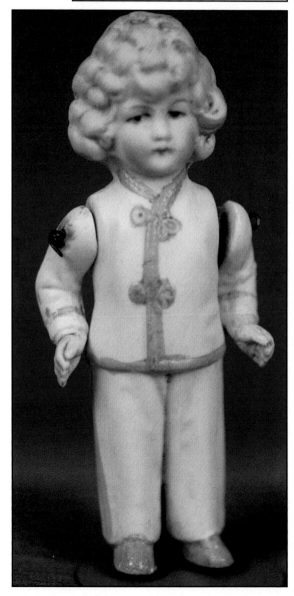

4-1/2in (12cm) all-bisque with molded clothes. *H & J Foulke, Inc.*

Doll is shown larger than actual size.

ALL-BISQUE DOLLS (GERMAN) *continued*

All-Bisque Slender Dolls: Ca. 1900 on. Stationary neck, slender arms and legs, glass eyes, molded shoes or boots and stockings; many in regional costumes; all in good condition, with proper parts.

3-3/4-4in (9-10cm)	$	**175 - 195**
5-6in (13-15cm)		**300**
Swivel neck:		
4in (10cm) 10a or 39/11		**225 - 250**
5-1/2in (14cm) 13a		**325 - 350**
Black or Mulatto:		
4-4-1/2in (10-12cm)		**325 - 375**
Swivel neck, 5in (13cm)		**500**

All-Bisque with painted eyes: Ca. 1880-1910. Stationary neck, painted eyes, molded and painted shoes and stockings; fine quality work; all in good condition, with proper parts.

1-1/4in (3cm) crocheted clothes		
	$	**65 - 85**
1-1/2-2in (4-5cm)		**75 - 85**
4-5in (10-13cm)		**175 - 200**
6-7in (15-18cm)		**225 - 275**
Swivel neck, 4-5in (10-13cm)		**225 - 275**
Early style, bootines, yellow boots or shirred hose:		
4-5in (10-13cm)	$	**275 - 300**
6–6-1/2in (15-16cm)		**350 - 400**
8in (20cm)		**675 - 725**
Black stockings, tan slippers, 6in (15cm)		**400 - 450**

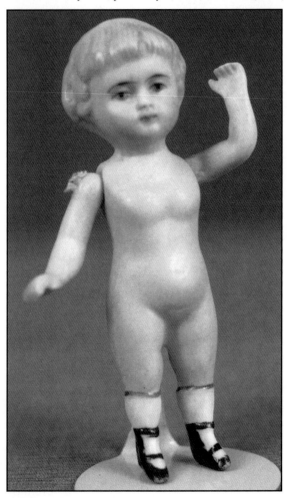

4in (10cm) early style all-bisque with bootines and molded hair. *H & J Foulke, Inc.*

Doll is shown larger than actual size.

ALL-BISQUE DOLLS (GERMAN) *continued*

 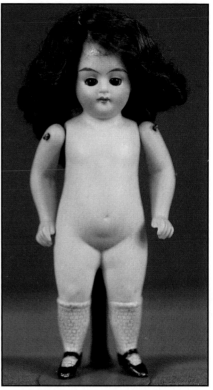

8-1/2in (21cm) early style all-bisque with stiff hips and bootines. *H & J Foulke, Inc.*

5-1/2in (14cm) early style all-bisque with shirred hose. *H & J Foulke, Inc.*

All-Bisque with glass eyes: Ca. 1890-1910. Stationary neck, glass eyes, molded and painted shoes and stockings; all in good condition, with proper parts, fine quality.

3in (8cm)	$ 275 - 325*
4-1/2–5in (11-13cm)	275 - 325*
6in (15cm)	350 - 375*
7in (18cm)	400 - 450*
8in (20cm)	500 - 550*
9in (23cm)	700 - 800
10in (25cm)	900 -1000
12in (31cm)	1300 -1400

Early style model, stiff hips, shirred hose or bootines:

3in (8cm)	$	325
4-1/2in (11cm)		325 - 350
6in (15cm)		500 - 550
7in (18cm)		650 - 700
8-1/2in (21cm)		950 - 1000

Long black or white stockings, tan shoes:

5in (13cm)	500 - 550
7-1/2in (19cm)	800 - 850

*Allow $50-100 extra for yellow boots or unusual footwear and/or especially fine quality.

ALL-BISQUE DOLLS (GERMAN) *continued*

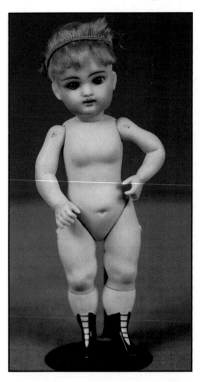

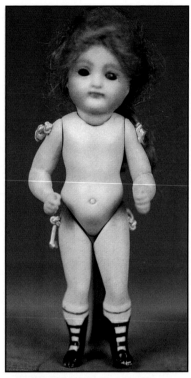

9in (23cm) #102, so-called "Wrestler".
H & J Foulke, Inc.

4-1/2in (12cm) early pouty Kestner.
H & J Foulke, Inc.

All-Bisque with swivel neck and glass eyes: Ca. 1880-1910. Swivel neck, glass eyes, molded and painted shoes or boots and stockings; all in good condition, with proper parts, fine quality.

3-1/4in (8cm)	$ 350 - 375
4–4-1/2in (10-12cm)	375 - 425*
5-6in (13-15cm)	550 - 650*
7in (18cm)	750 - 800*
8in (20cm)	900 - 1000*
9in (23cm)	1100 - 1200*
10in (25cm)	1300 - 1500
Early Kestner or S&H-type:	
4-1/2–5in (12-13cm)	1350 - 1400
6in (15cm)	1500 - 1650
8in (20cm)	2100 - 2300
10in (25cm)	2800 - 3000
With swivel waist,	
5-1/2–6in (14-15cm)	5000**
With jointed knee,	
8in (20cm)	4000 - 4200

#102 (so-called: "Wrestler"):

8-1/2–9in (22-23cm)	$ 2200 - 2500
#120 (Bru-type face),	
8-1/2in (22cm)	3000-3250**
Bare feet:	
5-1/2–6in (14-15cm)	2000
8in (20cm)	2800 - 3000
12in (31cm)	4500 - 5000**
Round face, bootines:	
6in (15cm)	1100 - 1250
8in (20cm)	1650 - 1850
Long black stockings, tan slippers,	
7-1/2in (19cm)	1050

Simon & Halbig **886** and **890**: See page 186.

*Allow $100-150 extra for yellow boots or unusual footwear.

**Not enough sample prices to compute a reliable range.

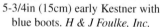

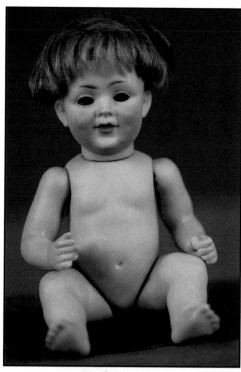

5-3/4in (15cm) early Kestner with
blue boots. *H & J Foulke, Inc.*

8in (20cm) SWC #391 all-bisque character baby.
H & J Foulke, Inc.

All-Bisque Character Baby: Ca. 1910. Jointed at shoulders and hips, curved arms and legs; molded hair, painted eyes; all in good condition, with proper parts, very good quality.

3-1/2in (9cm)	$ 95 - 110
4-1/2–5-1/2in (11-14cm)	175 - 225
7in (18cm)	275 - 325
8in (20cm)	375 - 425

#830, #391, and others with glass eyes:

4-5in (10-13cm)	275 - 325
6in (15cm)	400 - 450
8in (20cm)	600 - 650

Swivel neck, glass eyes:

6in (15cm)	550 - 575
8in (20cm)	725 - 775
10in (25cm)	950 - 1000

Swivel neck, painted eyes:

5-6in (13-15cm)	325 - 375
8in (20cm)	475 - 525
11in (28cm)	775 - 875

Mildred, the Prize Baby,

5in (13cm) at auction	4600

Baby Darling #497,

6in (15cm)	$ 850

Limbach (clover mark):

4-5in (10-13cm)	55 - 85
7in (18cm)	110 - 135
11-12in (28-31cm) fine quality	550 - 650

All-Bisque Character Dolls with Glass Eyes: Ca. 1910. Excellent quality with proper parts.

#150, 155, 156:

5-6in (13-15cm)	$ 350 - 450
7in (18cm)	550

#602, swivel neck,

5-1/2–6in (14-15cm)	550 - 650

#79, pierced nose,

4-1/2in (12cm)	500

All-Bisque Character Dolls: 1913-on. Painted eyes; all in good condition with proper parts.
Pink bisque:

2-3in (5-8cm)	$ 50 - 60
5in (13cm)	95
Thumbsucker, 3in (8cm)	225 - 250
Girl with molded hair bow loop,	
2-1/2in (6cm)	65 - 75
Chubby, 4-1/2in (11cm)	200 - 210
6in (15cm)	325 - 375
HEbee, SHEbee, 5in (13cm)	600
7in (18cm)	800
Peterkin, 5-6in (13-15cm)	275 - 375
Little Imp, 5in (13cm)	125 - 150
Orsini girls, 5in (13cm)	
glass eyes	1350 - 1550
painted eyes	900
Happifats,	
4in (10cm) boy and girl	500 - 600 pair
Happifats Baby,	
3-3/4in (10cm)	275 - 300
Wide Awake, 5in (13cm)	225
Little Annie Rooney, 4in (10cm)	$ 300

September Morn, Grace Drayton,	
7in (18cm) at auction	4000
Moritz, 6-1/2in (16cm) swivel neck,	
pedestal legs, at auction	2100
#222 Our Fairy, glass eyes:	
5in (13cm)	650 - 700
10in (25cm)	1200 - 1500
#790, 791, 792,	
5-1/2–6in (14-15cm)	450 - 500
#160, 5-1/2–6in (14-15cm)	300 - 350

Later All-Bisque with painted eyes: Ca. 1920. Many by Limbach (clover mark) and Hertwig; some of pretinted bisque; mohair wig or molded hair, molded and painted one-strap shoes and white stockings; all in good condition, with proper parts.

3-1/2in (9cm)	$ 70 - 80
4-1/2–5in (12-13cm)	100 - 110
6-7in (15-18cm)	160 - 185
8in (20cm)	225 - 250

7-1/2in (19cm) Hertwig all-bisque girl with painted eyes. *H & J Foulke, Inc.*

6in (15cm) *Chubby* with chest sticker. *H & J Foulke, Inc.*

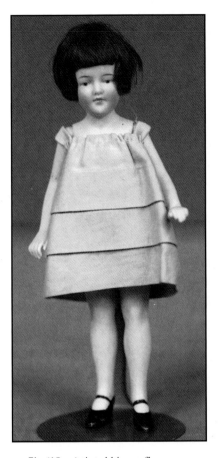

7in (18cm) tinted bisque flapper.
H & J Foulke, Inc.

3-1/2in (9cm) flapper with swivel waist.
H & J Foulke, Inc.
Doll is shown larger than actual size.

All-Bisque "Flapper" (tinted bisque): Ca. 1920. Molded bobbed hair with loop for bow, painted features; long yellow stockings, one-strap shoes with heels; all in good condition, with proper parts, very good quality.

5in (13cm)	**$275 - 300**
6-7in (15-18cm)	**375 - 425**
Standard quality,	
4-5in (10-13cm)	**135 - 165**

All-Bisque Baby: Ca. 1920. Pink bisque, so-called "Candy Baby," curved arms and legs; original factory clothes; all in good condition, with proper parts.

2-1/2–3in (6-8cm)	**$ 85 - 95**

All-Bisque "Flapper:" Ca. 1920. Pink bisque with molded bobbed hair; original factory clothes; all in good condition, with proper parts.

3in (8cm)	**$ 75 - 95**
Molded hats	**200 - 225**
Molded bunny ears cap	**350**
Aviatrix	**225**
Swivel waist, 3-1/2in (9cm)	**350**

ALL-BISQUE DOLLS (GERMAN) *continued*

3in (8cm) immobile children with animals on a string. *H & J Foulke, Inc.*
Dolls are shown larger than actual size.

All-Bisque Nodder Characters: Ca. 1920-on. Many made by Hertwig & Co. Nodding heads, elastic strung, molded clothes; all in good condition.

3-4in (8-10cm)	$	**35 - 50**
Comic characters		**45 up***
Dressed Animals		**150 - 175**
Dressed Teddy Bears		**200 - 225**
Santa		**200 - 225**
Dutch Girl, 6in (15cm)		**150 - 165**

All-Bisque Immobiles: Ca. 1920. Molded clothes, in good condition.

Adults and children,		
1-1/2–2-1/4in (4-6cm)	$	**35 - 45**
Children, 3-1/4in (8cm)		**55 - 65**

Santa, 3in (8cm)	$	**125 - 135**
Children with animals on string,		
3in (8cm)		**150 - 165**

Jointed Animals: Ca. 1910-on. All-bisque animals, wire-jointed shoulders and hips; original crocheted clothes, in good condition.

Rabbit, 2–2-3/4in (5-7cm)	$	**475 - 525**
Bear, 2–2-1/2in (5-6cm)		**500 - 550**
Frog, Monkey, Pig		**600 - 700**
Bear on all fours,		
3-1/4in (8cm)		**225**

*Depending upon rarity.

ALL-BISQUE DOLLS (MADE IN JAPAN)

Baby:		
White, 4in (10cm)	$	30 - 33
All original elaborate outfit		50 - 65
Black, 4-5in (10-13cm)		55 - 65
Betty Boop-type:		
4-5in (10-13cm)		20 - 25
6-7in (15-18cm)		32 - 38
Child:		
4-5in (10-13cm)		25 - 28
6-7in (15-18cm)		35 - 45
With animal on string,		
4-1/2in (12cm)		38 - 42
Comic Characters,		
3-4in (8-10cm)		30 up*
Mickey Mouse		175 - 225
Bride & Groom, boxed set,		
4in (10cm)		50 - 60
Stiff Characters:		
3-4in (8-10cm)	$	5 - 10
6-7in (15-18cm)		30 - 35

Cho-Cho San, 4-1/2in (12cm)	$	70 - 80
Nodders, 4in (10cm)		25 - 35
Orientals, 3-4in (8-10cm)		20 - 25
Queue San, 4in (10cm)		70 - 80
Marked "Nippon" Characters,		
4-5in (10-13cm)		85 - 95
Three Bears, boxed set		175 - 200
Snow White, boxed set		350 - 450
Black Character Girl, molded hair bow		
loop 4-1/2in (12cm)		40 - 50
Old Woman in Shoe,		
boxed set		150 - 175
Two-face Baby,		
(crying and sleeping)		150 - 175
Shirley Temple, 5in (13cm)		95 - 110
Circus Set, boxed, 11 pieces		150 - 175
Three Little Pigs		40 - 50 each
Teddy Bear, 3in (8cm)		40 - 50

*Depending upon rarity.

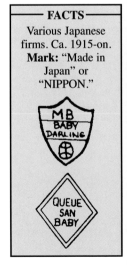

—— FACTS ——
Various Japanese
firms. Ca. 1915-on.
Mark: "Made in
Japan" or
"NIPPON."

MB
BABY
DARLING

QUEUE
SAN
BABY

3in (8cm) kneeling
Queue San Baby.
H & J Foulke, Inc.

*Doll is shown larger than
actual size.*

ALT, BECK & GOTTSCHALCK

China Shoulder Heads: Ca. 1880. Black or blonde-haired china head; old cloth body with china limbs; dressed; all in good condition. Mold numbers such as 784, 1000, 1008, 1028, 1046, 1142, 1210 and others.

Mark:

1008 ⋕9

16-18in (41-46cm)	$ 325 - 375
22-24in (56-61cm)	450 - 500
28in (71cm)	550 - 600

Bisque Shoulder Head: Ca. 1880. Molded hair, closed mouth; cloth body with bisque lower limbs; dressed; all in good condition. Mold numbers, such as 890, 990, 1000, 1008, 1028, 1064, 1142, 1254, 1288, 1304.

Painted eyes:

15-17in (38-43cm)	$ 375 - 425*
22-23in (56-58cm)	525 - 575*

Glass eyes:

14-16in (36-41cm)	550 - 650*
22in (56cm)	1100*

#926, molded pink and white scarf on head,
16in (41cm) at auction — **2000**
#990,
   pink mob cap, 20in (51cm) — **800 - 900**
#894, blue scarf, glass eyes,
   21in (52cm) — **1650 - 1750**
#1024, molded orange bonnet
   17-1/2in (44cm) — **2100**

*Allow extra for unusual or elaborate
  hairdo or molded hat.

─── **FACTS** ───
Alt, Beck &
Gottschalck, porcelain
factory, Nauendorf near
Ohrdruf, Thüringia,
Germany. 1854-on.

27in (69cm) 890 china
head. *H & J Foulke, Inc.*

ALT, BECK & GOTTSCHALCK *continued*

Bisque Shoulder Head: Ca. 1885-on. Turned shoulder head, wig, glass eyes, closed mouth; kid or cloth body; dressed; all in good condition. Mold numbers, such as 639, 698, 912, 1032, 1123, 1235.
Mark:

639 ✗ 6

with DEP after 1888

17-19in (43-48cm)	$	800 - 950
23-25in (58-64cm)		1100 - 1300
With open mouth:		
16-18in (41-46cm)		525 - 575
21-23in (53-58cm)		625 - 700

#911, 916, swivel neck, closed mouth,
20-23in (51-58cm) $ **1500 - 1650**

Child Doll: Perfect bisque head; open mouth; ball-jointed body in good condition; appropriate clothes.
Mark:

2 ½

A B ₈ G

Made in Ger many

#1362 Sweet Nell*:

14-16in (36-41cm)	$	425 - 475
19-21in (43-53cm)		525 - 550
23-25in (58-64cm)		650 - 750
29-30in (74-76cm)		1000 - 1100
36in (91cm)		1600 - 1700

*Allow 10-15% extra for Flapper body.

#911, closed mouth, 16in (41cm)
  composition body   **1500 - 1600**
#938, closed mouth,
  24in (61cm) at auction   **2800**

All-Bisque Girl: 1911. Chubby body, molded white stockings, blue garters, black Mary Janes.

Mold #83 over #100, 125, 150 or 225:

5-6in (13-15cm)	$	250 - 275
7in (18cm)		325 - 375
8in (20cm)		475 - 525

All-Bisque Baby,
  8-1/2in (21cm) swivel neck $ **850 - 900**

Character: 1910-on. Perfect bisque head, good wig, sleep eyes, open mouth; some with open nostrils; composition body; all in good condition; suitable clothes.
Mark:

#1322, 1352, 1361:

10-12in (25-31cm)	$	400 - 450*
16-18in (41-46cm)		575 - 625*
22-23in (56-58cm)		850 - 900*
Toddler:		
10in (25cm) 5-piece body		750 - 800
14-16in (36-41cm)		900 - 1000
#1357,		
16-18in (46-51cm)		1250 - 1500
#1407 Baby BoKaye:		
8in (20cm)		1350 - 1500
#1431 Orsini, earthenware baby,		
24in (61cm)		900 - 1100

*Allow $50 extra for flirty eyes.

See photographs on following page.

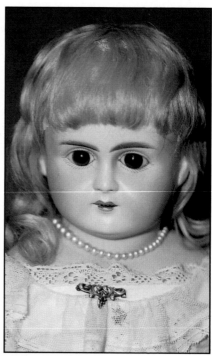

Top: Left: 23in (58cm) 911 with shoulder plate on kid body. *H & J Foulke, Inc.* *Right:* 24in (61cm) shoulder head with open mouth. *Jensen's Antique Dolls.*

Left: 19in (48cm) 1361 character baby. *H & J Foulke, Inc.*

LOUIS AMBERG & SON

Newborn Babe: 1914, reissued 1924. Designed by Jeno Juszko. Perfect bisque head, painted hair, sleep eyes, soft cloth body; appropriate clothes; all in good condition. Mold **886** by Recknagel. Mold **371** with open mouth by Marseille.

Mark: *L·A·&·S·*
371·3/0 D·R·G·M·
Germany

Length:

9-10in (23-25cm)	**$ 375 - 425**
13-14in (33-36cm)	**500 - 600**
17in (43cm)	**700 - 750**

FACTS
Louis Amberg & Son, New York, N.Y., U.S.A. 1907-on.

THE ORIGINAL
NEWBORN BABE
(C) Jan. 9th 1914 — No. G 45520
AMBERG DOLLS
The World Standard

16in (41cm) *Mibs*, repainted hair.
H & J Foulke, Inc.
(For information see page 34.)

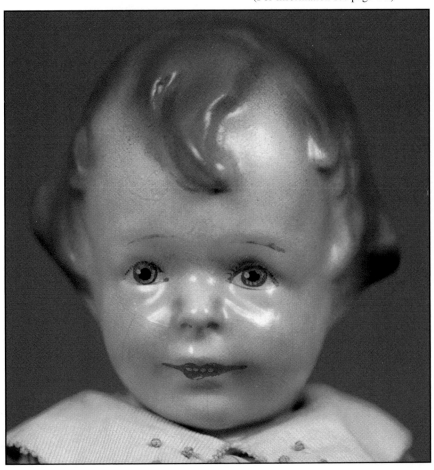

LOUIS AMBERG & SON *continued*

Charlie Chaplin: 1915. Composition portrait head molded mustache; straw-filled cloth body with composition hands; original clothes; all in good condition with wear.
Mark: cloth label on sleeve.
14in (36cm)   **$600**

Mibs: 1921. Composition shoulder head designed by Hazel Drucker with wistful expression, molded blonde or reddish hair; cloth body with composition arms and legs with painted shoes and socks; appropriate old clothes; all in good condition. (See photograph on page 33.)
Mark: None on doll; paper label only:

> "Amberg Dolls
> Please Love Me
> I'm Mibs"

16in (41cm)   **$ 850 - 950****

Baby Peggy: 1923. Composition head, molded brown bobbed hair, smiling closed mouth; appropriately dressed; all in good condition.
20in (51cm)   **$ 650 - 750****

Baby Peggy: 1924. Perfect bisque head by Armand Marseille with character face; brown bobbed mohair wig, brown sleep eyes, closed mouth; composition or kid body, fully-jointed; dressed or undressed; all in very good condition.
Mark:

> "19 © 24"
> LA & S NY
> Germany
> —50—
> 982/2"

#982 or 983 shoulder head,
20in (51cm)   **$ 1800 - 2000**

#972 or 973 socket head,
18-22in (46-56cm)   **2200 - 2500**

**Not enough price samples to compute a reliable range.

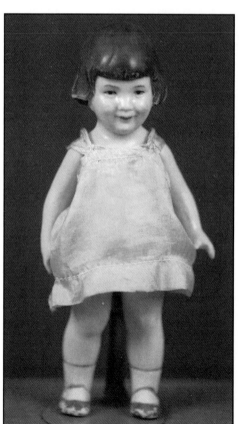

5-1/2in (14cm) *Baby Peggy*.
H & J Foulke, Inc.

LOUIS AMBERG & SON *continued*

All-Bisque Character Children: 1920s. Made by a German porcelain factory; pink pretinted bisque.

4in (10cm)	$	125
5-6in (13-15cm)		160 - 185
Girl with molded bow,		
6in (15cm)		350 - 400
Girl with downward gaze, glass eyes, wig,		
5-1/2in (14cm)		450 - 475
7in (18cm)		600
Mibs:		
3in (8cm)		250 - 275
4-3/4in (12cm)		350 - 375
6in (15cm)		575
Baby Peggy:		
3in (8cm)		275 - 300
5-1/2in (14cm)		450 - 500
4-1/2in (12cm) wigged		450 - 475

Mibs-type girl with molded flowers in hair,
4-3/4in (12cm)   **225**

Vanta Baby: 1927. A tie-in with Vanta baby garments. Composition or bisque head with molded and painted hair, sleep eyes, open mouth with two teeth, suitably dressed; all in good condition.

Mark: Bisque Head

Vanta Baby
L ABS · 3/0 D·R·G·M·
Germany.

Bisque head,		
20-22in (51-56cm)	$	900 - 1100
Composition head,		
20in (51cm)		325 - 375

Sue, Edwina or It: 1928. All-composition with round ball joint at waist.

14in (36cm)	$	425 - 475

Tiny Tots Body Twists: 1928. All-composition with large round ball joint at the waist.

8in (20cm)	$	135 - 150

4-3/4in (12cm) *Mibs*-type girl with molded flowers in hair.
H & J Foulke, Inc.

GEORGENE AVERILL (MADAME HENDREN)

Bonnie Babe: 1926. Bisque heads by Alt, Beck & Gottschalck; cloth bodies by K & K Toy Co.; distributed by George Borgfeldt, New York. Perfect bisque head with smiling face, open mouth with two lower teeth; cloth body with composition arms (sometimes celluloid) and legs often of poor quality; all in good condition. Mold #1386 or 1402

Mark:

Copr. by
Georgene Averill
Germany
1005/3652
1386

Length:

12-13in (31-33cm)	$	1000 - 1100
16-18in (41-46cm)		1400 - 1600
22-23in (56-58cm)		1800 - 1900

Composition body,
8in (20cm) tall   1250**

Celluloid head,
16in (41cm) tall $ 550 - 650**

All-Bisque Bonnie Babe: 1926.

5in (13cm)	$	750 - 850
7in (18cm)		1050 - 1150

Sunny Boy and Girl: Ca. 1927. Celluloid "turtle" mark head; stuffed body with composition arms and legs; appropriate or original clothes; all in good condition.

15in (38cm) $ 350 - 400
19in (48cm) all original and mint,
  at auction.   550

**Not enough price samples to compute a reliable range.

┌─── FACTS ───┐
Averill Mfg. Co. and Georgene Novelties, Inc., New York, N.Y., U.S.A. 1915-on.
Designer: Georgene Averill.
Trademarks: Madame Hendren, Georgene Novelties.

22in (56cm)
Bonnie Babe.
H & J Foulke, Inc.

Composition Dolls: All appropriately dressed in good condition.

Mme. Hendren Character: Ca. 1915 on. Original tagged felt costume, including Dutch children, Indians, cowboys, sailors.
10-14in (25-36cm) $ **125 - 150**

Mama and **Baby Dolls:** Ca. 1918 on. Composition with cloth bodies, Names such as *Baby Hendren* and *Baby Georgene*
15-18in (38-46cm) $ **250 - 300**
22-24in (56-61cm)   **400 - 450**

Dolly Reckord: 1922. Record-playing mechanism in torso, with records.
26in (66cm) $ **550 - 650**

Grace Drayton: 1920s. Black *Chocolate Drop* with yarn pigtails,
14in (36cm) $ **575**

Whistling Doll: 1925-1929. Doll whistles when feet are pushed up or head is pushed down:
14-15in (36-38cm) *Dan*, sailor or
   cowboy $ **250 - 275**
Black Rufus or **Dolly Dingle**   **400 - 450**

Little Brother and **Little Sister:** 1927. Grace Corry Rockwell,
14in (36cm) $ **450 - 500**

Snookums: 1927.
14in (36cm) $ **350 - 375**

Baby Twists: 1927. **Dimmie** and **Jimmie** with a large round ball joint at waist,
14-1/2in (37cm) $ **425 - 475**

Patsy-type Girl: 1928.
14in (36cm) $ **275 - 325**
17-18in (43-46cm)   **375 - 400**

Lenci-type Girl: Ca. 1930. Lenci-style, composition face; original felt and organdy clothes,
19in (48cm) $ **350 - 400**

Little Cherub: 1937. Designed by Harriet Flanders.
16in (41cm) $ **275 - 300**
12in (31cm) painted eyes   **160 - 175**

19in (48cm) *Baby Georgene* all original.
H & J Foulke, Inc.

Cloth Dolls: Original clothes; all in excellent condition, clean with bright color.

Children or Babies:

12in (31cm)	$	**125 - 150**
24-26in (61-66cm)		**225 - 275**
Girl Scout, 12in (31cm)		**200 - 225**

International and Costume Dolls:

12in (31cm)	$	**90 - 100**
Mint in box with wrist tag		**115 - 135**

Uncle Wiggily or Nurse Jane,

18-20in (46-51cm)	$	**550 - 600**

Characters, 14in (36cm),
Little Lulu, Nancy, Sluggo,1944.

	$	**400 - 500**

Topsy & Eva, 10in (25cm) $ **150- 175**

Maud Tousey Fangel,1938. Snooks, Sweets, Peggy-Ann. Marked "M.T.F." Bright color, all original.

12 - 14in (31 - 36cm)	$	**550 - 650**
17in (43cm)		**800 - 850**
22in (56cm)		**1100**

Grace G. Drayton: good clean condition, some wear acceptable.

Chocolate Drop,1923. Brown cloth with three yarn pigtails.

11in (28cm)	**$ 450 - 500****
16in (41cm)	**650 - 750****

Dolly Dingle,1923.

11in (28cm)	**$ 400 - 450****
16in (41cm)	**600 - 650****
10in (25cm) double face	**750****

**Not enough price samples to compute a reliable range.

(Note: These are Drayton dolls.)

19in (48cm) composition head girl in Lenci style, all original. *H & J Foulke, Inc.*

16in (41cm) cloth doll designed by Maud Tousey Fangel. *Courtesy of Richard W. Withington.*

BABY BO KAYE

Baby Bo Kaye: Perfect bisque head with flange neck marked as at right, molded hair, glass eyes, open mouth with two lower teeth; cloth torso with composition limbs; dressed; all in good condition.

16-19in (41-48cm)	$ 2400 - 2800
Celluloid head, 16in (41cm)	750
#1407 (ABG) bisque head, composition body, 7-1/2in (19cm)	1300 - 1400

All-Bisque Baby Bo Kaye: Molded hair, glass sleep eyes, open mouth with two teeth; swivel neck, jointed shoulders and hips; molded pink or blue shoes and socks; unmarked but may have sticker on torso:

┌─────────── FACTS ───────────┐
Bisque heads made in Germany by Alt,
Beck & Gottschalck;
bodies by K & K Toy Co., New York,
N.Y., U.S.A. 1925.
Designer: J.L. Kallus.
Distributor:
George Borgfeldt Co., N.Y.
Mark:
Mark: "Copr. by
J.L. Kallus
Germany
1394/30"

5in (13cm)	$ 1400 - 1500
6in (15cm)	1800 - 1900

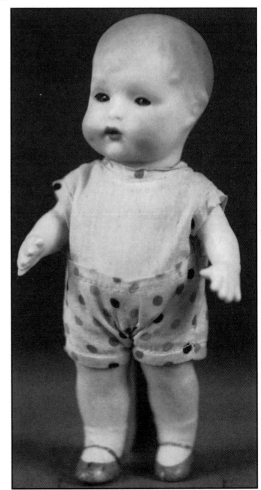

5in (13cm) all-bisque *Baby Bo Kaye*. *H & J Foulke, Inc.*

BABYLAND RAG

Babyland Rag: Cloth face with hand-painted features, sometimes mohair wig; cloth body jointed at shoulders and hips; original clothes.

Early face:

13-15in (33-38cm)		
Very good	$	750 - 850*
Fair		400 - 500
22in (56cm)		
Very good		900 - 1000*
Fair		550 - 600
30in (76cm) very good		2000 - 2200**

Topsy Turvy,
13-15in (33-38cm) very good
700 - 800*

Black:

15in (38cm) fair	$	650 - 700*
20-22in (51-56cm) very good		1100 - 1300*

Life-like face (printed features):

13-15in (33-38cm)		
Very good	$	600 - 650*

Babyland Rag-type (lesser quality),
White, 14in (36cm) good $ 375 - 475

Topsy Turvy,
14in (36cm) good   450 - 550

Brückner Rag Doll:
Mark:

PAT'D. JULY 8ᵀᴴ 1901

Stiffened mask face, cloth body, flexible shoulders and hips; appropriate clothes; all in good condition.

12-14in (31-36cm)		
White	$	210 - 235
Black		275 - 300
Topsy Turvy		500 - 550
Dollypop		250**

*Allow more for mint condition doll.
**Not enough price samples to compute a reliable range.

FACTS
E. I. Horsman, New York, N.Y., U.S.A. Some dolls made for Horsman by Albert Brückner. 1901-on.
Mark: None.

13in (33cm) girl with early hand-painted features.
H & J Foulke, Inc.

BÄHR & PRÖSCHILD

Marked Belton-type Child Doll: Ca. 1880. Perfect bisque head, solid dome with flat top having two or three small holes, paperweight eyes, closed mouth with pierced ears; wood and composition jointed body with straight wrists; dressed; all in good condition. Mold numbers in 200 series.

Mark: 204

12-14in (30-36cm)	$	1750 - 2000
18-20in (46-51cm)		2500 - 3000
24in (61cm)		3600 - 3800

Marked Child Doll: 1888-on. Perfect bisque socket head, set or sleeping eyes, open mouth with four or six upper teeth, good human hair or mohair wig; jointed composition body (many of French-type); dressed; all in good condition. Mold numbers in 200 and 300 series. (See photograph on page 42.)

Mark: 224
dep
#204, 239, 273, 275, 277, 289, 297, 300, 325, 340, 379, 394 and other socket heads:

12-13in (30-33cm)	$	600 - 700
16-18in (41-46cm)		800 - 900
22-24in (56-61cm)		1150 - 1250

#224 (dimples):

14-16in (36-41cm)	$	875 - 925
22-24in (56-61cm)		1250 - 1500

```
┌──────────── FACTS ────────────┐
│ Bähr & Pröschild, porcelain factory, │
│ Ohrdruf, Thüringia, Germany. Made │
│ heads for Bruno Schmidt, Heinrich Stier, │
│ Kley & Hahn and others. │
│ 1871- on. │
└──────────────────────────────┘
```

#246, 309 and other shoulder heads on kid bodies:

16-18in (41-46cm)	$	525 - 575
22-24in (56-61cm)		675 - 725

#302, swivel neck, kid body,

20in (51cm)	$	750 - 800

All-Bisque Girl, yellow stockings (Heart mark):

5in (13cm)	$	325 - 350
7in (18cm)		450

#513, possibly by B.P.,

22-26in (56-66cm)	$	850 - 900

12-1/2in (31cm)
204 Belton-type
child. *H & J
Foulke, Inc.*

Marked B.P. Character Baby: Ca. 1910 on. Perfect bisque socket head, solid dome or good wig, sleep eyes, open mouth; composition bent-limb baby body; dressed; all in good condition. Mold #585, 604, 624, 678, 619, 620 and 587.

Mark:

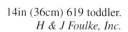

10-12in (25-31cm)	$	400 - 500
15-17in (36-43cm)		650 - 750
20-21in (51-53cm)		800 - 900

Toddler, fully jointed body:

12in (31cm)	$	950
22in (56cm)		1650

Toddler, 5-piece body:

10-12in (25-31cm)	675 - 750
14in (36cm)	850 - 950

#425, All-bisque baby,

5-1/2–6in (13-15cm)	250 - 300

#642, character child,

17in (43cm) at auction	2700

18in (46cm) 300 child with barely open mouth. *H & J Foulke, Inc.* (For information see page 41.)

14in (36cm) 619 toddler. *H & J Foulke, Inc.*

BELTON-TYPE (SO-CALLED)

Belton-type Child Doll: Perfect bisque socket head, solid but flat on top with two or three small holes for stringing; paperweight eyes, closed mouth, pierced ears; wood and composition ball-jointed body with straight wrists; dressed; all in good condition.

TR 809, 17in (43cm) $ **1600 - 1650**

Bru-type face, 12in (30cm) $ **2500 - 2700**

Fine early quality, French-type face (some mold #137 or #183):
13-15in (33-38cm)	$ **2400 - 2700**
18-20in (46-51cm)	**3100 - 3400**
22-24in (56-61cm)	**3600 - 4000**

Good quality, German-type face:
12in (31cm)	$ **1250 - 1450**
15-17in (38-43cm)	**1600 - 1800**
20in (51cm)	**2200 - 2400**

Tiny with 5-piece body (pretty),
8-9in (20-23cm) $ **850 - 950**

#200 Series, see Bähr & Pröschild, page 41.

FACTS
Various German firms, such as Bähr & Pröschild. 1875-on.
Mark:
None, except sometimes numbers.

13-1/2in (34cm) Belton-type boy with German-style face, all original. *H & J Foulke, Inc.*

16-1/2in (42cm) Belton-type girl with French-style face, all original. *H & J Foulke, Inc.*

C. M. BERGMANN

Bergmann Child Doll: Ca. 1889-on.
Marked bisque head, composition ball-jointed body, good wig, sleep or set eyes, open mouth; dressed; all in nice condition.
Heads by A.M. and unknown makers:

10in (25cm)	$	400
14-16in (36-41cm)		375 - 425
20in (51cm)		475 - 525
23-24in (58-61cm)		550
28-29in (71-74cm)		700 - 800
32-33in (81-84cm)		1100 - 1200
35-36in (89-91cm)		1400 - 1600
39-42in (99-111cm)		2200 - 2600

Heads by Simon & Halbig

10in (25cm)	$	450 - 500
13-15in (33-38cm)		400 - 450
18-20in (46-51cm)		525 - 575
23-24in (58-61cm)		650 - 700
29-30in (74-76cm)		1000 - 1100
35-36in (81-91cm)		1600 - 1800
39in (99cm)		2500
Eleonore, 25in (64cm)		800 - 900

#612 Character Baby, open closed mouth,
14-16in (36-41cm) $ **1500 - 1800****

**Not enough price samples to compute a
reliable range.

FACTS

C. M. Bergmann doll factory of
Waltershausen, Thüringia, Germany;
heads manufactured for this company by
Armand Marseille, Simon & Halbig,
Alt, Beck & Gottschalck and
perhaps others. 1888-on.
Distributor: Louis Wolfe & Co.,
New York
Trademarks: Cinderella Baby (1897),
Columbia (1904), My Gold Star (1926).
Mark:

CM BERGMANN

A - H ½ - M.

Made in Germany

C. M. Bergmann
Waltershausen
Germany
1916
6½a

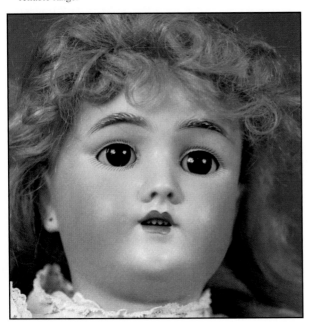

25in (64cm) *Eleonore.*
H & J Foulke, Inc.

BISQUE, FRENCH*

(Unmarked or Unidentified Marks and Unlisted Small Factories)

Marked H Bébé: Ca. late 1870s. Possibly by A. Halopeau. Perfect pressed bisque socket head of fine quality, paperweight eyes, pierced ears, closed mouth, cork pate, good wig; French wood and composition jointed body with straight wrists; appropriate clothing; all in excellent copndition.

Mark:

$$2 \cdot H$$

Size 0 = 16-1/2in (42cm)
        2 = 19in (48cm)
        3 = 21in (56cm)
        4 = 24in (61cm)

21-24in (53-61cm)   **$ 65,000 - 75,000**

Marked J.M. Bébé: Ca. 1880s. Perfect pressed bisque socket head, paperweight eyes, closed mouth, pierced ears, good wig; French composition and wood body; appropriate clothing; all in good condition.

Mark:

5

$$\text{J 유 M}$$

19-21in (48-53cm)   **$ 20,000****

Marked B.M. Bébé: 1880-1895. Alexandre Mothereau. Perfect pressed bisque socket head, closed mouth, paperweight eyes; French wood and composition jointed body; appropriate clothing; all in good condition.
    16in (41cm)   **$ 15,000 -18,000****
    27-29in (69-74cm)   **25,000****

Marked A.L. Bébé: Ca. 1875. Possibly Alexander Lefebvre & Cie. Perfect pressed bisque socket head, closed mouth, paperweight eyes; French wood and composition jointed body; appropraite clothing; all in good condition.
    22in (56cm) at auction   **$ 35,000**

Marked C.P. Bébé: Ca. 1875. Possibly Pannier. Perfect pressed bisque socket head, closed mouth, paperweight eyes; French wood and composition body; appropriate clothing; all in good condition.
    20in (51cm) at auction   **$ 58,500**

**Not enough price samples to compute a reliable range.

17in (43cm) P.G. *Bébé*.
H & J Foulke, Inc. (For information see page 46.)

12-1/2in (32cm) unmarked ***Bébé***. *Private Collection.* (For information see page 46.)

*For lady and fashion dolls (*poupées*), see pages 85 and 86.

BISQUE, FRENCH* *continued*

Marked M. Bébé: Mid 1890s. Perfect bisque socket head, closed mouth, paperweight eyes, pierced ears, good wig; French jointed composition and wood body; appropriate clothing; all in good condition. Some dolls with this mark may be **Bébé Mascottes.**

Mark:

$$\frac{M}{4}$$

18-21in (46-53cm) $ **3200-3800**

Marked PAN Bébé: Ca. 1887. Henri Delcroix, Paris and Montreuil-sous-Bois (porcelain factory). Perfect bisque socket head, paperweight eyes, closed mouth, pierced ears, good wig; French composition and wood body; appropriate clothes; all in good condition.

Mark:

$$\frac{PAN}{2}$$

Size   2 = 12in (31cm)
       10 = 27in (68cm)
       11 = 28-1/2in (72cm)

29in (74cm) at auction $ **16,500**

Marked J Bébé: Ca. 1880s. Perfect pressed bisque socket head, paperweight eyes; closed mouth; French wood and composition body; appropriate clothing; all in good condition.

15-16in (38-41cm) $ **5000 - 6000**

Huret Child: Ca. 1878. Maison Huret. Perfect bisque head; appropriate clothing; all in excellent condition. Gutta-percha body,

18in (46cm) at auction	$	**62,000**
Wood body, 18in (46cm)		**34,000**

Unmarked Bébé: Ca. 1880-1890. Perfect bisque socket head, paperweight eyes; closed mouth; jointed French composition and wood body; appropriate clothing; all in good condition. (See photograph on page 45.)

Jumeau quality:

12-14in (31-36cm)	$	**3100 - 3400**
20-22in (51-56cm)		**4400 - 4600**

Marked P.G. Bébé: Ca. 1880-1899. Pintel & Godchaux, Montreuil, France. Perfect bisque socket head, paperweight eyes, closed mouth, good wig; jointed French composition and wood body; appropriate clothing; all in good condition. (See photograph on page 45.)

Trademark: Bébé Charmant

Mark:

B	A
P9G	P7G

20-22in (51-56cm) $ **2500-3000**
Open mouth, 18-20in (46-51cm)
                        1600-1800

---

*For lady and fashion dolls (*poupées*), see pages 85 and 86.

BISQUE, GERMAN

(Unmarked or Unidentified Marks and Unlisted Small Factories)

American Schoolboy: Ca. 1880. Tinted bisque shoulder head with beautifully molded hair (usually blonde), glass eyes, closed mouth; original kid or cloth body; bisque lower arms; appropriate clothes; all in good condition.

12-14in (31-36cm)	$	550 - 650
17-20in (43-51cm)		750 - 850
Composition body,		
11-12in (28-31cm)		550 - 650

Hatted or Bonnet Doll: Ca. 1880-1920. Bisque shoulder head, molded bonnet; original cloth body with bisque arms and legs; good old clothes or nicely dressed; all in good condition. (See photograph on page 48.)

Standard quality:

8-9in (20-23cm)	$	185 - 225*
12-15in (31-38cm)		275 - 325*
Fine quality,		
18-22in (46-56cm)		1000 up*
All bisque,		
4-1/2in (12cm)		175 - 195*
7in (18cm)		250 - 300*

*Allow extra for unusual style.

Doll House Doll: 1890-1920. Man or lady bisque shoulder head; cloth body, bisque lower limbs; original clothes or suitably dressed; all in nice condition. 4-1/2-7in (12-18cm)

Victorian man with mustache $	175 - 225
Victorian lady, all original	200
Lady with glass eyes and wig	350 - 400
Man with mustache, original military uniform	750 up
Molded hair, glass eyes, Ca. 1870	450 - 500
Girl with bangs, Ca. 1880	150 - 165

Chauffeur with molded cap	$	250 - 300
Black man		650 - 700
Soldier, molded hat, goatee and mustache		1250
Soldier, all original with helmet at auction		2035
1920s man or lady		100 - 125

Child Doll with closed mouth: Ca. 1880-1890. Perfect bisque head; glass eyes; good wig; nicely dressed; all in good condition. Kid or cloth body. (See photographs on pages 48 and 49.)

17-19in (43-48cm)	$	800 - 950*
23-25in (58-64cm)		1100 - 1300*
#50 shoulder head,		
14-16in (35-41cm)		1100 - 1200
#132, 120 Bru-type face:		
13-14in (33-36cm)		1600 - 1800
19-21in (48-53cm)		2800 - 3000
#51 swivel neck shoulder head,		
17-19in (43-48cm)		1550 - 1750

*Allow 30% extra for swivel neck fashion-type model.

FACTS

Various German firms. 1860s-on.
Mark: Some numbered, some "Germany," some both.

Above: Left: 14in (35cm) bisque bonnet head doll. *H & J Foulke, Inc.* (For information see page 47.) ***Right:*** 12-1/2in (32cm) early child with closed mouth. *H & J Foulke, Inc.* (For information see page 47.)

13-1/2in (34cm) 50/3 shoulder head child with closed mouth. *Jensen's Antique Dolls.* (For information see page 47.)

23in (58cm) 444 child doll.
H & J Foulke, Inc. (For information see page 50.)

4-1/2in (12cm) child doll with closed mouth, all original.
H & J Foulke, Inc. (For information see page 47.)

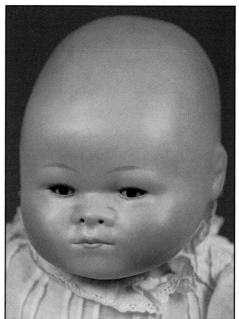

17in (43cm) **Arthur A. Gerling** Baby.
H & J Foulke, Inc. (For information see page 50.)

Composition body:

11-13in (28-33cm)	$	1450 - 1650
16-19in (41-48cm)		1950 - 2250
#136:		
12-15in (31-38cm)	$	2200 - 2400
19-21in (48-53cm)		2800 - 3200
#111,		
25in (64cm) at auction	$	3000

Child Doll with open mouth "Dolly Face": 1888-on. Perfect bisque head, ball-jointed composition body or kid body with bisque lower arms; good wig, glass eyes, open mouth; dressed; all in good condition. Very good quality; including dolls marked G.B., and K inside H, L.H.K., P.Sch., D&K.

12-14in (31-35cm)	$	400 - 450
18-20in (46-51cm)		600 - 700
23-25in (58-64cm)		800 - 900
30-32in (76-81cm)		1300 - 1500
#50, 51, square teeth,		
14-16in (36-41cm)		950 - 1050
#444 (See photograph on page 49.), 478:		
23-25in (58-64cm)		900 - 1000
35in (81cm)		2000 - 2200

Standard quality; including My Sweetheart, Princess, My Girlie, My Dearie, Pansy, Viola, Goebel, G & S, MOA, and A.W. (See photograph of *Pansy II* on page 9.):

14-16in (35-41cm)	$	350 - 400
20-23in (51-58cm)		525 - 550
30-32in (76-81cm)		1000 - 1100

Small Child Doll: 1890 to World War I. Perfect bisque socket head, 5-piece composition body, set or sleep eyes, cute clothes; all in good condition. Very good quality (Simon & Halbig type):

5-6in (13-15cm)	$	300 - 350
8-10in (20-25cm)		400 - 450
Fully-jointed body,		
7-8in (18-20cm)		500 - 550

Closed mouth (See photograph on page 49.):

4-1/2–5-1/2in (12-14cm) all original	500
8in (20cm)	750 - 825

Standard quality:

5-6in (13-15cm)	100 - 125
8-10in (20-25cm)	150 - 175

#39-13, 5-piece mediocre body, original clothes:

5in (13cm) glass eyes		200 - 225
Painted eyes		90 - 100

Globe Baby. 1898. Carl Hartmann.

8in (20cm)	$	325 - 350
8in (20cm) all original clothes and		
wig		375 - 425
12in (31cm)		450 - 475

Character Baby: 1910 on. Perfect bisque head, good wig or solid dome with painted hair, sleep eyes, open mouth; composition bent-limb baby body; suitably dressed; all in good condition. Including dolls marked G.B., S&Q, and Goebel.

9-10in (23-25cm)	$	300 - 350
14-16in (35-41cm)		500 - 550*
19-21in (48-53cm)		600 - 700*
23-24in (58-61cm)		800 - 900*
Toddler,		
12-14in (31-35cm)		650 - 850

My Sweet Baby:

23in (58cm) toddler	$	1000 - 1200

Character Child: 1910-on. Perfect bisque head; jointed composition body; dressed; all in good condition.

#820, PM shoulder head,		
12in (31cm)	$	350
#2-22, black molded hair,		
18in (46cm) at auction		2400
#111, 18-20in (46-51cm)		15,000
#128, 18-20in (46-51cm)		17,500
#159, 23in (58cm)		1150
#660, PR, 23in (58cm) at auction		2100

Infant, unmarked or unidentified maker: 1924-on. Perfect bisque head; cloth body; dressed; all in good condition.

10-12in (25-31cm) long	$	325 - 375*
15-18in (38-46cm) long		525 - 625*
#800, 11-12in (28-31cm)		550 - 600

HvB:

15in (38cm) long	$	450

Gerling Baby, 17in (43cm) long (see photograph on page 49) $ 550 - 600

#697, 12in (31cm) at auction $ 1200

BISQUE JAPANESE (CAUCASIAN DOLLS)

Character Baby: Perfect bisque socket head with solid dome or wig, glass eyes, open mouth with teeth, dimples; composition bent-limb baby body; dressed; all in good condition.

9-10in (23-25cm)	$	175 - 200*
13-15in (33-38cm)		275 - 325*
19-21in (48-53cm)		450 - 500*
24in (61cm)		600 - 650*

Hilda look-alike, 19in (48cm)   750 - 850*

Child Doll: Perfect bisque head, mohair wig, glass sleep eyes, open mouth; jointed composition or kid body; dressed; all in good condition.

14-16in (36-41cm)	$	250 - 300*
20-22in (51-56cm)		350 - 400*

*Do not pay as much for doll with inferior bisque head.

---FACTS---
Various Japanese firms; heads were imported by New York distributors, such as Morimura Brothers, Yamato Importing Co. and others. 1915-on.
Marks:

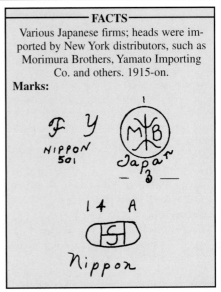

16in (41cm) Nippon
character baby.
H & J Foulke, Inc.

BLACK DOLLS*

Black Bisque Doll: Ca. 1880-on. Various French and German manufacturers from their regular molds or specially designed ones with Negroid features. Perfect bisque socket head either painted dark or with dark coloring mixed in the slip, running from light brown to very dark; composition or sometimes kid body in a matching color; cloth bodies on some baby dolls; appropriate clothing; all in good condition.

French Makers —

Bru, Circle Dot, 17in (43cm)	$ 30,000
E.D., open mouth, 16in (41cm)	2200
Jumeau:	
19in (48cm) early E. J.	
at auction	31,000
Bébé, open mouth,	
15in (38cm)	2700 - 2900
Exhibition Doll (1876), 25in (64cm)	
at auction $	88,000
Paris Bébé, closed mouth,	
15-1/2in (39cm)	4800 - 5000
Poupée shoulder head, jointed wood	
body, original ethnic clothes	13,000
Steiner, Figure A, open mouth,	
27-1/2in (69cm) at auction	6325
Van Rozen, 15in (38cm), all original,	
at auction	17,000
With crack behind ear	5100

German Makers —

Belton-type, 14in (36cm) 179 $	2700
Gebr. Heubach #7671,	
18in (46cm)	3500
H. Handwerck, 12in (31cm)	1000
18in (46cm)	1600 - 1800

4in (10cm) S & H-type
unmarked child.
H & J Foulke, Inc.

*Also see entry for specific maker of doll or for
material of doll.

Doll is shown larger than actual size.

E. Heubach, #399, 414, 452:
7-1/2in (19cm) toddler $	**425 - 450**
10-12in (25-30cm) baby	**500 - 550**
#444, 13in (33cm)	**650**
#463, 12in (30cm)	**700**
#300, 6in (15cm)	**450 - 500**

Kämmer & Reinhardt:
Child, 16in (41cm) $	**1800 - 2000**
#100 Baby, 14in (36cm)	**1000 - 1100**
#101, 11in (28cm)	**3500 - 3600**
#126, toddler, 8-9in (20-23cm)	**1250**

J. D. Kestner:
Child, 18in (46cm) $	**1900 - 2100**
Hilda, 12-13in (31-33cm)	**3800 - 4200**

Kuhnlenz #34:
7-8in (18-20cm) fully jointed $	**500 - 600**
8-1/2in (21cm) 5-piece body all original Mammy with baby	**700**
21in (53cm)	**5500 - 6500**

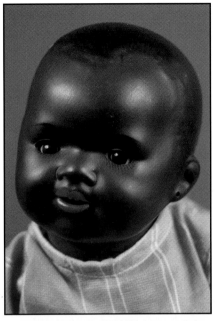

12-1/2in (32cm) A.M. 362 character baby.
H & J Foulke, Inc.

Armand Marseille:
#341, cloth body, 10-12in (25-31cm) $	**400 - 425**
#351, composition body:	
8-12in (20-31cm)	**500 - 525**
14-16in (38-41cm)	**650 - 750**
#362, composition body, 15in (38cm)	**900**

S PB H:
Hanna, 7-8in (18-20cm) $	**375 - 425**
#1923 child,	
19-20in (48-51cm)	**900 - 1000**

Simon & Halbig
#739, 19-22in (48-56cm) $	**2900 - 3100**
#949, open mouth,	
16in (41cm)	**2600 - 2900**
#970, 16-1/2in (42cm)	**1600 - 1700**
#1009, 18in (46cm)	**2100 - 2200**
#1249, 20in (51cm)	**1900 - 2100**
#1349 Jutta, 13in (33cm)	**1750**
#1358, 19-20in (48-51cm)	**8000 - 9000**

Franz Schmidt 1272,
22-1/2in (57cm)	**2600**

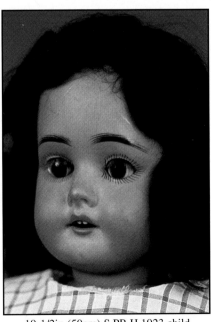

19-1/2in (50cm) S PB H 1923 child.
H & J Foulke, Inc.

BLACK DOLLS *continued*

Unmarked Child:
10-13in (25-33cm)
jointed body   **$**   **400 - 500**
8-9in (20-23cm) 5-piece body   **300 - 350**
4-5in (10-14cm)
   S & H quality   **450 - 500**

All-Bisque:
5in (14cm) glass eyes   **$**   **500 - 550**
6in (15cm) Kestner, swivel neck,
   bare feet   **1500 - 1600**
2-1/2in (6cm) French,
   swivel neck   **250**

Cloth Black Doll*: 1880s on. American-made cloth doll with black face, painted, printed or embroidered features; jointed arms and legs; original clothes; all in good condition.

Primitive, painted or embroidered
   face   **$ 1000 - 2000+**
Stockinette (so-called Beecher-type).
   20in (51cm)   **2000 - 2500**

1930s Mammy,
   18-20in (46-51cm)   **250 - 350+**

*Also check under manufacturer if known.
+Greatly depending upon appeal.

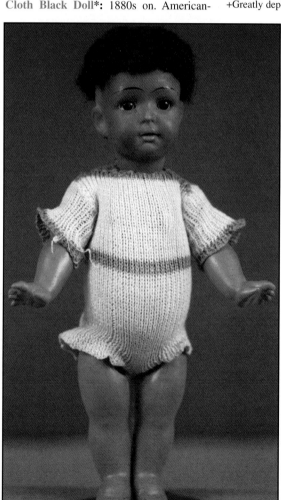

8-3/4in (22cm) K&R 126 toddler. *H & J Foulke, Inc.*

BLACK DOLLS *continued*

WPA, molded cloth face,
  22in (56cm)   **$ 1100 - 1200**
Alabama-type, 24in (61cm)   **2500 - 3500**
Chase Mammy, 26in (66cm)   **10,000**

Golliwogg: 1925-1930. English cloth character; all original; very good condition.
  18in (46cm)   **425 - 525**
Ca. 1950,
  16-18in (41-46cm)   **225 - 325**

Black Papier-Mâché Doll: Ca. 1890. By various German manufacturers. Papier-mâché character face, arms and legs, cloth body; glass eyes; original or appropriate clothes; all in good condition.
  12-14in (31-36cm)   **$ 350 - 450**
  18-20in (46-51cm) character with broad smile   **1200**

Black Low-Fired Pottery: Ca. 1930. English and German. 16in (41cm) molded curly hair.   **$ 850**
  K&R, 24in (61cm) flirty eyes   **1250**

6in (15cm) Kestner child
with bare feet, swivel neck.
H & J Foulke, Inc.

BRU

Poupée (Fashion Lady): 1866 on. Perfect bisque swivel head on shoulder plate, cork pate, appropriate old wig, closed mouth, paperweight eyes, pierced ears; gusseted kid lady body; original or appropriate clothes; all in good condition.
Smiling face, sizes A (11in, 28cm) to O (36in, 91cm):

14-16in (35-41cm)	$	3200 - 3800*
20-21in (51-53cm)		5500 - 6000*
Wood arms,		
13-14in (33-35cm)		3800 - 4000*
Wood body, naked:		
15-17in (38-43cm)		6000 - 6800*
14in (36cm) in original box		10,500*

Oval face, incised with numbers only. Shoulder plate sometimes marked "B. Jne & Cie."

12-13in (31-33cm)	$	2500 - 2800*
15-17in (38-43cm)		3200 - 3600*

20-21in (51-53cm)	$	4200 - 4700*
Wood body, naked,		
16in (41cm)		5000 - 5200

Candy Container: 1867. 2 faces (crying and smiling).
14in (36cm) at auction $ 7400*

All-Bisque: 1867. 2 faces.
9-1/2in (24cm) $ 4500 - 5500**

*Allow extra for original clothes.
**Not enough samples to compute a reliable range.

--- FACTS ---
Bru Jne. & Cie, Paris, and Montreuil-sous-Bois, France. 1866-1899.

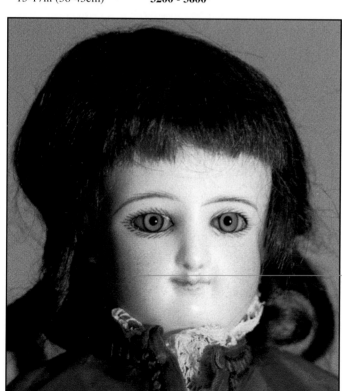

12in (31cm) smiling Bru poupée *B*. *Private Collection.*

BRU *continued*

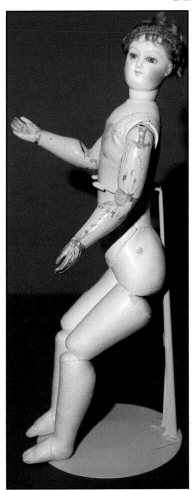

21-1/2in (54cm) Circle Dot Bru. *Private Collection.* (For information see page 58.)

17in (43cm) smiling Bru *poupée* E with wood jointed arms. *Kay & Wayne Jensen Collection.* (For information see page 56.)

25in (64cm) Bru Jne 10. *Private Collection.* (For information see page 58.)

58

BRU *continued*

Marked Breveté Bébé: 1879-1880. Perfect bisque swivel head on shoulder plate, cork pate, skin wig, paperweight eyes with shading on upper lid, closed mouth with white space between lips, full cheeks, pierced ears; gusseted kid body pulled high on shoulder plate and straight cut with bisque lower arms (no rivet joints); original or appropriate old clothes; all in good condition.
Mark: Size number only on head.
Oval sticker on body:

```
   ┌─────────────┐
   │   BÉBÉ       │
   │ Breveté Sdbe │
or │   PARIS      │
   └─────────────┘
```

or
rectangular sticker like Bébé Bru one, but with words "Bébé Breveté."

Size 5/0 = 10-1/2in (27cm)
Size 2/0 = 14in (36cm)
Size 1   = 16in (41cm)
Size 2   = 18in (46cm)
Size 3   = 19in (48cm)

11in (28cm)	$	**11,000**
14-16in (35-41cm)		**14,000 - 16,000**
19-22in (48-56cm)		**19,000 - 22,000**
4-1/2in (12cm) head and shoulderplate, 2 hairlines		**4000**
12in (31cm) body only		**1000**

Bébé Modele: 1880. Breveté face, wood body, 21in (53cm) $ **22,500**

Marked Crescent or Circle Dot Bébé: 1879-1884. Perfect bisque swivel head on a deep shoulder plate with molded breasts, cork pate, attractive wig, paperweight eyes, closed mouth with slightly parted lips, molded and painted teeth, plump cheeks, pierced ears; gusseted kid body with bisque lower arms (no rivet joints); original or appropriate old clothes; all in good condition. (See photograph on page 57.)
Mark: ⌒ ◉

Sometimes with "BRU J^{ne}"

Approximate size chart:
0 = 11in (28cm)
1 = 12in (31cm)
2 = 13in (33cm)
5 = 17in (43cm)
8 = 22in (56cm)

10 = 26in (66cm)
12 = 30in (76cm)
14 = 35in (89cm)

10-1/2in (26cm)	$	**8000 - 9000**
13-14in (33-35cm)		**13,000 - 15,000**
18-19in (46-48cm)		**18,000 - 20,000**
24in (61cm)		**24,000 - 25,000**
12in (31cm) missing arms		**5750**
31in (79cm) repaired shoulder plate and hand, at auction		**15,500**

Marked Nursing Bru (Bébé Têteur): 1878 -1898. Perfect bisque head, shoulder plate, open mouth with hole for nipple, mechanism in head sucks up liquid, operates by turning key; nicely clothed; all in good condition.
13-15in (33-38cm):

Early model	$	**8500 - 9500**
Later model		**5500 - 6500**

Marked Bru Jne Bébé: 1884-1889. Perfect bisque swivel head on deep shoulder plate with molded breasts, cork pate, attractive wig, paperweight eyes, closed mouth, pierced ears; gusseted kid body with scalloped edge at shoulder plate, bisque lower arms with lovely hands, kid over wood upper arms, hinged elbow, all kid or wood lower legs (sometimes on a jointed wood body); original or appropriate clothes; all in good condition. (For color photograph see page 57; for body photograph see *6th Blue Book*, page 79.)
Mark: "BRU J^{ne}"
Body Label:

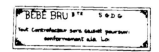

12-13in (31-33cm)	$	**12,000 - 14,000***
15-17in (38-43cm)		**15,500 - 17,500***
23-24in (58-61cm)		**22,000***
27in (69cm)		**23,000 - 24,000***

Marked Bru Shoes: $ **800 - 900**

Bru factory dress and hat: $ **1700 - 2000**

*Allow extra for original clothes.

BRU *continued*

Marked Bru Jne R Bébé: 1889-1899.
Perfect bisque head on a jointed composition
body. (See also photogrpah on page 57.)

Mark: BRU JⁿᵉR
         11

Body Stamp: "Bebe Bru" with size number

Closed mouth:
11-13in (28-33cm)	$	2200 - 2600
19-21in (48-53cm)		6000 - 7000

Open mouth:
12in (31cm)	1500 - 1800
20-21in (51-53cm)	3000 - 4000

22in (56cm) Bru Jne 8. *Private Collection.*

BUCHERER

Bucherer Doll: Composition character head sometimes with molded hat; metal ball-jointed body with large composition hands and composition molded shoes; original clothes, often felt; all in good condition. 8in (20cm) average

Man and woman in provincial costumes	**$ 200 each**
Fireman, clown, black man, aviator, rabbit, baseball player. **Becassine** and others	**275 - 325**

Characters: *Mutt, Jeff, Maggie, Jiggs, Katzenjammers, Happy Hooligan, Charlie Chaplin, Aggie, Jimmy Dugan, Puddin' head* and others.   **400 - 500**

FACTS
A. Bucherer, Amriswil,
Switzerland. 1921.
Mark:
"MADE IN
SWITZERLAND
PATENTS
APPLIED FOR"

The *Katzenjammers*, all original.
Wayne Jensen Collection.

BYE-LO BABY

Bisque Head Bye-Lo Baby: Ca. 1923. Perfect bisque head, cloth body with curved legs (sometimes with straight legs), composition or celluloid hands; sleep eyes; dressed. Made in seven sizes, 9-20in (23-51cm). (May have purple "Bye-Lo Baby" stamp on front of body.) Sometimes Mold **#1373** (ABG).
Mark:

© 1923 *by*
Grace S. Putnam
MADE IN GERMANY

Head circumference:

7-1/2–8in (19-20cm)	$	**500 - 525***
9-10in (23-25cm)		**475 - 500***
12-13in (31-33cm)		**550 - 600***
15in (38cm)		**900***
17in (43cm)		**1100 - 1300***
18in (46cm)		**1400 - 1600***

Tagged Bye-Lo gown	**50**
Bye-Lo pin	**95**
Bye-Lo type, incised "45," open mouth 12in (31cm) h.c.	**800**

*Allow extra for original tagged gown and button.

FACTS
Bisque heads — J.D. Kestner; Alt, Beck
& Gottschalck; Kling & Co.; Hertel,
Schwab & Co.; all of
Thüringia, Germany.
Composition heads — Cameo Doll
Company, New York, N.Y.
Celluloid heads — Karl Standfuss,
Saxony, Germany.
Wooden heads (unauthorized) —
Schoenhut of Philadelphia, Pa.
All-Bisque Baby — J.D. Kestner.
Cloth Bodies and Assembly — K & K
Toy Co., New York, N.Y.
Composition Bodies — König &
Wernicke. 1922-on.
Designer: Grace Storey Putnam.
Distributor: George Borgfeldt,
New York, N.Y., U.S.A.

Mold #1369 (ABG) socket head on composition body, some marked "K&W."
  12-13in (30-33cm) long **$**   **700 - 900**

Mold #1415, smiling with painted eyes,
  13-1/2in (34cm) h.c.   **4000****
Composition head, 1924.
  12-13in (31-33cm) h.c.,
    all original   **400 - 425**
Celluloid head,
  10in (25cm) h.c.   **350 - 375**
Painted bisque head, late 1920s.
  12-13in (31-33cm) h.c.,   **325 - 350**
Wooden head, (Schoenhut), 1925.
                 1700 - 2000
Vinyl head, 1948.
  16in (41cm)   **150 - 200**

Wax head, 1922.   **700 - 800**

Baby Aero or **Fly-Lo Baby** bisque head
Mold #1418,
  11in (28cm)   **$ 3800 - 4200**
Composition head, original costume,
  12in (31cm)   **800 - 900**

**Not enough price samples to
  compute a reliable average.

13in (33cm) ***Bye-Lo Baby***.
H & J Foulke, Inc.

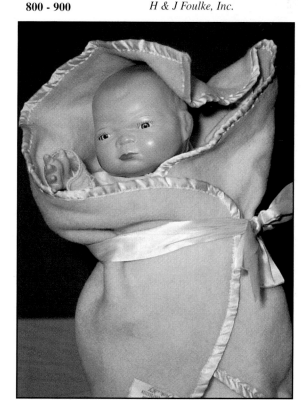

Composition head ***Bye-Lo
Baby***, all original with label.
Jensen's Antique Dolls.

BYE-LO BABY *continued*

Marked All-Bisque Bye-Lo Baby: 1925-on.
Solid head with molded hair and painted eyes, jointed shoulders and hips:

4-5in (10-13cm)	$	325 - 395
6in (15cm)		475 - 525
8in (20cm)		675 - 725

Solid head with swivel neck, glass eyes, jointed shoulders and hips:

4-5in (10-13cm)	$	550 - 625
6in (15cm)		725 - 825
8in (20cm)		1100 - 1200

Head with wig, glass eyes, jointed shoulders and hips:

4-5in (10-13cm)	650 - 750
6in (15cm)	850 - 950
8in (20cm)	1250 - 1450

Action Bye-Lo Baby, immobile in various positions, painted features,

3in (8cm)	$	400
All-Celluloid 4in (10cm)		250 - 300

8in (20cm) all-bisque *Bye-Lo Baby*. *H & J Foulke, Inc.*

CATTERFELDER PUPPENFABRIK

C.P. Child Doll: Ca. 1902-on. Perfect bisque head, good wig, sleep eyes, open mouth with teeth; composition jointed body; dressed; all in good condition.
#264 (made by Kestner):
17-19in (43-48cm)	$	**800 - 850**
22-24in (56-61cm)		**950 - 1000**
35-36in (89-91cm)		**2000 - 2500****

C.P. Character Child: Ca. 1910-on. Perfect bisque character face with wig, painted eyes; composition jointed body; dressed; all in good condition. Sometimes mold #207 or #219.
15-16in (38-41cm)	$	**3000 - 4000****
#217, 18in (46cm)		**9750****
#220, 14in (36cm) glass eyes,		**7500****
#210, 14in (36cm)		**5000****

C.P. Character Baby: Ca. 1910-on. Perfect bisque character face with wig or molded hair, painted or glass eyes; jointed baby body; dressed; all in good condition.
#200, 201:
14-16in (36-41cm)	$	**500 - 550**
19-21in (48-53cm)		**750 - 850**

#201, toddler, 10in (25cm)	$	**700 - 900****

#262, 263, (made by Kestner):
15-17in (38-43cm)	$	**525 - 625**
20-22in (51-56cm)		**800 - 900**

#262, toddler, 5-piece body,
16-1/2in (42cm)	$	**1000 - 1200**

#208:
15-17in (38-43cm)	$	**525 - 575**
22-24in (56-61cm)	$	**800 - 900**

**Not enough price samples to compute a reliable range.

FACTS
Catterfelder Puppenfabrik, Catterfeld, Thüringia, Germany. Heads by J.D. Kestner and other porcelain makers. 1902-on. Bisque head; composition body. **Trademark:** My Sunshine.
Mark:

C. P.
2 0 8
45
N

24in (61cm) 264 child with head made by Kestner. *H & J Foulke, Inc.*

CELLULOID DOLLS

Celluloid Shoulder Head Child Doll: Ca. 1900-on. Cloth or kid body, celluloid or composition arms; dressed; all in good condition.

Painted eyes, 16-18in (41-46cm) **$160 - 185**
Glass eyes:
19-22in (48-56cm) child   **225 - 250**
Original provincial costume,
12-14in (30-36cm)   **210 - 235**
Boy/girl pair   **525 - 550**

All-Celluloid Child Doll: Ca. 1900-on. Jointed at neck, shoulders, and hips; all in good condition.

Painted eyes:
4in (10cm) $ **45 - 60***
7-8in (18-20cm)   **75 - 85***
10-12in (25-31cm)   **110 - 135***
14-15in (36-38cm)   **175 - 200***
5in (12cm) googly   **135 - 150**
Flocked celluloid, Lenci-type
6-1/2in (17cm)   **300 - 350**

*Allow extra for unusual dolls.

─ FACTS ─

Germany: Rheinische Gummi und Celluloid Fabrik Co. (Turtle symbol); Buschow & Beck, *Minerva* trademark (Helmet symbol); E. Maar & Sohn, *Emasco* trademark (3 M symbol); Cellba (Mermaid symbol).
Poland: P.R. Zask (ASK in triangle).
France: Petitcolin (Eagle symbol); Société Nobel Francaise (SNF in diamond); Neumann & Marx (Dragon symbol); Société Industrielle de Celluloid (Sicoine).
United States: Parsons-Jackson Co., Cleveland, Ohio, and other companies.
England: Cascelloid Ltd. (Palitoy). 1895-1940s.
Marks: Various as indicated above: may also be in combination with the marks of J. D. Kestner, Kämmer & Reinhardt, Bruno Schmidt, Käthe Kruse and König & Wernicke.

6-1/2in (17cm) flocked celluloid child with turtle mark, all original in Lenci-style. *H & J Foulke, Inc.*

10in (25cm) turtle mark boy, all original. *H & J Foulke, Inc.*

CELLULOID DOLLS *continued*

SNF pair with molded provincial costumes,
9in (23cm) $ 225
Tommy Tucker-type character:
12-14in (31-36cm)   200 - 225

Glass Eyes:
12-13in (31-33cm)   175 - 200*
15-16in (38-41cm)   250 - 275*
18in (46cm)   350 - 400*
21in (53cm)   450 - 475*

*Allow extra for unusual dolls.

K★R 717 or 728,
14-16in (36-41cm) $ 550 - 650

All-Celluloid Baby: Ca. 1910-on. All in
good condition.
6-8in (15-20cm) $ 65 - 85
10-12in (25-31cm)   110 - 135*
15in (38cm)   175 - 200*
21in (53cm)   250 - 300*

SNF black with African features
10in (25cm)   450

*Allow $25-35 extra for glass eyes.

All-Celluloid, Made in Japan: Ca. 1920s.
Molded clothes:
4-5in (10-12cm) $ 60 - 80
8-9in (20-23cm)   150 - 175
Baby, 13in (33cm)   175
24in (61cm)   350 - 400

Occupied Japan, 6-1/2in (17cm)
chubby toddler character   85 - 95

Parsons-Jackson, Stork Mark:
11-1/2in (29cm) baby $ 165 - 185*
14in (36cm) toddler   300 - 350*

*Allow extra for molded shoes and socks.

Celluloid Head Infant: Ca. 1920s-on. Baby
head with glass eyes, cloth body, appropriate
clothes; all in good condition.
12-15in (31-38cm) $ 150 - 200

Celluloid Socket Head Doll: Ca. 1910-on.
Wig, glass eyes, sometimes flirty, open
mouth with teeth; ball-jointed or bent-limb
composition body; dressed; all in good condition.

K★R 701 child,
12-13in (31-33cm) $ 900 - 1100
K★R 717 child, flapper body:
12in (31cm)   350
16-18in (41-46cm)   600 - 650
K★R 700 baby,
14-15in (36-38cm)   325 - 375
K★R 728:
12-13in (31-33cm) baby   350 - 400
20in (51cm) toddler   550 - 650
18in (46cm) flapper   850
F.S. & Co. 1276,
20in (51cm) baby   550 - 600

13in (33cm) celluloid baby
with *Minerva* mark.
H & J Foulke, Inc.

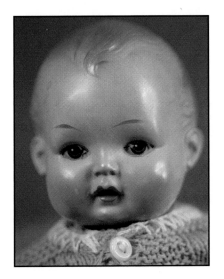

CHAD VALLEY

Chad Valley Doll: All-cloth, usually felt face and velvet body, jointed neck, shoulders and hips; mohair wig, glass or painted eyes; original clothes; all in excellent condition.

Characters, painted eyes,
10-12in (25-31cm) $ 85 - 115
Characters, glass eyes,
17-20in (43-51cm)   1000 - 2000*
Children, painted eyes:
9in (23cm)   135 - 150
13-14in (33-36cm)   375 - 475
16-18in (41-46cm)   550 - 650
Children, glass eyes,
16-18in (41-46cm)   700 - 800
Royal Children, glass eyes,
16-18in (41-46cm)   1650
Mabel Lucie Attwell, glass inset side-glancing eyes, smiling watermelon mouth.
15-17in (38-43cm) $ 750 - 800

Snow White Set:
Dwarfs, 10in (25cm)   **250 - 275 each**
Snow White, 16in (41cm) and
seven 6-1/4in (16cm) dwarfs, all
excellent and boxed, at auction   **4500**

*Depending upon rarity.

FACTS
Chad Valley Co. (formerly Johnson
Bros., Ltd.), Birmingham, England.
1917-on.
Mark: Cloth label usually on foot:
"HYGIENIC TOYS
Made in England by
CHAD VALLEY CO. LTD."

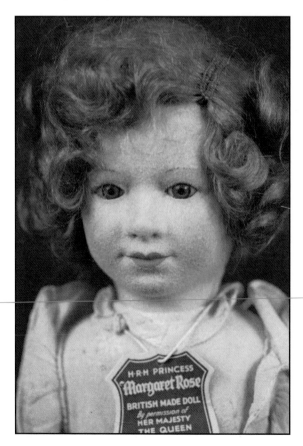

16in (41cm) *Princess Margaret Rose*, all original. *H & J Foulke, Inc.*

MARTHA CHASE

Martha Jenks Chase, Pawtucket, R.I., U.S.A. 1889-on.
Designer: Martha Jenks Chase.
Mark: "Chase Stockinet Doll" stamp on left leg or under left arm, paper label on back (usually gone).

Chase Doll: Head and limbs of stockinette, treated and painted with oils, large painted eyes with thick upper lashes, rough-stroked hair to provide texture, cloth bodies jointed at shoulders, hips, elbows and knees, later ones only at shoulders and hips; some bodies completely treated; appropriate clothing; showing wear, but no repaint.

Baby:

9in (23cm)	$	6000**
13-15in (33-38cm)		575 - 675*
17-20in (43-51cm)		750*
24-26in (61-66cm)		850*

Hospital Baby, 19-20in (49-51cm)	750
Child. molded bobbed hair:	
12-15in (31-38cm)	1200 - 1600
20in (51cm)	2000
Lady,	
13-15in (33-38cm)	1500 - 1600

*Allow extra for a doll in excellent condition or with original clothes.
**Very rare. Not enough price samples to compute a reliable average.

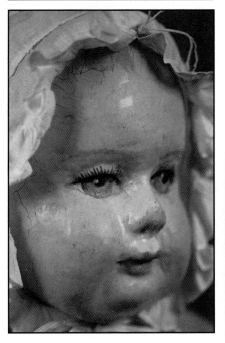

19in (49cm) Chase baby with unusual face. *H & J Foulke, Inc.*

16-1/2in (42cm) Chase baby. *H & J Foulke, Inc.*

MARTHA CHASE *continued*

Man, 15-16in (38-41cm) $ **3000**

Black, Mammy or child
$ **$ 10,000 - 11,000**
Boy with side part and side curl,
    15-16in (38-41cm)   **3000**

Hospital Lady, 64in (163cm) $ **900 - 1200**

Chase black "Mammy".
Nancy A. Smith Collection.

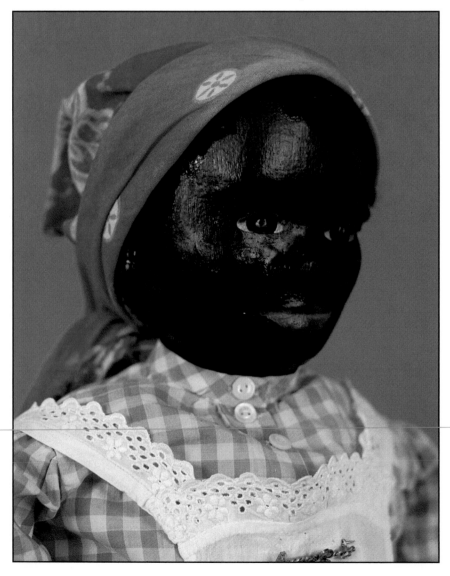

CHINA HEADS

(French)

FACTS
Various French doll firms; some heads sold through French firms may have been made in Germany. 1850s.
Mark: None.

French China Head Doll: China shoulder head, glass or beautifully painted eyes, painted eyelashes, feathered eyebrows, closed mouth, open crown, cork pate, good wig; shapely kid fashion body (may have china arms curved to above elbow); appropriately dressed; all in good condition.

16-17in (41-43cm) $ **3200 - 3700**
15-16in (38-41cm), naked   **2200 - 2500**
16in (41cm) Rohmer-type with trunk,
   wardrobe and accessories   **5000**
Painted short black hair, pink kid body,
   13in (33cm) all original at auction **3630**
Brown hair, extended pierced ear lobes,
   lovely painted eyes with eyelashes,
   15in (38cm)   **4000**

(Attributed to England)

FACTS
Unidentified English firm, possibly Rockingham area. Ca. 1840-1860.
Mark: None.

English China Doll: Flesh-tinted shoulder head with bald head (some with molded slit for inserting wig), painted features, closed mouth; human hair wig. Cloth torso and upper arms and legs, china lower limbs with holes to attach them to cloth, bare feet. Appropriately dressed; all in good condition.

19-22in (48-56cm) $ **2500 - 3000**
   without china limbs   **1200**

13-1/2in (34cm) French china head lady.
Private Collection.

CHINA HEADS (German)

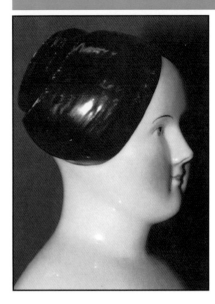

China head with high molded bun.
Jensen's Antique Dolls.

1840s Hairstyles: China shoulder head with black molded hair; may have pink tint complexion; old cloth body; (may have china arms); appropriate old clothes; all in good condition.

Hair swept back into bun:

13-15in (33-38cm)	$	2000 - 2600
18-21in (46-53cm)		3000 - 5500

Fancy braided bun,

22-24in (56-61cm)		5000 - 6000

Long curls, early face

21in (53cm)		3400

K.P.M.:

Brown hair with bun,

16-18in (41-46cm)	$	4000 up*

Young man, brown hair,

16-18in (41-46cm)		3500 up

Kinderkopf (child head),

18-22in (46-56cm)	2200 - 2800

Wood jointed body, china lower limbs:

5-6in (13-15cm)	$	1600 - 1800
11in (28cm)		3500 - 4000

*Depending upon quality, hairdo and rarity.

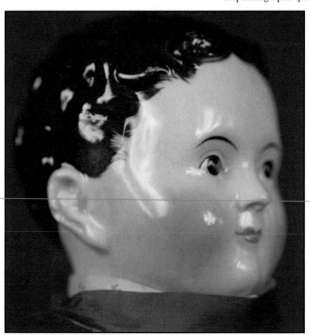

20in (51cm) *Kinderkopf* china head boy. *H & J Foulke, Inc.*

1850s Hairstyles: China shoulder head (some with pink tint), molded black hair (except bald), painted eyes; old cloth body with leather or china arms; appropriate old clothes; all in good condition.

Bald head, some with black areas on top, proper wig. Allow extra for original human hair wig in fancy style.

Fine quality:
15-17in (38-43cm)	$	1000 - 1200
22-24in (56-61cm)		1700 - 1900

Standard quality:
13in (33cm)	$	500 - 550
16-17in (41-43cm)		700 - 800
20-22in (51-56cm)		900 - 1000
4-1/2in (12cm) head only		310

Covered wagon with blue eyes:
6-1/2in (17cm) head only	$	350
15-17in (38-43cm)		675 - 775
21-23in (53-58cm)		1000 - 1100

Covered wagon with brown eyes,
20-22in (51-56cm)	1100 - 1200

Greiner-style with brown eyes:
14-15in (36-38cm)	1000 - 1200
19-22in (48-56cm)	1700 - 2000

Greiner-style with glass eyes:
15-16in (38-41cm)	3850**
22in (56cm)	4800**

**Not enough price samples to compute a reliable average.

25in (64cm) china head with covered wagon hairdo, brown eyes, pink complexion. *H & J Foulke, Inc.*

20in (51cm) china head with Greiner-style hairdo, brown eyes. *H & J Foulke, Inc.*

CHINA HEADS (GERMAN) *continued*

Top: Left: 10in (25cm) child china with *Alice* hairstyle and taüfling-style body. *Kay & Wayne Jensen Collection.* (For information see page 74.)
Right: 14-1/2in (37cm) china with 1860s plain style hairdo. *H & J Foulke, Inc.* (For information see page 74.)

24in (61cm) *Alice* hairdo with molded hairband. *H & J Foulke, Inc.* (For information see page 74.)

CHINA HEADS (GERMAN) *continued*

26in (66cm) china with *Adelina Patti* hairdo. *H & J Foulke, Inc.* (For information see following page.)

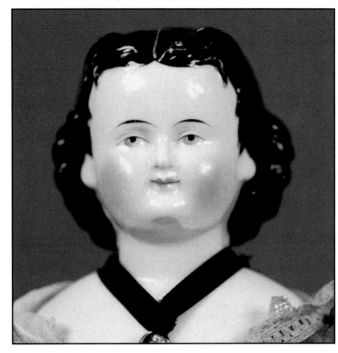

17in (43cm) china with *Dolley Madison* hairdo. *H & J Foulke, Inc.* (For information see following page.)

Waves framing face, brown eyes:
20-21in (51-53cm) $ **1200 - 1500**
With glass eyes,
  18-21in (46-53cm)   **2400 - 2800**

Alice Hairdo, with molded headband (See photograph on page 72.),
  22-24in (56-61cm)   **850 - 950**

Child or Baby, flange swivel neck; taüfling body with china or papier-mâché shoulder plate and hips, china lower limbs; cloth midsection (may have voice box) and upper limbs.
10in (25cm)   **3000 - 3500****

Child with Alice Hairstyle (See photograph on page 72.),
  8-11in (20-28cm) $ **4000****

1860s and 1870s Hairstyles: China shoulder head with black molded hair (a few blondes); old cloth body may have leather arms or china lower arms and legs; appropriate old clothes; all in good condition.
Plain style with center part (so-called flat top and high brow) (See photograph on page 72.):
6-7 in (15-18cm) $ **110 - 115**
14-16in (36-41cm)   **265 - 295**
19-22in (48-56cm)   **375 - 400**
24-26in (61-66cm)   **425 - 525**
28in (71cm)   **625 - 650**
34-35in (86-89cm)   **800**
Molded necklace,
  22-24in (56-61cm)   **600 - 700**
Blonde hair,
  18in (46cm)   **425 - 475**
Brown eyes,
  20-22in (51-56cm)   **600 - 700**
Swivel neck,
  15-1/2in (40cm)   **2000****

Mary Todd Lincoln with snood,
  18-21in (46-53cm) $ **900 - 1000**

Conta and Boehme,
  19in (48cm)   **700 - 800**

Young Man,
  16in (41cm)   **900 - 1100**

Dolley Madison with molded bow (See photograph on page 73.):
14-16in (36-41cm) $ **425 - 475**
21-24in (53-61cm)   **625 - 700**

Adelina Patti (See photograph on page 73.):
13-15in (33-38cm) $ **425 - 475**
19-22in (48-56cm)   **650 - 725**

Jenny Lind,
  21-24in (53-61cm) $ **1600 - 1800**
Curly Top:
  14in (36cm) black hair   **600**
  19in (48cm) tan hair   **900**
Grape Lady, 18in (46cm) $ **2200 - 2500**
Spill Curl, 19-22in (48-56cm)   **900 - 1100**
Morning Glory,
  21in (53cm)   **5500 - 6500****

Fancy hairdo with pierced ears, all original,
  21in (53cm)   **2000**
Fancy hairdo with molded rose, brown eyes, pierced ears, 20in (51cm)   **2425**
Hair pulled back into cascading curls, brown eyes, 22in (56cm)   **2000**
Fancy hairdo with snood,
  23in (58cm)   **2200**

1880s Hairstyles: China shoulder head with black or blonde molded hair; appropriate old clothes; all in good condition. Many made by Alt, Beck & Gottschalck or Kling & Co. (For photograph, see page 5.)
14-16in (36-41cm) $ **325 - 375**
21-23in (53-58cm)   **475 - 525**
28in (71cm)   **700 - 750**

Youth and Old Age, double-faced,
  10in (25cm) at auction   **1600**
Bawo and Dotter, "Pat. Dec. 7/80."
  18-20in (46-51cm)   **400 - 450**

**Not enough price samples to compute a reliable range.

CHINA HEADS (GERMAN) *continued*

*5in (8cm) china head
with lustre snood.
Courtesy of Richard W.
Withington, Inc.*

*Doll is shown larger than
actual size.*

Dressel & Kister: 1890-1920. China shoulder head with varying hairdos and brush stroked hair, delicately painted features; cloth body with china having beautifully molded fingers. Often used as ornamental dolls in only half form as for a boudoir lamp or candy box. (For photograph, see *12th Blue Book*, page 129.)

13in (33cm) tall	$	**1500 up****
Heads only		**675 -750**

1890s Hairstyles: China shoulder head with black or blonde molded wavy hair; appropriate clothes; all in good condition.

8-10in (20-25cm)	$	**100 - 125**
13-15in (33-38cm)		**150 - 195**
19-21in (48-53cm)		**235 - 285**
24in (61cm)		**350**

Molded bonnet, 8in (20cm)	**150 - 165**
Molded "Jewel" necklace, 22in (56cm)	**400**

Pet Name: Ca. 1905. Made by Hertwig & Co. for Butler Bros., N.Y. China shoulder head, molded yoke with name in gold; black or blonde painted hair (one-third were blonde). Used names such as **Agnes, Bertha, Daisy, Dorothy, Edith, Esther, Ethel, Florence, Helen, Mabel, Marion** and **Pauline**.

12-14in (30-36cm)	$	**200 - 250**
18-21in (46-53cm)		**350 - 400**
24in (61cm)		**450**

**Not enough price samples to compute a
reliable average.

CLOTH, PRINTED

━━━━━━━━━ FACTS ━━━━━━━━━

Various American companies, such as Cocheco Mfg. Co., Lawrence & Co., Arnold Print Works, Art Fabric Mills and Selchow & Righter and Dean's Rag Book Company in England. 1896-on.

Mark: Mark could be found on fabric part, which was discarded after cutting.

Cloth, Printed Doll: Names such as: **Dolly Dear, Merry Marie, Improved Foot Doll, Standish No Break Doll,** and others:

7-9in (18-23cm)	$	60 - 70
16-18in (41-46cm)		110 - 125
22-24in (56-61cm)		135 - 165

Uncut sheet, bright colors:

13in (33cm) doll	110 - 125
20in (51cm) doll	135 - 165

Brownies: 1892. Designed by Palmer Cox; marked on foot.

8in (20cm)	75 - 85
Uncut sheet of six	250

Boys and Girls with printed outer clothes, Ca. 1903.

12-13in (31-33cm)	100 - 125
17in (43cm)	150 - 175

Darkey Doll, made up,

16in (41cm)	225 - 250

Aunt Jemima Family,

(four dolls)	65 - 75 each
Punch & Judy,	350 pair
Pitti Sing, uncut	65

Hen and Chicks, uncut sheet	$	65
Tabby Cat		70 - 80
Tabby's Kittens		45 - 55
Ball, uncut		250 - 275
Peck 1886 Santa		225
Topsy, uncut,		
8-1/2 (22cm) two dolls on sheet		195

E.T. Gibson, 1912.

Red bathing suit	165 - 185

George & Martha Washington   **350 pair**

Pillow-type, printed and hand embroidered,

1920s - 1930s, 16in (41cm)	65 - 85

Hug-Me-Tight, 1916. Grace Drayton.

Mother Goose Characters,

11in (28cm)	225 - 250

Orphan Annie, oil cloth		
17in (43cm)		185
Sandy, oil cloth	$	75 - 85
Smitty, oil cloth		60 - 70
Skeezix, oil cloth		60 - 70
Buster Brown and Tige,		325

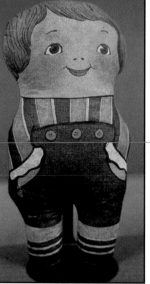

8-1/2in (22cm) printed cloth boy. *H & J Foulke, Inc.*

16-1/2in (42cm) printed and hand-embroidered girl. *H & J Foulke, Inc.*

CLOTH, RUSSIAN

Russian Cloth Doll: All-cloth with stockinette head and hands, molded face with hand-painted features; authentic regional clothes; all in very good condition.

6-1/2in (16cm) child	$	**50 - 55**
11in (28cm) child		**110 - 125**
15in (38cm)		**200 - 250**
Tea Cosy, 20in (51cm)		**250 - 275**

---FACTS---
Unknown craftsmen. Ca. 1930.
Mark: "Made in Soviet Union" sometimes with identification of doll, such as "Ukrainian Woman," "Village Boy," "Smolensk District Woman."

15in (38cm) *Ryasan District Woman*, all original. *H & J Foulke, Inc.*

COLUMBIAN DOLL

Columbian Doll: All-cloth with hair and features hand-painted on a flat face; treated limbs; appropriate clothes; all in very good condition, no repaint or touch up.

15in (38cm)	$	**5000**
20-22in (51-56cm)		**6000 - 7000**
Some wear,		
20-22in (51-56cm)		**4000 - 4200**
Worn,		
29in (74cm)		**2000**

---FACTS---
Emma and Marietta Adams.
1891-1910 or later.
Mark: Stamped on back of body.
Before 1900:
"COLUMBIAN DOLL
EMMA E. ADAMS
OSWEGO CENTRE
N.Y."
After 1906:
"THE COLUMBIAN DOLL
MANUFACTURED BY
MARIETTA ADAMS RUTTAN
OSWEGO, N.Y."

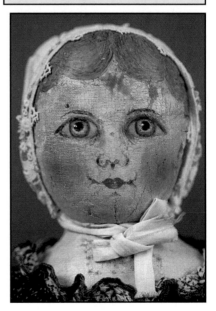

15in (38cm) *Columbian Doll*.
Private Collection.

DANEL (LATER JUMEAU)

Marked Paris Bébé: 1889-1892. Perfect bisque socket head with Jumeau look, good wig, paperweight eyes, closed mouth, pierced ears; composition jointed body; appropriately dressed; all in good condition. This doll was a copy of a Jumeau.

Mark: On Head

TÊTE DÉPOSÉ PARIS BEBE

On Body

PARIS BEBE
Breveté

16-18in (41-46cm)	$ 3800 - 4000
22-24in (56-66cm)	4200 - 4500

Marked Paris Bébé: 1892-on. Character face developed by Jumeau for use with this trademark after he won a lawsuit against Danel. (For photograph see *11th Blue Book*, page 144.)

18-19in (46-48cm)	$ 4800 - 5100
23-25in (58-64cm)	5500 - 6500

Marked B.F.: Ca. 1891. Bébé Français was used by Jumeau after 1892. Perfect bisque head, appropriate wig, paperweight eyes, closed mouth, pierced ears; jointed composition body; appropriate clothes; all in good condition.

Mark:

16-19in (41-48cm)	$ 4400 - 4700
23-25in (58-64cm)	5200 - 5500

FACTS

Danel & Cie., Paris & Montreuil-sous-Bois, France. 1889-1895. **Trademarks:** Paris Bébé, Bébé Français. Both used by Jumeau after winning an 1892 lawsuit.

25in (64cm) *Paris Bébé* with Jumeau character face. *Private Collection.*

DEP

DEP Closed Mouth: Ca. 1890. Perfect bisque head, swivel neck, lovely wig, set paperweight eyes, upper and lower painted eyelashes, closed mouth, pierced ears; jointed French composition and wood body; pretty clothes; all in good condition.

Mark: **DEP**
        (size number)

15in (38cm)	$ 2200 -2500*
18-20in (46-51cm)	2900 - 3200*
25-27in (63-68cm)	4200 - 4500*
Open mouth, 22in (56cm)	1000 - 1200

*Allow more for an especially lovely sample.

Jumeau DEP: Ca. 1899-on. Heads possibly by Simon & Halbig. Perfect bisque socket head (sometimes with **Tête Jumeau** stamp), human hair wig, deeply molded eye socket, sleeping eyes, painted lower eyelashes, upper hair eyelashes (sometimes gone), pierced ears; jointed French composition and wood body (sometimes with Jumeau label or stamp); lovely clothes; all in good condition.

Mark: **DEP**
        8

11-1/2in (29cm)	$	750 - 850
13-15in (33-38cm)		800 - 900
18-20in (46-51cm)		1050 - 1200
23-25in (58-64cm)		1400 - 1700
29-30in (74-76cm)		2200 - 2500
35in (89cm)		3000 - 3200
28in (71cm) all original, in Jumeau box		3400

15in (38cm) *DEP* with walking body, all original. *H & J Foulke, Inc.*

DOOR OF HOPE

Door of Hope: Carved wooden head with painted and/or carved hair; cloth body, some with stubby arms, some with carved hands; original handmade clothes, exact costuming for different classes of Chinese people; all in excellent condition. 25 dolls in the series.

Adult,
 11-13in (28-33cm) $ **450 - 650**
Child,
 7-8in (18-20cm)   **550 - 650**
Amah and **Baby**   **700 - 800**
Manchu Lady,
 carved headdress   **1100 - 1200**

Kindergarten Girl,
 6in (15cm)   **600 - 675**
Bride and **Groom**   **1500 - 1600**
Women or **Girls** with special carving in the hair   **750 - 850**

FACTS
Door of Hope Mission, China; heads by carvers from Ning-Po. 1901-on.
Mark: Sometimes
"Made in China" label.

Door of Hope man, all original. *H & J Foulke, Inc.*

DRESSEL

Marked Holz-Masse: 1875-on. Papier-mâché or composition shoulder head; cloth/composition body. See page 164.

┌─────── **FACTS** ───────┐
Cuno & Otto Dressel verlager & doll factory of Sonneberg, Thüringia, Germany. Bisque heads by Armand Marseille, Simon & Halbig, Ernst Heubach, Gebrüder Heubach. 1700-on. **Trademarks:** Fifth Ave. Dolls (1903), Jutta (1907), Bambina (1909), Poppy Dolls (1912), Holz-Masse (1875).
└─────────────────────────┘

19in (48cm) Jutta 1914 character toddler. *Anna May Case Collection.* (For information see page 83.)

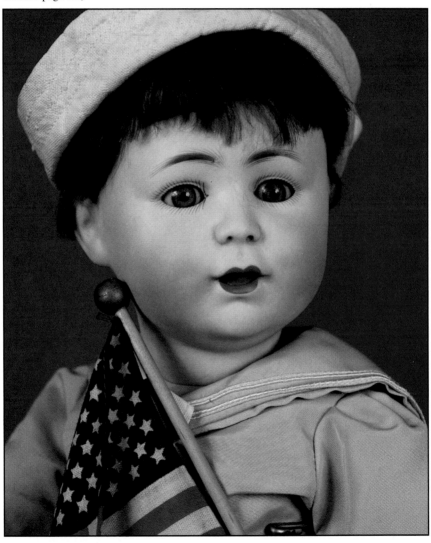

DRESSEL *continued*

Child Doll: 1893-on. Perfect bisque head, good wig, glass eyes, open mouth; suitable clothes; all in good condition.
Mark:

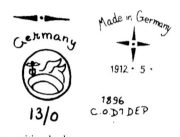

13/0

Composition body:

15-16in (38-41cm)	$	375 - 400
19-21in (48-53cm)		450 - 500
24in (61cm)		525 - 550
32in (81cm)		1100
38in (96cm)		2000 - 2200

#93, 1896 Kid body,

19-22in (48-56cm)	$	500 - 550

Character-type face, similar to **K★R 117n.** (For photograph see *12th Blue Book*, page 151.):

14in (36cm)	950
26in (66cm)	1300 - 1500

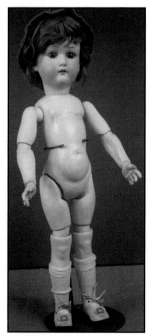

21in (53cm) 1349, flapper body. *H & J Foulke, Inc.*

Portrait Series: 1896. Perfect bisque heads with portrait faces, glass eyes, some with molded mustaches and goatees; composition body; original clothes; all in good condition. Some marked "S" or "D" with a number.

13in (33cm) Uncle Sam	$	1200 - 1500
15in (38cm) Admiral Dewey and		
Officers		1200 - 1600
8in (20cm) Old Rip		600 - 700
10in (25cm) Farmer		700 - 800
10in (25cm) Buffalo Bill		750

Marked Jutta Child: Ca. 1906-1921. Perfect bisque socket head, good wig, sleep eyes, open mouth, pierced ears; ball-jointed composition body; dressed; all in good condition. Head made by Simon & Halbig. (See photograph on page 5.)
Mold **1348** or **1349**
Mark:

1349
Jutta
S &H
11

14-16in (36-41cm)	$	675*
19-21in (43-53cm)		700 - 800*
24-26in (61-66cm)		900 - 1000*
30-32in (76-81cm)		1600 - 1800
38-39in (96-99cm)		3000 - 3500

*Allow $150 extra for flapper body with high knee joint.

14in (36cm) character from Portrait Series. *Kay & Wayne Jensen Collection.*

Character Child: 1909-on. Perfect bisque socket head, ball-jointed composition body; mohair wig, painted eyes, closed mouth; suitable clothes; all in good condition. Glazed inside of head. (For photograph see *10th Blue Book*, page 179.)

Mark:

C.O.D.
A/2

10-12in (25-31cm)	$ 1250 - 1400**
16-18in (41-46cm)	2200 - 2500**

Composition head:

19in (48cm)	2600 - 3000**
13in (33cm) wear on nose and lips	1300

Marked C.O.D. Character Baby: Ca. 1910-on. Perfect bisque character face with marked wig or molded hair, painted or glass eyes; jointed baby body; dressed; all in good condition.

12-13in (31-33cm)	$ 350 - 375
16-18in (41-46cm)	450 - 500
22-24in (56-61cm)	675 - 775

Marked Jutta Character Baby: Ca. 1910-1922. Perfect bisque socket head, good wig, sleep eyes, open mouth; bent-limb composition baby body; dressed; all in good condition. (See photograph on page 81.)

Simon & Halbig:

16-18in (41-46cm)	$ 650 - 750
23-24in (58-61cm)	1300 - 1500

Other Makers: (Armand Marseille, E. Heubach):

16-18in (41-46cm)	450 - 500
23-24in (58-61cm)	700 - 800

Mark:

Heubach 6½ Koppelsdorf
Jutta · Baby
Dressel
Germany
1922
10 ½

Jutta
1914
8

Toddler:

16-18in (41-46cm)	1150 - 1250
22in (56cm)	1600 - 1800

**Not enough price samples to compute a reliable range.

Lady Doll: Ca. 1920s. Bisque socket head with young lady face, good wig, sleep eyes, closed mouth; jointed composition body in adult form with molded bust, slim waist and long arms and legs, feet modeled to wear high-heeled shoes; all in good condition.

Mark:

1469
C O. Dressel
Germany
2

#1469:

14in (36cm)

Naked	$ 2000 - 2300
Original clothes	3000 - 4200

14in (36cm) 1469 lady doll.
H & J Foulke, Inc.

E. D. BÉBÉ

Marked E. D. Bébé: Perfect bisque head, wood and composition jointed body; good wig, beautiful blown glass eyes, pierced ears; nicely dressed; good condition.

Closed mouth:

15-18in (38-46cm)	$	2800 - 3200*
22-24in (56-61cm)		3600 - 4000*
28in (71cm)		4200 - 4400*

Open mouth:

18-20in (38-51cm)	1800 - 2000*
25-27in (64-69cm)	2500 - 2700*

*For a pretty face.

Note: Dolls with Jumeau look but signed E. D. are Jumeau factory dolls produced when Emile Douillet was director of the Jumeau firm, 1892-1899. They do not have the word "Déposé" under the E. D. They should be priced as Jumeau dolls. (For photograph see *10th Blue Book*, page 181.)

FACTS

Etienne Denamur of Paris, France.
1889-on.

Mark:

E 8 D
DÉPOSÉ

15in (38cm) E.D. child.
H & J Foulke, Inc.

EDEN BÉBÉ

Marked Eden Bébé: Ca. 1890. Perfect bisque head, fully-jointed or 5-piece composition jointed body; beautiful wig, large set paperweight eyes, closed or open/closed mouth, pierced ears; lovely clothes; all in nice condition.

Closed mouth:

14-16in (36-41cm)	$	2200 - 2400
21-23in (53-58cm)		2800 - 3000
5-piece body, 12in (31cm)		1200 - 1500

Open mouth,

19-20in (48-51cm)	1900 - 2000

FACTS

Fleischmann & Bloedel, doll factory,
Paris, France. 1890, then into
S.F.B.J. in 1899.
Trademark: Eden Bébé (1890), Bébé
Triomphe (1898).
Mark: "EDEN BEBE, PARIS"

20in (51cm) *Eden Bébé.*
Jensen's Antique Dolls.

FRENCH FASHION-TYPE (POUPÉE)

French Fashion Lady (Poupée): Perfect unmarked bisque shoulder head, swivel or stationary neck, kid body *poupée peau* or cloth body with kid arms — some with wired fingers; original or old wig, lovely blown glass eyes, closed mouth, earrings; appropriate old clothes; all in good condition. Fine quality bisque.

12-13in (31-33cm)	$	**1800 up***
15-16in (38-41cm)		**2500 up***
18-19in (46-48cm)		**3200 up***
21in (53cm)		**3500 up***
33in (84cm)		**6750**

Dainty oval face,
12-14in (31-36cm)	**2300 - 2500**

Round face, cobalt eyes (shoulder head),
13-15in (33-38cm)	**2300 - 2500**

Fully-jointed wood body (*poupée bois*), naked,
15-17in (38-43cm)	$	**5000 - 5500+**

Benoit Martin, wood body, naked,
18in (46cm) at auction	**17,500**

Portrait face, wood body,
18in (46cm)	**30,000 up**

Twill-over-wood body (Simon & Halbig-type):
9-10in (23-25cm)	**4000 - 4500**
15-17in (38-43cm)	**5000 - 6000**

*Allow extra for fancy original clothing. Value of doll varies greatly depending upon the appeal of the face. Also, allow additional for kid-over-wood upper and bisque lower arms.
+Allow extra for joints at ankle and waist.

FACTS
Various French firms. Ca. 1860-1930.
(See also *Bru, Jumeau, Gaultier,* and *Gesland.*)

23in (58cm) Barrois-type *poupée peau.*
H & J Foulke, Inc. (For information see page 86.)

20in (51cm) *poupée peau.*
Private Collection. (See also photograph on page 8.)

FRENCH FASHION-TYPE (Poupée) *continued*

E.B. Poupée: E. Barrois 1862-1877. Perfect bisque shoulder head (may have a swivel neck), glass eyes (may be painted with long painted eyelashes), closed mouth; appropriate wig; adult kid body, some with jointed wood arms or wood and bisque arms; appropriate clothing. All in good condition. (See photograph on page 85.)

Mark:

$$E . I \text{ DÉPOSÉ } B.$$

14-16in (36-41cm)	$	2500 - 3000
20-22in (51-56cm)		3200 - 3500

Marked Huret Poupée: Ca. 1850. China or bisque shoulder head, good wig, painted eyes, closed mouth; kid body; beautifully dressed; all in good condition.

17in (43cm)	$15,000 - 20,000
Swivel neck	32,000
Gutta-percha body	20,000**
Boots, 2in (5cm)	1000

Radiquet and Cordonnier: molded breasts, bisque arms, one bent at elbow, bisque lower legs, original signed stand.

17in (43cm)	$13,000 - 15,000

L.D.:

19in (48m) at auction	6000

Period Clothes, Fashion Lady clothing:

Dress	$ 500 - 1000 up
Boots	300 - 350
Elaborate wig	300 - 400
Nice wig	150 - 250

Rohmer Poupée: Ca. 1857-1880. China or bisque swivel or shoulder head, jointed kid body, bisque or china arms, kid or china legs; lovely wig, set glass eyes, closed mouth, some ears pierced; fine costuming; entire doll in good condition.

16-18in (41-46cm)	$	4000 - 4500*

Mark:

Parasol Doll, original silk outfit,

18in (46cm) tall	2200

Rochard Head, with Stanhope necklace 1868. 6-3/4in (17cm)

at auction	24,300

A. Dehors, 1860.
17in (43cm) shoulder head,

at auction	18,000

*Allow extra for fancy original clothing. Value of doll varies greatly depending upon the appeal of the face. Also, allow additional for kid-over-wood upper and bisque lower arms.
**Not enough price samples to compute a reliable average.

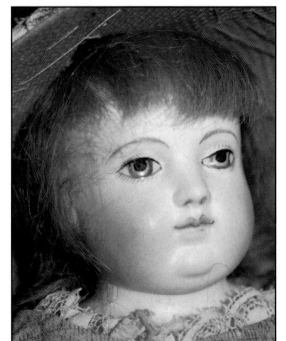

16in (41cm) *poupée peau* with painted eyes. *Courtesy of Richard W. Withington, Inc.*

FROZEN CHARLOTTE

(Bathing Doll)

Frozen Charlotte: All-china doll, black or blonde molded hair, painted features; hands extended, legs separated but not jointed; no clothes; perfect condition. Good quality.

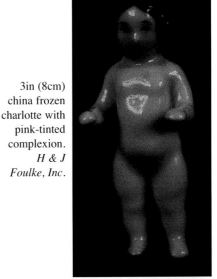

2-3in (5 - 8cm) $	**50 - 65***
4-5in (10-13cm)	**110 - 135***
6-7in (15-18cm)	**165 - 185***
9-10in (23-25cm)	**275 - 325***
14-15in (36-38cm)	**550 - 600**
Pink tint, early hairdo:	
2-1/2–3-1/2in (6-9cm)	**200 - 225**
5in (13cm)	**350 - 375**
10in (25cm)	**750**
Pink tint with bonnet:	
3-1/2 (9cm)	**400 - 450**
5in (13cm)	**525 - 575**
Black china, 5in (13cm)	**165 - 195**
Black boy, molded turban and pants,	
3in (8cm)	**275 - 300**
Black boy, molded shift,	
5in (13cm)	**300 - 350**
Blonde hair, molded bow,	
5-1/2in (14cm)	**175 - 200**
Wig, lovely boots, 5in (13cm)	**175 - 195**

3in (8cm) china frozen charlotte with pink-tinted complexion. *H & J Foulke, Inc.*

All-Bisque:	
5in (13cm) $	**135 - 160**
Parian-type (1860s style),	
5in (13cm)	**195 - 225**
Alice style with pink boots,	
5in (13cm)	**325 - 350**
Fancy hairdo and boots,	
4-1/2in (11cm)	**275 - 300**
Molded clothes,	
3-1/4in (9cm)	**225**
Early boy, blonde hair,	
9in (23cm)	**450**

*Allow extra for pink tint, fine decoration and modeling, unusual hairdo.

```
――――――― FACTS ―――――――
      Various German firms.
      Ca. 1850s-early 1900s.
Mark: None, except for "Germany," or
         numbers or both.
```

5in (13cm) parian-type frozen charlotte. *H & J Foulke, Inc.*

FULPER

Fulper Child Doll: Perfect bisque head, good wig; kid jointed or composition ball-jointed body; set or sleep eyes, open mouth; suitably dressed; all in good condition. Good quality bisque.

Kid body,
  18-21in (46-53cm) $ 375 - 425*
Composition body:
  16-18in (41-46cm)   450 - 500*
  22-24in (56-61cm)   550 - 600*

Fulper Baby:
  16-18in (41-46cm)   550 - 650*
  22-24in (56-61cm)   750 - 850*
Toddler,
  15-17in (38-43cm) very cute   800 - 900

*Allow more for an especially pretty or cute doll.

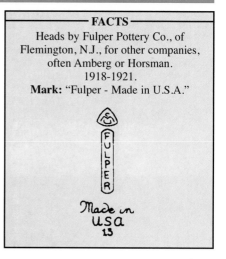

┌──────── FACTS ────────┐
Heads by Fulper Pottery Co., of
Flemington, N.J., for other companies,
often Amberg or Horsman.
1918-1921.
Mark: "Fulper - Made in U.S.A."

20-1/2in (52cm)
Fulper character.
Keifer Collection.

GAULTIER

Marked F.G. Fashion Lady (Poupée Peau): 1860 to 1930. Perfect bisque swivel head on bisque shoulder plate, original kid body, kid arms with wired fingers or bisque lower arms and hands; original or good French wig, lovely glass stationary eyes, closed mouth, ears pierced; appropriately dressed; all in good condition.

Mark: "F.G." on side of shoulder.

12-13in (30-33cm)	**$ 1800 - 2100***
16-17in (41-43cm)	**2500 - 2600***
20in (51cm)	**2800 - 2900***
23in (58cm)	**3200 -3400***
35in (89cm)	**6750****
Wood body, *(Poupée Bois)*,	
16-18in (41-46cm)	**$ 4200 - 4500**
Late doll in ethnic costume,	
8-9in (20-23cm)	**750 - 850**
Painted eyes,	
16-17in (41-43cm)	**1600 - 1800**

Approximate size chart:
Size 3/0 = 10-1/2in (27cm)
    2/0 = 11-1/2in (29cm)
      1 = 13-1/2in (34cm)
      2 = 15in (38cm)
      3 = 17in (43cm)
      5 = 20in (51cm)
      6 = 22in (56cm)

*Allow extra for original clothes.

**Not enough price samples to compute a reliable average.

FACTS

François Gauthier (name changed to Gaultier in 1875); St. Maurice, Charenton, Seine, Paris, France. (This company made only porcelain parts, not bodies.) 1860 to 1899 (then joined S.F.B.J.)

18-1/2in (47cm) *poupée bois* (wood jointed body). *Kay & Wayne Jensen Collection.*

Marked F.G. Bébé: Ca. 1879-1887. Perfect bisque swivel head, large bulgy paperweight eyes, closed mouth, pierced ears; dressed; all in good condition. So-called "Block letters" mark.

Mark:

F . 7.G

Composition body:

13-15in (33-38cm)	$	4000 - 4400
18-20in (46-51cm)		5000 - 5200
22-23in (56-58cm)		5400 - 5700
27-28in (69-71cm)		6500 - 7200
33-35in (84-89cm)		7500 - 8000

Kid body:

13in (33cm)	4200 - 5200
16in (41cm)	5500 - 5750
20-22in (51-56cm)	6500 - 7000

Marked F.G. Bébé: Ca. 1887-1900. Bisque head, beautiful large set eyes; well dressed; all in good condition. So-called "Scroll" mark.

Mark:

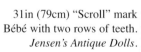

Closed mouth:

5-6in (13-15cm)	$	750 - 800
15-17in (38-43cm)		2800 - 3100
22-24in (56-61cm)		3600 - 3900
27-28in (69-71cm)		4300 - 4600

Open mouth:

15-17in (38-43cm)	1750 - 1950
20-22in (51-56cm)	2100 - 2400
31in (79cm)	3300 - 3600

28in (71cm) F 12 G block letters. *Kay & Wayne Jensen Collection.*

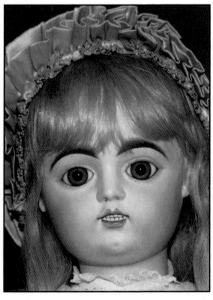

31in (79cm) "Scroll" mark Bébé with two rows of teeth. *Jensen's Antique Dolls.*

GESLAND

Fashion Lady (Poupée): Perfect bisque swivel head, good wig, paperweight eyes, closed mouth, pierced ears; stockinette body on metal frame with bisque hands and legs; dressed; all in good condition.

Early face,
16-20in (41-51cm)	**$ 5500 - 6200***

F.G. face:
14in (36cm)	**3600 - 3800***
16-20in (41-51cm)	**4000 - 4500***
28in (71cm)	**5500 - 6000***
Body only for 14in (36cm)	**900**

*Allow extra for original clothes.

Man with molded black hair and hat,
18-1/2in (47cm) at auction	**22,500**

Bébé: Perfect bisque swivel head; composition shoulder plate, good wig, paperweight eyes, closed mouth, pierced ears; stockinette body on metal frame with composition lower arms and legs; dressed; all in good condition.

Beautiful early face:
14-16in (36-41cm)	**$ 4900 - 5100**
22-24in (56-61cm)	**5900 - 6400**

"Scroll" mark face:
14-16in (36-41cm)	**2800 - 3100***
22-24in (56-61cm)	**4000 - 4500***

*Deduct 25% for ruddy bisque.

FACTS

Heads: Francois Gaultier, Paris, France.
Bodies: E. Gesland, Paris, France.
1860-1928.
Mark: Head: **F G**

Body: Sometimes stamped E. Gesland

18-1/2in (47cm) F.G. head on Gesland body. *H & J Foulke, Inc.*

GOOGLY-EYED DOLLS

All-Bisque Googly: Jointed at shoulders and hips, molded shoes and socks; mohair wig, glass eyes, impish mouth; undressed; in perfect condition.

#217, 501, 330 and others:

4-1/2–5in (11-13cm)	$	550 - 600
5-1/2–6in (14-15cm)		700 - 800

#189, 192 swivel necks:

4-1/2–5in (11-13cm)	750 - 850
5-1/2–6in (14-15cm)	900 - 1000
7in (18cm)	1200 - 1300

S.W.C. #405 (glass eyes), 6-1/2in (17cm)	950
S.W.C. #408 (painted eyes), 5in (13cm)	250

Jointed elbows and knees (Kestner), swivel neck,

5in (13cm)	$	2500
6-7in (15-18cm)		3000 - 3500
Baby, 4-1/2in (12cm)		450 - 475

Painted eyes, molded hair:

4-1/2 (12cm)	400 - 425
6in (15cm)	550 - 600

K & R 131, 7in (18cm)	$2600 - 3000**

**Not enough price samples to compute a reliable range.

Painted eyes, composition body: Perfect bisque swivel head; 5-piece composition toddler or baby body; cute clothes; all in good condition.

A.M., E. Heubach, Goebel, R.A.:

6-7in (15-18cm)	$	500 - 550*
9-10in (23-25cm)		900 - 950*

#252 A.M. Kewpie-type baby,

9in (23cm)	1200 - 1300

Gebrüder Heubach:

6-7in (15-18cm)	575 - 625*
7in (18cm) Winker	850 - 900
9in (23cm) with top knot	1350 - 1450

*Allow extra for unusual models.

Glass eyes, composition body: Perfect bisque head; original composition body; cute clothes; all in nice condition.

JDK 221:

12-15in (30-38cm) toddler	$5500 - 6500
19in (48cm)	8600
JDK 112, 7in (18cm)	1250 - 1350

A.M. #323 and other similar models by H. Steiner, E. Heubach, Goebel and Recknagel:

6-7in (15-18cm)	$	900 - 1100
10-11in (25-28cm)		1400 - 1600
13in (33cm)		2000
Baby body, 10-11in (25-28cm)		1200 - 1300

A.M. #253 (watermelon mouth):

6-7in (15-18cm)	1000 - 1200
9in (23cm)	1600

A.M. #200, 241:

8in (20cm)	1200 - 1500
11-12in (28-31cm)	2100 - 2300

A.M. #240,

10in (25cm) toddler	3000 - 3200

B.P. 686, 12in (31cm), at auction	3600

Demalcol (Dennis, Malley, & Co. London, England),

9-10in (23-25cm)	750 - 850

E. Heubach:

#419, 7in (18cm), at auction	2750
#322, 8-1/2in (21cm)	1100

FACTS

J.D. Kestner, Armand Marseille, Hertel, Schwab & Co., Heubach, H. Steiner, Goebel and other German and French firms. Ca. 1911-on.

GOOGLY-EYED DOLLS *continued*

7in (18cm) A.M. 254 googly.
H & J Foulke, Inc.

7in (18m) Kestner 112 googly
H & J Foulke, Inc.

11-3/4in (30cm) SFBJ 245 googly.
Kay & Wayne Jensen Collection. (For information see page 94.)

14in (36cm) 165 googly.
Geri & Ralph Gentile. (For information see page 94.)

Hertel, Schwab & Co. —
#163, toddler, 15-16in (38- 41cm)
$ **5000 - 5600**
#165, baby (see photograph on page 93):
12-13in (31-33cm)	**3900 - 4100**
16in (41cm)	**4800 - 5000**
19in (48cm)	**5500**
Toddler 15in (38cm)	**3800 - 4200**

#172, 173:
Baby, 16in (41cm)	**5000****
Toddler,	
10-12in (25-31cm)	**4000 - 5000****
16in (41cm)	**6000 - 6500****

G. Heubach —
Einco:
11in (28cm) 5-piece body $	**3200**
14-15in (36-38cm)	**4000 - 5000**
Elizabeth, 7-9in (18-23cm)	**1650 - 1850**

#8678, 9573:
6-7in (15-18cm)	**900 - 1100**
9in (23cm)	**1250 - 1500**

Handwerck, Max:
Molded hat,
10-13in (25-33cm)	**2100 - 2300**
Double-faced	**2200 - 2400**

K ★ R 131:
8in (20cm), 5-piece body	**$2500 - 3500****
15-16in (38-41cm)	**7500**

Kley & Hahn 180,
16-1/2in (43cm) $ **3500****

Limbach SK, 10in (25cm) $ **1350 - 1450**

P.M. 950,
11in (28cm) $ **1600****

SFBJ #245 (see photograph on page 93):
8in (20cm), 5-piece body $ **1500 - 1700****
11in (28cm) jointed body, with wardrobe
at auction **3750**
15in (38cm) **4200 - 4600****

Schieler, 9in (23cm) at auction **1650**

Disc Eyes,
DRGM 954642 black or white,
11-12in (28-31cm) $ **1250 - 1500****

Composition face: 1911-1914.
Hug Me Kids, Little Bright Eyes, and other trade names. Round all-composition or composition mask face, wig, round glass eyes looking to the side, watermelon mouth; felt body; original clothes; all in very good condition.
10in (25cm) $	**650 - 700**
14in (36cm)	**850 - 950**

**Not enough price samples
to compute a reliable range.

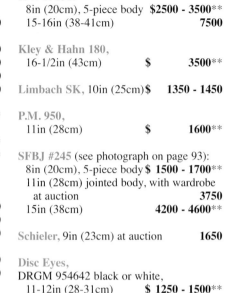

Shoulder head
googly 9232.
*Richard Wright
Antiques.*

GREINER

Marked Greiner: Papier-mâché shoulder head with blonde or black molded hair, painted features; homemade cloth body, leather arms; nice old clothes; entire doll in good condition, some wear acceptable.

'58 label:

15-17in (38-43cm)	$	800 - 950
20-23in (51-58cm)		1150 - 1350
28-30in (71-76cm)		1500 - 1800
38in (97cm)		2500
Much worn:		
20-23in (51-58cm)		650 - 750
28-30in (71-76cm)		850 - 950
Glass eyes,		
20-23in (51-58cm)		2200 - 2500

'72 label:

19-22in (48-56cm)	$	500 - 550
29-31in (71-79cm)		800 - 900
35in (89cm)		1100 - 1200

FACTS

Ludwig Greiner of Philadelphia, Pa., U.S.A. 1858-1883, but probably as early as 1840s.

Mark: Paper label on back shoulder:

GREINER'S
IMPROVED
PATENTHEADS
Pat. March 30th '58

or

GREINER'S
PATENT DOLL HEADS
No 7
Pat. Mar. 30'58. Ext.'72

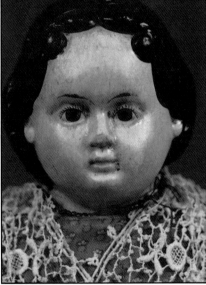

24in (61cm) Greiner with '58 label.
H & J Foulke, Inc.

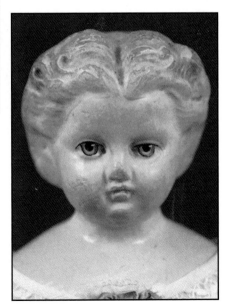

20in (51cm) Greiner
with '72 label.
H & J Foulke, Inc.

HEINRICH HANDWERCK

Marked Handwerck Child Doll: Ca. 1885 -on. Perfect bisque socket head, original or good wig, sleep or set eyes, open mouth, pierced ears; composition ball-jointed body with Handwerck stamp; dressed; entire doll in good condition.

#69, 89, 99 or no mold #:

10-12in (25-31cm)	$	500 - 600*
14-16in (36-41cm)		650 - 700*
19-21in (43-53cm)		700 - 800*
23-25in (58-64cm)		800 - 900*
28-30in (71-76cm)		1200 - 1400*
32-33in (79-84cm)		1700 - 1800*
36in (91cm)		2200 - 2500
42in (107cm)		3800 - 4200
29in (74cm) totally original with exceptional clothes, at auction		2100

#79, 109, 119:

14-16in (36-41cm)	$	700 - 750
22-24in (56-61cm)		900 - 1000
41in (104cm)		4300

*Allow extra for original wig, clothes and shoes.

#139 and other shoulder heads, kid body :

16-18in (41-46cm)	$	350 - 400
22-24in (56-61cm)		450 - 500

#79, 89 closed mouth:

18-20in (46-51cm)	$	2300 - 2500
24in (61cm)		2800 - 3200

#189, open mouth,

18-20in (46-51cm)	900 - 950
6-1/2in (17cm) at auction	660

Bébé Cosmopolite, 19in (48cm),
all original and boxed   **1000**

FACTS

Heinrich Handwerck, doll factory, Waltershausen, Thüringia, Germany. Heads by Simon & Halbig. 1855-on. **Trademarks:** Bébé Cosmopolite, Bébé de Réclame, Bébé Superior.
Mark:

Germany   HANDWERCK

HEINRICH HANDWERCK   109-11
SIMON B HALBIG

Germany

20in (51cm) 109
child, all original.
H & J Foulke, Inc.

MAX HANDWERCK

Marked Max Handwerck Child Doll: Perfect bisque socket head, original or good wig, set or sleep eyes, open mouth, pierced ears; original ball-jointed body; well dressed; all in good condition. Some mold **#283, 297** or **421**.

16-18in (41-46cm)	$	375 - 400
22-24in (56-61cm)		525 - 575
31-32in (79-81cm)		1000 - 1100
38-39in (97-99cm)		2000 - 2200

Bébé Elite Character Baby,
19-21in (48-53cm)	$	550 - 650

---FACTS---
Max Handwerck, doll factory, Waltershausen, Thüringia, Germany. Some heads by Goebel. 1900-on.
Trademarks: Bébé Elite, Triumph-Bébé.
Mark:

33in (84cm) 421 child. *H & J Foulke, Inc.*

HERTEL, SCHWAB & Co.

Marked Character Baby: Perfect bisque head; bent limb baby body; dressed; all in good condition.
#130, 142, 150, 151, 152:

10-12in (25-31cm)	$	425 - 500
15-17in (38-43cm)		575 - 675
19-21in (48-53cm)		700 - 750
24-25in (61-64cm)		900 - 1000

---FACTS---
Hertel Schwab & Co., porcelain factory, Stutzhaus, near Ohrdruf, Thüringia, Germany. 1910-on.
Mark:

26in (66cm) 152 character baby.
H & J Foulke, Inc.

HERTEL, SCHWAB & Co. *continued*

#142 all-bisque, painted eyes,
11in (28cm) $ 850 - 900
#169 (open mouth),
18-20in (46-51cm)   1000 - 1200**
#125 (so-called Patsy Baby),
11-12in (28-31cm)   800 - 900**
#126 (so called Skippy),
10-12in (25-31cm)   900 - 1100**

Child Doll: Ca. 1910. Perfect bisque head, mohair or human hair wig, sleep eyes, open mouth with upper teeth; good quality jointed composition body (some marked K & W); dressed; all in good condition. Mold **#136.**

14-17in (36-43cm) $ 475 - 525
20-22in (51-56cm)   575 - 625
24-25in (61-64cm)   700 - 750

Marked Character Child: Perfect bisque head, painted or sleeping eyes, closed mouth; jointed composition body; dressed; all in good condition.

#134, 149, 141:
13in (33cm) $ 3500 - 3800
16-18in (41-46cm)   6500 - 8500**
#154 (closed mouth):
14-16in (36-41cm)   2300 - 2500
19in (48cm)   3100
#154, 166 (open mouth):
16-18in (41-46cm)   1200 - 1400
31in (79cm) at auction   4000
#169 (closed mouth),
19-21in (48-53cm) toddler   3500 - 4000
#127 (so-called Patsy):
17in (43cm) $ 2000**

**Not enough price samples to compute a reliable range

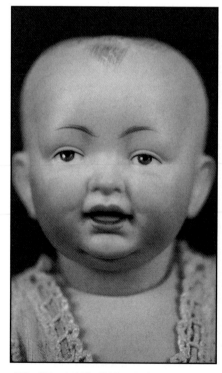

12in (31cm) 142 all-bisque character baby.
H & J Foulke, Inc.

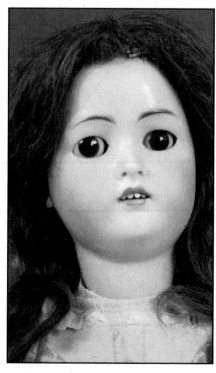

25in (64cm) 136 child, all original.
H & J Foulke, Inc.

ERNST HEUBACH

D.E.P. 1902   Heubach · Kopplesdorf.
300·14/0
2/0   Germany

Heubach Child Doll: Ca. 1888-on. Perfect
bisque head; dressed; all in good condition.
#275 or horseshoe, kid or cloth body:

19-21in (48-53cm)	$	**275 - 325**
24in (61cm)		**425 - 450**

#250, 251, composition body:

8-9in (20-23cm) 5-piece body	**210 - 235**
16-18in (41-46cm)	**350 - 400**
23-24in (58-61cm)	**500 - 550**

Painted bisque, **#250, 407,**

7-8in (18-20cm)	**110 - 135**

#312 SUR (for Seyfarth & Reinhard):

14in (36cm)	**375 - 400**
28in (71cm)	**850 - 900**
45-46in (113-115cm)	**3500**

Character Children: 1910-on. Perfect
bisque shoulder head with molded hair in various styles, some with hair bows, painted
eyes, open/closed mouth; cloth body with
composition lower arms,
#261, 262, 271 and others,

12in (31cm)	$	**400 - 450****

**Not enough price samples to compute a
reliable range.

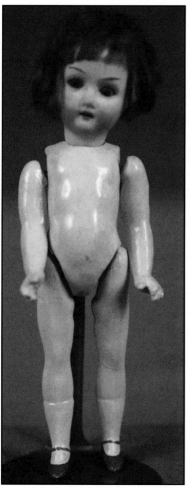

7-1/2in (19cm) 250 flapper girl.
H & J Foulke, Inc.

13in (33cm) 271 character.
H & J Foulke, Inc.

ERNST HEUBACH *continued*

Character Baby: 1910-on. Perfect bisque head, good wig, sleep eyes, open mouth (sometimes also wobbly tongue and pierced nostrils); composition bent-limb baby; dressed; all in good condition.

#300, 320, 342 and others:

5-1/2–6in (14-15cm)	$ 250 - 275
8-10in (20-25cm)	250 - 275
14-17in (36-43cm)	425 - 500
19-21in (48-53cm)	550 - 650
24-25in (61-64cm)	850 - 900

Toddler:

9-10in (23-25cm) 5-piece body	375 - 450

15-17in (38-43cm)	650 - 750
23-25in (58-64cm)	1250 - 1500

Infant: Ca. 1925. Perfect bisque head; cloth body.

#349, 339, 350,

13-16in (33-41cm)	$ 575 - 675**

#338, 340,

14-16in (36-41cm)	725 - 825**

**Not enough price samples to compute a reliable range.

22in (56cm) 300 character baby, *Jensen's Antique Dolls.*

GEBRÜDER HEUBACH

Heubach Character Child: Ca. 1910. Perfect bisque head; jointed composition or kid body; dressed; all in good condition. (For photographs of Heubach dolls see *Focusing On Dolls*, pages 30-68 and previous *Blue Books*.)

#5636, 7663, laughing child, glass eyes:
12-13in (31-33cm)	$ **1600 - 1900**
15-18in (38-46cm)	**2500 - 2800**

#5689 smiling child,
27in (69cm)	**3500 - 4000**

#5730 Santa,
19-21in (48-53cm)	**1800 - 2200**

#5777 Dolly Dimple:
19-22in (48-56cm)	**3000 - 3200**
Shoulder head,	
21in (53cm) with hairline	**1000**

#6969, 6970, 7246, 7347, 7407, 8017, pouty child (must have glass eyes):
12-13in (31-33cm)	$ **2000 - 2500**
16-19in (41-48cm)	**3500 - 4000**
24in (61cm)	**5500 - 6000**

#6692 and other shoulder head pouties,
14-16in (36-41cm)	**750 - 950**

#7407 painted eye, wigged,
16in (41cm)	**2100**

─── **FACTS** ───
Gebrüder Heubach, porcelain factory, Licht and Sonneberg, Thüringia, Germany. 1820-on; doll heads, 1910-on.
Mark:

11in (28cm) 7711 character girl.
Jensen's Antique Dolls.

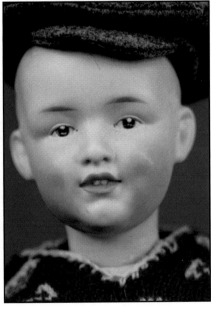

15in (38cm) 7820 character boy.
H & J Foulke, Inc.

GEBRÜDER HEUBACH *continued*

#7604, 7820 and other smiling socket heads,
14-16in (36-41cm) $ 800 - 1000
#7602, 6894 and other socket head pouties,
14-16in (36-41cm)   750 - 950
#7622 and other socket head pouties (wide
lips), 14-17in (36-43cm)   1000 - 1250
#7661 squinting eyes, crooked mouth,
19in (48cm)   6750
#7665 Smiling, 16in (41cm)   1800
#7679 Whistler socket head:
10in (25cm)   800 - 900
14in (36cm)   1100 - 1300
#7684 Screamer,
16-19in (41-48cm)   2500 - 3000
#7711 12-14in (31-36cm)   1200 - 1400
#7743 big ears, 17in (43cm)   5500 - 6000
#7764 singing girl, 16in (41cm)   10,000
#7788, 7850 Coquette (See photograph on
page 8.),
14in (36cm)   1200
Shoulder head, 12in (31cm)   700 - 775
#7865, 14in (36cm)   3000

#7852 shoulder head, molded coiled
braids, 16in (41cm)   2200
#7853 shoulder head, downcast eyes,
14in (36cm)   1650 - 1850
#7911, 8191 grinning:
11in (28cm)   850 - 900
15in (38cm)   1200 - 1250
#7925, 7926 lady,
18-19in (46-48cm)   2800 - 3100
#8050 smiling girl with hairbow,
18in (46cm)   10,000
#8192:
9-11in (23-28cm)   450 - 550
14-16in (36-41cm)   800 - 900
18-22in (46-56cm)   1100 - 1300
#8381 Princess Juliana,
16in (41cm)   10,000 - 12,000
#8550, molded tongue sticking out:
13in (33cm) intaglio eyes   950 - 1050
17in (43cm) glass eyes   1300 - 1500
#8556, googly-type face   11,500

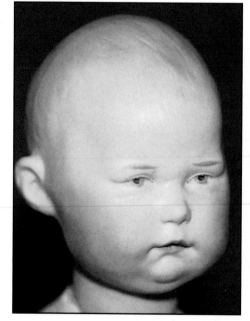

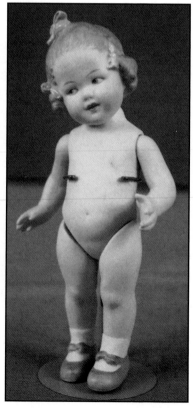

16in (41cm) 7744 character boy.
Private Collection.

9in (23cm) all-bisque girl with rare
swivel neck. *H & J Foulke, Inc.*

GEBRÜDER HEUBACH *continued*

#9102 Cat, 6in (15cm) $ 1000 - 1150
#9141 Winker:
  9in (23cm) glass eye   1500
  7in (18cm) painted eye   850 - 950
#9467 Indian, 14in (36cm)   2500 - 3000
#10532, 20-22in (51-53cm)   1200 - 1300
#10586, 10633,
  18-20in (46-51cm)   750 - 850

#11173 Tiss Me,
  8in (20cm)   1850 - 2000
Baby Bokaye, Bonnie Babe,
  7-8in (18-20cm)   900 - 950
#1907 Jumeau,
  20-22in (51-56cm)   2400 - 2500

All-Bisque:
Position Babies and Action Figures,
  5in (13cm)   350 - 500
Girl with bobbed hair,
  9in (23cm)   900 - 1000*
Girl with head band,
  9in (23cm) 1100 - 1200*
Girl with three bows,
  9in (23cm) 1500 - 1800*
Boy, 8in (20cm)
   1200 - 1300
Boy or girl,
  4-1/2in (11cm) 300 - 400

*Allow extra for swivel neck.

Heubach Babies: Ca. 1910. Perfect bisque head; composition bent-limb body; dressed; all in nice condition.
#6894, 7602, 6898, 7759 and other pouty babies; #7604 laughing:
  4-1/2in(12cm) $ 225 - 275
  6in (15cm)   275 - 300
  10-12in (25-31cm)   500 - 700
  14in (36cm)   750 - 800
#7877, 7977 Baby Stuart:
  12in (31cm) glass eyes   2100
  13-15in (33-38cm),
    painted eyes   1300 - 1500

#8420, glass eyes,
  14in (36cm)   1250 - 1300
#7959, molded pink cap,
  14in (36cm) at auction   4200

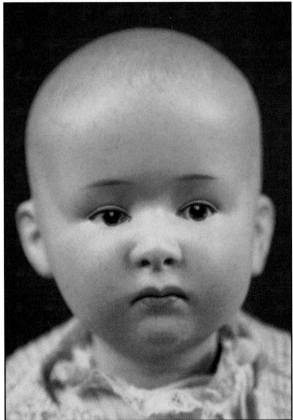

12in (31cm) 6894 character baby. *H & J Foulke, Inc.*

JULLIEN

Marked Jullien Bébé: Perfect bisque head, lovely wig, paperweight eyes, closed mouth, pierced ears; jointed wood and composition body; pretty old clothes; all in good condition.

17-19in (43-48cm)	$	3500 - 3700
24-26in (61-66cm)		4200 - 4500
Open mouth:		
19-21in (48-53cm)		1600 - 1800
29-30in (74-76cm)		2600 - 2900

FACTS

Jullien, Jeune of Paris, France.
1875- 1904 when joined with S.F.B.J.
Mark: "JULLIEN" with size number

JuLLiEN
1

27in (69cm) *Jullien Bébé. H & J Foulke, Inc.*

JUMEAU

Poupée Peau Fashion Lady: Late 1860s-on. Perfect bisque swivel head on shoulder plate, old wig, paperweight eyes, closed mouth, pierced ears; all-kid body; appropriate old clothes; all in good condition.

Mark on body: JUMEAU
                    MEDAILLE D'OR
                    PARIS

Standard face:

11-1/2–13in (29-33cm)	$	2600 - 3000*
17-18in (43-46cm)		3200 - 3800*
20in (51cm)		3800 - 4000*

Very pretty face,

15-17in (38-43cm)	3500 - 4000*

Poupée Bois, wood body with bisque limbs,

18in (46cm)	5000 - 6000*

Later face with large eyes:

10-12in (25-31cm)	1800 - 2000*
14-15in (36-38cm)	2400 - 2500*

So-called "Portrait Face" (see *11th Blue Book*, page 221):

19-21in (48-53cm)	6000 - 7000*

Wood body (*poupée bois*),

19-21in (48-53cm)	9000 - 11,000*

Rare lady face,

29in (74cm) at auction	39,000

Period Clothes for Bébés:

Jumeau shift	$	400 - 600
Jumeau shoes		350 - 400
Jumeau dress and hat		900 up

*Allow extra for original clothes.

FACTS

Maison Jumeau, Paris, France. 1842- on.
Trademark: Bébé Jumeau (1886)
Bébé Prodige (1886)
Bébé Francais (1896)

20in (51cm)
Jumeau *poupée peau*, all original.
Courtesy of Richard W. Withington, Inc.

Long-Face Triste Bébé: 1879-1886. Designed by Carrier-Belleuse. Marked with size (9-16) number only on head, blue stamp on body. Perfect bisque socket head with beautiful wig, paperweight eyes, closed mouth, applied pierced ears; jointed composition body with straight wrists (separate ball joints on early models); lovely clothes; all in good condition. (See photograph on page 108.)

20-21in (51-53cm)	**$ 16,000 - 20,000**
28-30in (71-76cm)	**22,000 - 25,000**

Size	9 =	21in (53cm)
	11 =	24in (61cm)
	13, 14 =	29-30in (74-76cm)

Portrait Jumeau: 1877-1883. Usually marked with size number only on head, blue stamp on body; skin or other good wig; spiral threaded enamel paperweight eyes, closed mouth, pierced ears; jointed composition body with straight wrists and separate ball joints; nicely dressed; all in good condition.

Premiere Jumeau (for photograph see *12th Blue Book*, page 224):

10-12in (25-30cm)	**$ 5000 - 5500***	
14-15in (36-38cm)	**6000 - 7000***	
18-19in (46-48cm)	**7500 - 8000***	

*Expect dust specks, uneven eye cuts and uneven eyebrows.

Almond-Eyed (see photograph on page 108):

Sizes:	4/0 = 12in (30cm)
	3/0 = 13-1/2in (34cm)
	2/0 = 14-1/2in (37cm)
	0 = 16in (41cm)
	1 = 17in (43cm)
	2 = 18-1/2in (47cm)
	3 = 20in (51cm)
	4 = 23in (58cm)
	5 = 25in (64cm)

12-14-1/2in (30-37cm)	**$ 10,000 - 12,000**
16-18-1/2in (41-47cm)	**16,000 - 18,000**
20in (51cm)	**20,000***
23in (58cm)	**28,000***
25in (64cm)	**45,000***

*Allow extra for unusually large eyes.

21in (53cm) Portrait Jumeau, Size 10. *Mary Barnes Kelley Collection.*

JUMEAU *continued*

E.J.Bébé: 1881-1886. Perfect bisque socket head with good wig, paperweight eyes, closed mouth, pierced ears; jointed composition body with straight wrists, early models with separate ball joints; lovely clothes; all in good condition. (See photograph on page 108.)

Early Mark:

8
E.J.

17-18in (43-46cm) size 6	$		**10,500**
19-21in (48-53cm) size 8			**12,500**
23in (58cm) size 9			**17,500**
EJA, 25in (64cm)			**30,000 - 32,000**

Mid to Late Period Mark:
DEPOSÉ

E. 8 J.

10in (25cm)	$	**5200 - 5700**
14-16in (36-41cm)		**6100 - 6600**
19-21in (48-53cm)		**7000 - 7600**
25-26in (64-66cm)		**8800 - 9800**
30in (76cm)		**11,000 - 12,000**
Later Tête-style face:		
15-16in (38-41cm)		**4800 - 5000**
18-19in (46-48cm)		**5300 - 5800**
25-26in (64-66cm)		**7200 - 8000**
30in (76cm)		**8800 - 9200**

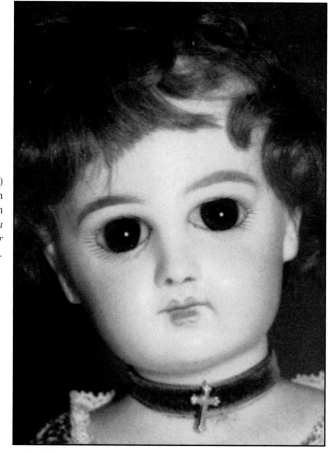

14-1/2in (37cm) *Deposé Jumeau* with kid child fashion body. *Rhoda Shoemaker Collection.*

JUMEAU *continued*

16in (41cm) E 6 J, standard face. *H & J Foulke, Inc.* (For information see page 107.)

23in (58cm) extreme almond-eyed Jumeau. *Private Collection.* (For information see page 106.)

24in (61cm) Jumeau *Triste*. *Private Collection.* (For information see page 106.)

Incised "Jumeau Déposé" Bébé: 1886-1889. Head incised as below, blue stamp on body. Perfect bisque socket head with good wig, paperweight eyes, closed mouth, pierced ears; jointed composition body with straight wrists; lovely clothes; all in good condition.

Mark: Incised on head: DÉPOSÉ
JUMEAU
8

14-15in (36-38cm)	$ 4500 - 5000
18-20in (46-51cm)	5500 - 6000
24-25in (61-64cm)	6800 - 7500
21in (53cm) all original	8250

Tête Jumeau Bébé: 1885-on, then through S.F.B.J. Red stamp on head as indicated below, blue stamp or "Bebe Jumeau" oval sticker on body. Perfect bisque head, original or good French wig, beautiful stationary eyes, closed mouth, pierced ears; jointed composition body with jointed or straight wrists; original or lovely clothes; all in good condition. (See also photograph on page 110.)

Mark:

DÉPOSÉ
TETE JUMEAU
BTE SGDG
6

10in (25cm) #1	$ 4200 - 4800*
12-13in (31-33cm)	3300 - 3600*
15-16in (38-41cm)	3900 - 4300*
18-20in (46-51cm)	4400 - 4800*
21-23in (53-58cm)	4800 - 5000*
25-27in (64-69cm)	5000 - 5500*
30in (76cm)	6000 - 6400*
34-36in (86-91cm)	7000 - 8000*
10in (25cm) #1 with trunk and wardrobe, at auction	6200
13in (33cm), all original factory clothes	5200
Lady body, 20in (51cm)	5200 - 5500*
Open mouth:	
14-16in (36-41cm)	2300 - 2700
20-22in (51-56cm)	2900 - 3200
24-25in (61-64cm)	3300 - 3500
27-29in (69-74cm)	3600 - 3800
32-34in (81-86cm)	4000 - 4200

*Allow extra for original clothes.

16-1/2in (42cm) *Déposé 7* Portrait-type Jumeau. *Kay and Wayne Jensen Collection.* (For information see page 106.)

25in (64cm) unmarked **Tête Jumeau**, open mouth. *H & J Foulke, Inc.*

Bébé Phonographe,
24-25in (61-64cm) **6500 - 7500**

Marked E.D. Bébé: Mark used during the Douillet management, 1892-1899. Perfect bisque head, closed mouth.
18-20in (46-51cm) $ **4500 - 4800**
Mark:

E.8.D

Marked B.L. Bébé: Ca. 1880. For the Louvre department store. Perfect bisque socket head, closed mouth.
Mark:

B.9 L.

18-21in (46-53cm) $ **4400 - 4800**

Marked R.R. Bébé: Ca. 1880s. Perfect bisque head, closed mouth.
Mark:

R 10 R

21-23in (53-58cm) $ **4900 - 5300**
22in (56cm) open mouth **3500**

Approximate sizes of E.J.s and Têtes:
1 = 10in (25cm)
2 = 11in (28cm)
3 = 12in (31cm)
4 = 13in (33cm)
5 = 14-15in (36-38cm)
6 = 16in (41cm)
7 = 17in (43cm)
8 = 19in (48cm)
9 = 20in (51cm)
10 = 21-22in (53-56cm)
11 = 24-25in (61-64cm)
12 = 26-27in (66-69cm)
13 = 29-30in (74-76cm)

#230 Character Child: Ca. 1910. Perfect bisque socket head, open mouth, set or sleep eyes, good wig; jointed composition body; dressed; all in good condition.
16in (41cm) $ **1600**
21-23in (53-58cm) **2000**

19in (48cm) **Tête Jumeau** *8. H & J Foulke, Inc.* (For information see page 109.)

JUMEAU *continued*

#1907 Jumeau Child: Ca. 1907-on.
Sometimes red-stamped "Tête Jumeau."
Perfect bisque head, open mouth.

14in (36cm)	$	**2000 - 2200**
16-18in (41-46cm)		**2300 - 2500**
24-25in (61-64cm)		**3000 - 3200**
33-34in (84-87cm)		**3800 - 4000**

Papier-mâché face,
22-24in (56-61cm) $ **800 - 1000****

DEP Jumeau: See page 79 for details.
SFBJ Tête Jumeau: See page 173 for details.
Jumeau Characters: Ca. 1900. Tête Jumeau mark. Perfect bisque head with glass eyes, character expression.

#203, 208 and others $ **50,000 up**
#221 Great Ladies, 10-11in (25-28cm)
all original **550 - 650**

Double-faced laughing and crying,
18in (46cm) at auction **14,500**
Princess Elizabeth Jumeau: 1938 through S.F.B.J. Perfect bisque socket head highly colored, glass flirty eyes.

Mark: **Body Incised:**

UNIS
FRANCE 149
306
JUMEAU
1938
PARIS

JUMEAU
PARIS
Princess

18-19in (46-48cm)	$	**1600 - 1800**
32-33in (81-84cm)		**2700 - 3200****

**Not enough price samples to compute a reliable range.

KAMKINS

Marked Kamkins: Molded mask face with painted features, wig; cloth body and limbs; original clothing; all in excellent condition.

18-20in (46-51cm)	$	**1200 - 1400**
Fair to good condition		**750 - 850**
With swivel joints or molded		
derriére,		**2000 - 2500**

FACTS

Louise R. Kampes Studios, Atlantic City, N.J. U.S.A. 1919-1928 and perhaps longer.
Mark: Red paper heart on left side of chest:

KAMKINS
A DOLLY MADE TO LOVE
PATENTED
FROM
L R KAMPES
ATLANTIC CITY,
N J

Also sometimes stamped with black on foot or back of head:
KAMKINS
A DOLLY MADE TO LOVE
PATENTED BY L.R. KAMPES
ATLANTIC CITY,   N.J.

18in (46cm) *Kamkins*, all original.
H & J Foulke, Inc.

KÄMMER & REINHARDT

Child Doll: 1886-1895. Perfect bisque head; ball-jointed composition body; appropriate clothes; all in good condition.
#192:
Closed mouth:

6-7in (15-18cm)	$	600 - 700*
10in (25cm)		900 - 1000
16-18in (41-46cm)		2800 - 3000
22-24in (56-61cm)		3200 - 3400

Open mouth:

7-8in (18-20cm)	550 - 600*
12in (31cm)	700 - 800
14-16in (36-41cm)	900 - 1000
20-22in (51-56cm)	1300 - 1500
26-28in (66-71cm)	1900 - 2100

*Allow $100-200 extra for a fully-jointed body.

FACTS

Kämmer & Reinhardt of Waltershausen, Thüringia, Germany. Bisque heads often by Simon & Halbig. 1886-on.
Trademarks: Majestic Doll, Mein Liebling (My Darling), Der Schelm (The Flirt), Die Kokette (The Coquette), My Playmate.
Mark: Size number is height in centimeters.

K ✡ R
SIMON & HALBIG
116/A
50

29in (74cm)
192 child.
*H & J
Foulke, Inc.*

KÄMMER & REINHARDT *continued*

Child Doll: 1895-1930s. Perfect bisque head, open mouth; K & R ball-jointed composition body; appropriate clothes; all in good condition.

#191, 290, 403 or size number only+:

5-piece body,

4-1/2-5in (12-13cm)	$	**450 - 495**
7-8in (18-20cm)		**425 - 475**

Fully-jointed body,

8-10in (20-25cm)	**650 - 750**
12-14in (31-36cm)	**600 - 700***
16-17in (41-43cm)	**750 - 800***
19-21in (48-53cm)	**850 - 950***
23-25in (58-64cm)	**1050 - 1150***
29-31in (74-79cm)	**1400 - 1600***
35-36in (89-91cm)	**2200 - 2500***
39-42in (99-107cm)	**3600 - 4200***

12in (31cm) in original box with exceptional clothes, at auction **1700**

Closed mouth, 6in (15cm) **600 - 650**

+Numbers 15-100 low on neck are centimeter sizes, not mold numbers.

*Allow $50-100 additional for flirty eyes; allow $200 extra for flapper body; allow $100 for walking body.

Child Doll: Shoulder head, kid body; all in good condition.

17-18in (41-46cm)	$	**450 - 500**
22in (56cm)		**550 - 650**

22in (56cm) child doll. *H & J Foulke, Inc.*

KÄMMER & REINHARDT *continued*

Character Babies or Toddlers: 1909-on.
Perfect bisque head; K & R composition
body; nicely dressed; all in good condition.
(See *Simon & Halbig Dolls, The Artful
Aspect* for photographs of mold numbers not
pictured here or on page 116.)

#100 Baby, painted eyes:

12in (31cm)	$	575 - 625
14-15in (36-38cm)		725 - 800
18-20in (46-51cm)		1000 - 1200
Glass eyes, 16in (41cm)		2000

#126, 22 baby body:

10-12in (25-31cm)	450 - 525*
14-16in (36-41cm)	550 - 600*
18-20in (46-51cm)	700 - 800*
22-24in (56-61cm)	850 - 950*
30-33in (76-84cm)	1800 - 2200*

#126 all-bisque baby:

6in (15cm)	750 - 800
8-1/2in (21cm)	1000 - 1100**

#126 all-bisque toddler,

7in (18cm)	1400 - 1500**

#126, 22 5-piece toddler body:

6-7in (15-18cm)	$	750 - 800+
9-10in (23-25cm)		850 - 900+
15-17in (38-43cm)		800 - 900
23in (58cm)		1050 - 1150

#126 toddler fully-jointed:

12in (31cm)	$	650 - 700*
15-17in (38-41cm)		1000 - 1200*
23-25in (58-64cm)		1400 - 1500*
28-30in (71-76cm)		1800 - 2000*

*Allow $50-75 extra for flirty eyes.

#128 baby body,

20in (51cm)	1500 - 1600

#128 toddler body,

16-18in (41-46cm)	1400 - 1500

#121, 122 baby body:

10-11in (25-28cm)	600 -650
15-16in (38-41cm)	800 - 1000
23-24in (58-61cm)	1300 - 1500

#121, 122, toddler body:

13-14in (33-36cm)	1050 - 1200
20-23in (51-58cm)	1500 - 1700

#118A baby body,

15in (38cm)	2100**

#119 baby body,

24in (61cm), at auction	16,000

#926, composition head
5-piece toddler body,

17in (43cm)	500 - 600*

"Puz": composition
head baby:

16-17in (41-43cm)	350 - 400*
25in (64cm)	650 - 750*

*Allow $50 additional for
flirty eyes.
+With "Star fish" hands.
**Not enough price samples
to compute a reliable range.

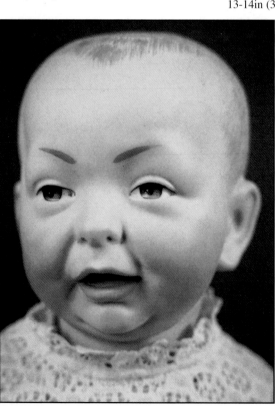

20in (51cm) 100 *Baby.*
H & J Foulke, Inc.

KÄMMER & REINHARDT *continued*

Character Children: 1909-on. Perfect bisque-socket head; K & R composition ball-jointed body; nicely dressed; all in good condition. (See *Simon & Halbig, The Artful Aspect* for photographs of mold numbers not pictured here or on pages 116 and 117.)

#101 (Peter or Marie):

8-9in (20-23cm)	
5-piece body	$ 1300
8-9in (20-23cm)	
jointed body	1800 - 2000
12in (31cm)	2500 - 2800
15-16in (38-41cm)	3800 - 4200
19-20in (48-51cm)	5000 - 5500
Glass eyes:	
15in (38cm)	11,500
20in (51cm)	14,000 - 15,000

#102:

12in (31cm)	25,000**
22in (55cm)	50,000 - 60,000**

#103, 104,

22in (56cm)	75,000 up**
#105, 22in (56cm)	170,000
#106, 22in (56cm)	145,000

#107 (Carl):

12in (30cm)	16,000 - 19,000
22in (56cm)	50,000 - 55,000
#108 at auction	277,095

#109 (Elise):

9-10in (23-25cm)	3000 - 3500
14in (36cm)	7500 - 8500
19-21in (48-53cm)	13,000 - 15,000
Glass eyes,	
20in (51cm)	18,000 - 20,000

#112, 112x,

16-18in (41-46cm)	$ 16,000

#114 (Hans or Gretchen):

8-9in (20-23cm) jointed body	1800 - 2200
12in (31cm)	3200
15-16in (38-41cm)	4200 - 4500
19-20in (48-51cm)	5500 - 6000

Glass eyes:

15in (38cm)	8000 - 9000
20in (51cm)	12,000 - 14,000

#115,

15-16in (38-41cm)	
toddler	5500 - 6000**

#115A:

Baby, 14-16in (36-41cm)	3500 - 3850
Toddler, 15-16in (38-41cm)	4500 - 5000
19-20cm (48-51cm)	5500 - 6000

#116,

16in (41cm) toddler	4500 - 5000**

#116A, open/closed mouth:

Baby, 10-11in (25-28cm)	1500 - 1800
Baby, 14-16in (36-41cm)	2300 - 2600
Toddler,16in (41cm)	3000 - 3500

#116A, open mouth:

Baby, 14-16in (36-41cm)	1800 - 2000
Toddler, 16-18in (41-46cm)	2000 - 2250

**Not enough price samples to compute a reliable range.

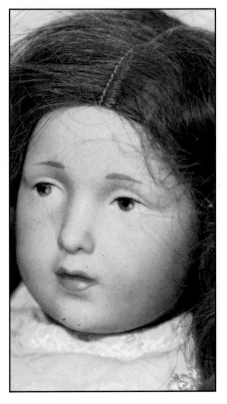

13-1/2in (34cm) 109 child. *Mary Barnes Kelley Collection.*

128 character baby. *H & J Foulke, Inc.*
(For information see page 114.)

15in (38cm) 115 toddler. *H & J Foulke, Inc.*
(For information see page 115.)

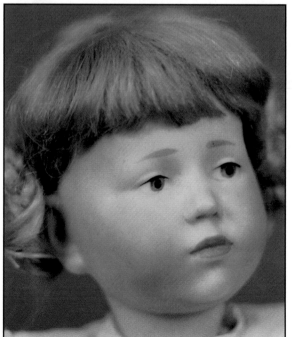

12in (31cm) 101 character
girl. *Private Collection.* (For
information see page 115.)

KÄMMER & REINHARDT *continued*

14in (36cm) 117a character child. *H & J Foulke, Inc.* (For information see page 118.)

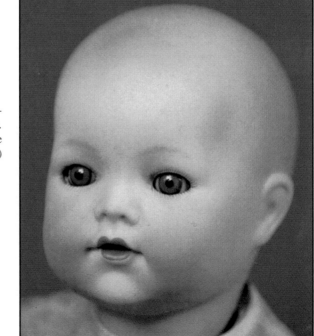

14in (36cm) 173 toddler. *H & J Foulke, Inc.* (For information see page 118.)

KÄMMER & REINHARDT *continued*

#117, 117A, closed mouth (may have an
H. Handwerck body):

8in (20cm)	$ 2400 - 2500
12in (30cm)	3200 - 3500
14-16in (36-41cm)	4000 - 4300
18in (46cm)	4800 - 5300
22-23in (56-58cm)	6300 - 6800
30-32in (76-81cm)	7500 - 8500
23in (58cm) all original, boxed,	
at auction	9500

#117n, flirty eyes:

14-16in (36-41cm)	1400 - 1500*
20-22in (51-56cm)	1900 - 2100*
28-30in (71-76cm)	2500 - 2600*

#117n, sleep eyes:

14-16in (36-41cm)	1000 - 1100
22-24in (56-61cm)	1500 - 1600
30-32in (76-81cm)	1900 - 2100

#117x flapper, 14in (36cm)   3700 - 3900**
#117, open mouth,
27in (69cm)   4700 - 5000**
#123, 124 (Max & Moritz),
17in (43cm) each   18,000 - 23,000**

#127:

Baby, 10in (25cm)	800 - 850
14-15in (36-38cm)	1300 - 1400
20-22in (51-56cm)	1800 - 2000
Toddler or child,	
15-16in (38-41cm)	1450 - 1600
Toddler, 25-27in (64-69cm)	2200 - 2500

#135 child,
14-16in (36-41cm)   1500 - 1900**
#201, 13in (33cm)   1500**
#214, 15in (38cm)   2100 - 2500**
Infant: 1924-on. Perfect bisque head; cloth
body, composition hands; nicely dressed; all
in good condition.
#171, 172,
14-15in (36-38cm) $ 3500**
#173, toddler (composition body),
14in (36cm)   1650**
#175,
11in (28cm) h.c.   1100 - 1200**

*Allow extra for flapper body.
**Not enough price samples to compute a
   reliable range.

18in (46cm) 117n
flapper with flirty
eyes. *H & J
Foulke, Inc.*

KESTNER

Child doll, early socket head: Ca. 1880. Perfect bisque head, plaster dome; Kestner composition ball-jointed body, some with straight wrists and elbows; well dressed; all in good condition. Many marked with size numbers only.

#169, 128, long-face and round face with no mold number, closed mouth:

12in (31cm)	$	1750 - 1850*
14-16in (36-41cm)		2000 - 2200*
19-21in (48-53cm)		2300 - 2500*
24-25in (61-64 cm)		2600 - 2800*
29in (74cm)		3000*

Face with square cheeks, face with white space between lips, no mold number, closed mouth (see photograph on page 120):

11-12in (28-30cm)	$	2000 - 2200*
14-16in (36-41cm)		2200 - 2500*
19-21in (48-53cm)		2600 - 2800*
24-25in (61-64cm)		3000 - 3200*

Very pouty face:

10-12in (25-31cm)	$	2600 - 2800*
14-16in (36-41cm)		3000 - 3300*
19-21in (48-53cm)		3600 - 3800*

#XI,

12-14in (31-36cm)	3000 - 3500
18-21in (46-53cm)	3600 - 3800

#103,

28-32in (71-78cm)	3500 - 4500

A.T.-type:

Closed mouth, 18in (46cm)	$	8000 up**
Open mouth, 19in (48cm)		2500

Bru-type, molded teeth, jointed ankles:

20in (51cm)	$	5000
Kid body, 24in (61cm)		3200

Open mouth, square cut teeth:

12-14in (31-36cm)	$	1000 - 1200
16-18in (41-46cm)		1400 - 1600
24-25in (61-64cm)		1900 - 2000

*Allow 20% more for original clothes, wig and shoes. Allow more for an especially beautiful face.
**Not enough price samples to compute a reliable average.

FACTS

J.D. Kestner, Jr., doll factory, Waltershausen, Thüringia, Germany. Kestner & Co., porcelain factory, Ohrdruf. 1816-on.

11in (28cm) closed-mouth pouty child. *H & J Foulke, Inc.*

KESTNER *continued*

20in (51cm) closed-mouth child with white space between lips. *H & J Foulke, Inc.* (For information see page 119.)

18in (46cm) 160 child. *H & J Foulke, Inc.* (For information see page 122.)

Early open-mouth child with chunky body. *Kay & Wayne Jensen Collection.* (For information see page 119.)

KESTNER *continued*

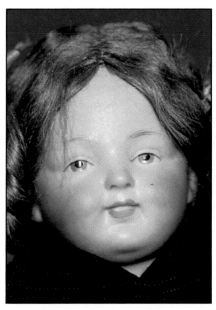

12in (31cm) 185 character child. Kay & Wayne Jensen Collection. (For information see page 123.)

13-1/2in (34cm) 167 child, all original. *H & J Foulke, Inc.* (For information see page 122.)

12-1/2in (32cm) 143 child. *H & J Foulke, Inc.* (For information see page 123.)

KESTNER *continued*

Child doll, early shoulder head: Ca. 1880s. Perfect bisque head, plaster dome, good wig, set or sleep eyes; sometimes head is slightly turned; kid body with bisque lower arms; marked with size letters or numbers. (No mold numbers.)

Closed mouth:

12in (31cm)	$ 650 - 675*
14-16in (36-41cm)	750 - 850*
20-22in (51-56cm)	900 - 950*
26in (66cm)	1100 - 1300*

A.T.-type, closed mouth,

18in (46cm)	7000 up**

Open/closed mouth,

16-18in (41-46 cm)	650 - 750

Open mouth (turned shoulder head):

16-18in (41-46cm)	500 - 600
22-24in (56-61cm)	700 - 750

Open mouth, square cut teeth,

14-16in (36-41cm)	1000 - 1200

*Allow $100-200 extra for a very pouty face or swivel neck.

Child doll, bisque shoulder head, open mouth: Ca. 1892. Kid body, some with rivet joints. Plaster dome, good wig, sleep eyes, open mouth; dressed, all in good condition. (See *Kestner, King of Dollmakers* for photographs of mold numbers not pictured here.)

HEAD MARK:

154 8 dep
D made in Germany

BODY MARK:

#145, 154, 147, 148, 166, 195:

12-13in (31-33cm)	$ 300 - 350*
16-18in (41-46cm)	450 - 500*
20-22in (51-56cm)	550 - 600*
26-28in (66-71cm)	800 - 900*

*Allow additional for a rivet jointed body and/or jointed composition arms.

Child doll, open mouth: Bisque socket head on Kestner ball-jointed body; dressed; all in good condition. (See *Kestner, King of Dollmakers* for photographs of mold numbers not pictured here.)

HEAD MARK: *made in Germany. 8. 162.*

BODY MARK:

Germany
5-1/2

or

Excelsior
DRP N. 70686
Germany

Mold numbers 142, 144, 146, 164, 167, 171, 214:

10-21in (25-31cm)	$ 550 - 650*
14-16in (36-41cm)	750 - 850*
18-21in (46-53cm)	850 - 950*
24-26in (61-66cm)	1000 - 1100*
30in (76cm)	1200 - 1500
36in (91cm)	2200 - 2500
42in (107cm)	3750 - 4250

#128, 129, 149, 152, 160, 161, 173, 174:

10-12in (25-31cm)	$ 700 - 800*
14-16in (36-41cm)	900 - 1000*
18-21in (46-53cm)	1100 - 1250*
24-26in (61-66cm)	1300 - 1400*

*Allow 30% additional for all original clothes, wig and shoes.

#155, fully-jointed body:

7-8in (18-20cm)	$ 800 - 900
10in (25cm) 5-piece body	750 - 800

#171: Daisy, blonde mohair wig,

18in (46cm) only	1000 - 1300

#168, 196, 215:

18-21in (46-53cm)	700 - 750
26-28in (66-71cm)	800 - 900
32in (81cm)	1000 - 1100

**Not enough price samples to compute a reliable average.

(See photographs on pages 120 and 121.)

Character Child: 1909-on. Perfect bisque head character face, plaster pate, wig, painted or glass eyes, closed, open or open/closed mouth; Kestner jointed composition body; dressed; all in good condition. (See *Kestner, King of Dollmakers* for photographs of mold numbers not pictured here.)

#143 (Pre 1897):

7in (18cm)	$	**725 - 750**
9-10in (23-25cm)		**800 - 850**
12-14in (31-36cm)		**900 - 1000**
18-20in (46-51cm)		**1300 - 1400**
27in (69cm)		**1800 - 2000**

#178-190:

Painted eyes:

12in (31cm)	**1800 - 2200**
15in (38cm)	**3000 - 3400**
18in (46cm)	**4000 - 4500**

Glass eyes:

12in (31cm)	**2800 - 3200**
15in (38cm)	**4000 - 4500**
18in (46cm)	**5000 - 5500**
Boxed set, 15in (38cm)	
painted eyes	**12,500****
Boxed set, 15in (38cm) glass eyes	**17,500****

#191, glass eyes, 19in (48cm)

at auction	**6200**

#206:

12in (31cm)	**4000 - 5000****
19in (48cm)	**12,000 - 15,000****

#208:

Painted eyes:

12in (31cm)	**4000 - 5000****
23-24in (58-61cm)	**12,000 - 15,000****

#220 toddler (See photograph on page 125.):

14-16in (36-41cm)	**5000 - 6000**
24in (61cm)	**7500 - 8000**

#239 toddler,

15-17in (38-43cm)	**4000****

#241,

21-22in (53-56cm)	**7000 - 7500****

#249:

13-14in (33-36cm)	**1100 - 1200**
20-22in (51-56cm)	**1800**

Max & Moritz:

12in (31cm) pair, at auction	**40,000**

****Not enough price samples to compute a reliable range.

#260:

Toddler:

8-10in (20-25cm)	$	**900 - 1000**
19in (48cm)		**1200 - 1400**

Jointed body:

12-14in (31-36cm)	**800 - 850**
18-20in (46-51cm)	**900 - 1100**
29in (75cm)	**1400 - 1500**
35in (88cm)	**1800 - 2000**
42in (107cm)	**4000**

Teenage body,

14in (36cm)	**900 - 1000**

Character Baby: 1910-on. Perfect bisque head, molded and/or painted hair or good wig, sleep or set eyes, open or open/closed mouth; Kestner bent-limb body; well dressed; nice condition. (See *Kestner, King of Dollmakers* for photographs of mold numbers not pictured here.)

Mark:

#211, 226, 257:

11-13in (28-33cm)	$	**700 - 775***
16-18in (41-46cm)		**900 - 1000***
20-22in (51-56cm)		**1150 - 1350***
25in (64cm)		**1650 - 2250***

*Allow $50-100 extra for an original skin wig.

JDK solid dome:

12-14in (31-36cm)	$	**600 - 700**
18in (46cm)		**800**
23-25in (58-64cm)		**1200 - 1500**

#262, 263:

16-18in (41-46cm)	**700 - 800**
21-23in (53-58cm)	**950 - 1050**
16in (41cm) 5-piece toddler body	**950**

#210, 234, 235, 238 shoulder heads,

14-16in (36-41cm)	**1300 - 1500**

Hilda, #237, 245, and solid dome baby **1070**

11-13in (28-33cm)	**2800 - 3200**
16-17in (41-43cm)	**3800 - 4200**
20-22in (51-56cm)	**4800 - 5300**
24in (61cm)	**6000 - 6500**

KESTNER *continued*

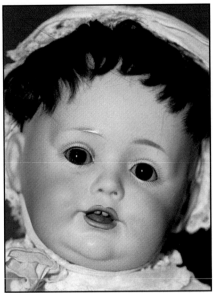

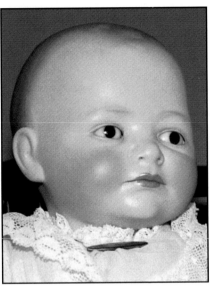

15in (38cm) 247 character baby. *H & J Foulke, Inc.* (For information see page 126.)

16in (41cm) long ***Siegfried***. *Jennifer Raybarn DeHay.* (For information see page 126.)

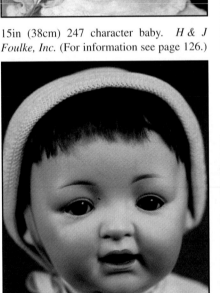

18in (46cm) 226 character baby, all original. *H & J Foulke, Inc.* (For information see page 123.)

15in (38cm) ***Hilda*** 1070. *H & J Foulke, Inc.* (For information see page 123.)

KESTNER *continued*

14-1/2in (37cm) 220 toddler. *H & J Foulke, Inc.* (For information see page 123.)

Toddler:

14in (36cm)	$ 4500 - 5000
17-19in (43-48cm)	5500 - 6000

#247:

11in (28cm)	1100
14-16in (36-41cm)	1800 - 2100
Toddler,	
13in (33cm)	2200 - 2300
20in (51cm)	3200

JDK solid dome, fat-cheeked (so-called Baby Jean):

12-13in (31-33cm)	$ 1200 - 1300
17-18in (43-46cm)	1500 - 1650
23-24in (58-61cm)	2000 - 2100
15in (38cm) toddler	1500 - 1600

All-bisque Baby:

Painted eyes, stiff neck,	
5-6in (13-15cm)	225 - 275
Swivel neck, painted eyes:	
7-1/2in (19cm)	425 - 450
9in (23cm)	600 - 650
12in (31cm)	850
Glass eyes, swivel neck,	
9-10in (23-25cm)	900 - 1000
#177 toddler, 8in (20cm)	1000
#178 toddler, 8in (20cm)	1250

All-Bisque Child: Perfect all-bisque child jointed at shoulders and hips. Very good quality.

#130, 150, 160, 184 and 208:

4-5in (10-13cm)	$ 225 - 325*
6in (15cm)	350 - 375*
7in (18cm)	400 - 450*
8in (20cm)	500 - 550*
9in (23cm)	700 - 800
11in (28cm)	1100 - 1200
12in (31cm)	1300 - 1400

*Allow 30-40% extra for swivel neck; allow $25-50 extra for yellow boots.

Early All-Bisque Dolls: see page 24.

Gibson Girl: Ca. 1910. Perfect bisque shoulder head with appropriate wig, closed mouth, up-lifted chin; kid body with bisque lower arms (cloth body with bisque lower limbs on small dolls); beautifully dressed; all in good condition; sometimes marked Gibson Girl on body.

#172:

10in (25cm)	$ 1100 - 1300
15in (38cm)	2000 - 2400
20-21in (51-53cm)	3200 - 3600

Lady Doll: Perfect bisque socket head, plaster dome, wig with lady hairdo; Kestner jointed composition body with molded breasts, nipped-in waist, slender arms and legs; appropriate lady clothes; all in good condition.

Mark:

D *made in Germany. 8. 162.*

#162:

16-18in (41-46cm)	$ 1600 - 1800
Naked, 16-18in (41-46cm)	1200
All original clothes,	
16-18in (41-46cm)	2300

O.I.C. Baby: Perfect bisque solid dome heads, wide open mouth with molded tongue; cloth body, dressed; all in good condition. Mold #255 (For photograph, see page 4.)

10in (25cm) h.c.	$ 1500 - 1800

Siegfried: Perfect bisque head; cloth body with composition hands; dressed; all in good condition. Mold #272 (See photograph on page 124.)

MARK:

Siegfried made in Germany 9

10in (25cm)	$ 1500**
14in (36cm)	2000**

Marked Century Doll Co. Infant: Ca. 1925. Perfect bisque head; cloth body. Some with smiling face are mold #227.

Head circumference:

10-11in (25-28cm)	$ 550 - 600
13-14in (33-36cm)	800 - 900
Double-face	2500**

Mama doll, bisque shoulder head #281,

21in (53cm)	$ 650 - 750**

**Not enough price samples to compute a reliable average.

KEWPIE

All-Bisque: 1913 on. Made by J. D. Kestner and other German firms. Often have imperfections in making. Sometimes signed on foot "O'Nei *ll*". Standing, legs together, arms jointed, blue wings, painted features, eyes to side.

2-1/2in (5-6cm)	$	110 - 125
4in (10cm)		135 - 150*
5in (13cm)		165 - 185*
6in (15cm)		210 -235*
7in (18cm)		250 - 300*
8in (20cm)		400 - 450*
9in (23cm)		550 - 600*
10in (25cm)		750 - 800*
12in (31cm)		1300 - 1500
Jointed hips:		
4in (10cm)		500 - 550
6in (15cm)		750
8in (20cm)		950
Shoulder head, 3in (8cm)		425
Perfume bottle,		
4-1/2in (11cm)		550 - 600
Black Hottentot,		
5in (13cm)		550 - 600

Button hole,	
2in (5cm)	165 - 175
Pincushion,	
2-3in (5-8cm)	250 - 300
Painted shoes and socks:	
5in (13cm)	600
11in (28cm)	1500 - 1800
With glass eyes and wig,	
6in (15cm) at auction	2400

*Allow extra for original clothes.

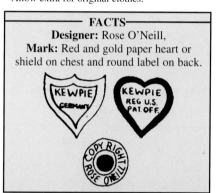

FACTS
Designer: Rose O'Neill,
Mark: Red and gold paper heart or shield on chest and round label on back.

4-1/4in (11cm) all-bisque *Kewpie* in original patriotic outfit. *H & J Foulke, Inc.*

KEWPIE *continued*

4-1/2in
(12cm)
Kewpie
German
soldier.
*H & J
Foulke, Inc.*

Action Kewpies (sometimes stamped: ©):
Thinker:

4in (10cm)	$	275 - 325
7in (18cm)		500 - 550

Kewpie with cat,
3-1/2in (9cm)   450 - 500
Kewpie holding pen,
3in (8cm)   425 - 475
Kneeling, 4in (10cm)   700 - 775
Reclining or sitting,
3-4in (8-10cm)   425 - 475
Farmer, Fireman (molded hats),
4in (10cm)   1000
Kewpie, 2in (5cm) with rabbit,
rose, turkey, pumpkin,
shamrock, etc.   325 - 375
Doodledog:
3in (9cm)   1500 - 1800
1-1/2in (4cm)   750 - 800
Huggers, 3-1/2in (9cm)   200 - 225
Guitar player, 3-1/2in (9cm)   350 - 400
Traveler, 3-1/2in (9cm)   325 - 350
Governor or Mayor,
4in (10cm)   450 - 500
Kewpie and Doodledog on bench,
3-1/2in (9cm)   3000 up
Kewpie sitting on inkwell,
3-1/2in (9cm)   650 - 750
Kewpie Traveler with Doodledog,
3-1/2in (9cm)   1250 - 1350
Kewpie Soldiers,
5-6in (13-15cm)   950
Kewpie on sled, 2-1/2in (6cm)   750
Two Kewpies reading book,
3-1/2in (9cm), standing   850 - 950
Kewpie at tea table   1800 up
Kewpie with basket, 4in (10cm)   1000
Kewpie Mountain with
17 figures   17,000 up
Kewpie holding teddy bear,
4in (10cm)   750
Kewpie in bisque swing,
2-1/2in (6cm)   4000
Glazed Kewpie shaker with animal,
2in (5cm)   275 - 300

3-1/2in (9cm) *Kewpies*
reading book. *H & J
Foulke, Inc.*

Bisque head on chubby jointed composition toddler body, glass eyes: Made by J.D. Kestner.

Mark: "Ges.gesch.
                   O'Neill J.D.K."

10in (25cm) 5-piece body $ **5000**
12-14in (31-36cm) **6000 - 6500**

Bisque head on cloth body: Mold **#1377** made by Alt, Beck & Gottschalck.
12in (31cm) glass eyes $ **2600 - 2800****
Painted eyes **1600 - 2000****

Celluloid: Made by Karl Standfuss, Saxony, Germany.
2-1/2in (6cm) $ **35 - 40**
5in (13cm) **85 - 90**
8in (20cm) **160 - 185**
12in (31cm) **300 - 350**
22in (56cm) **550 - 600**
Black, 2-1/2in (6cm) **85 - 90**
5in (13cm) **150 - 165**

Kewpie/Billiken double face,
2-1/2 (6cm) **85**

**Not enough price samples to compute a reliable range.

All-Composition: Made by Cameo Doll Co., Rex Doll Co., and Mutual Doll Co. All-composition, jointed at shoulders, some at hips; good condition.
8in (20cm) $ **150 - 175**
11-12in (28-31cm) **225 - 275**
Black, 12-13in (31-33cm) **350 - 400**
Talcum container, 7in (18cm) **175 - 225**
Composition head, cloth body,
12in (31cm) **250 - 275**
All-Cloth: Made by Richard G. Krueger, Inc., or King Innovations, Inc., New York. Patent number 1785800. Mask face with fat-shaped cloth body.
10-12in (25-31cm) $ **200 - 225**
18-22in (46-56cm) **375 - 425**

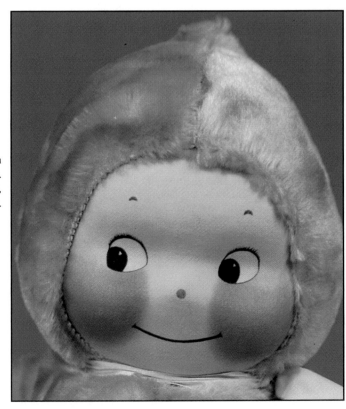

15in (38cm) cloth
Cuddle Kewpie.
H & J Foulke,
Inc.

KEWPIE *continued*

Hard Plastic: Ca. 1950s.
  Standing Kewpie, 1-piece with jointed
    arms, 8in (20cm) $ **125 - 135**
  Boxed   **200 - 250**
  Fully-jointed with sleep eyes; all original
    clothes, 13in (33cm)   **450 - 500**
Vinyl: Ca. 1960s, Cameo Dolls. All original
and excellent condition.
  12-13in (31-33cm) $ **100 -110***
  16in (41cm)   **135 - 165***
Kewpie Baby with hinged body,
  16in (41cm)   **225 - 250**

Kewpie Gal:
  8in (20cm)   **65 - 75***
  14in (36cm)   **125***
Ragsy, molded clothes, 8in (20cm)   **40***

*Allow extra for label and box.

Jesco Dolls, 1980s.
  12in (31cm)   **40 - 60**
  18in (46cm)   **75 - 85**
  26-1/2in (67cm)   **110 - 135**

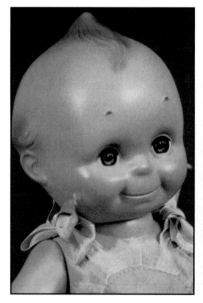

13in (33cm) hard plastic *Kewpie* with
sleep eyes. *H & J Foulke, Inc.*

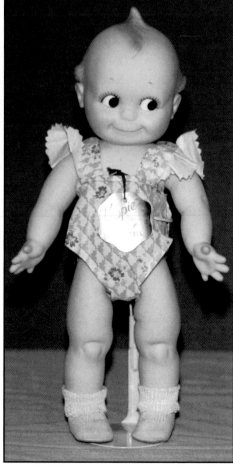

13in (33cm) vinyl *Kewpie*,
all original. *Jensen's
Antique Dolls.*

KLEY & HAHN

FACTS
Kley & Hahn, doll factory, Ohrdruf,
Thüringia, Germany. Heads by Hertel,
Schwab & Co. (100 series), Bähr &
Pröschild (500 series) and J.D. Kestner
(200 Series, 680 and Walküre). 1902-on.
Trademarks: Walküre, Meine Einzige,
Special, Dollar Princess.
Mark:

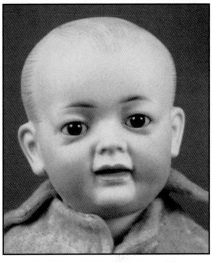

16in (41cm) 525 character toddler.
H & J Foulke, Inc.

Character Baby: Perfect bisque head; bent-limb baby body; nicely dressed; all in good condition.

#138, 158, 160, 167, 176, 458, 525, 531, 680 and others:

11-13in (28-33cm)	$	500- 525
18-20in (46-51cm)		750 - 850
24in (61cm)		1100 - 1200
28in (71cm)		1600
Toddler, 14-16in (36-41cm)		1200 - 1400

#525, Toddler, glass eyes:

15-16in (38-41cm)	1500 - 1650
22-23in (56-58cm)	1900 - 2200

Two-face baby,
13in (33cm)	2000 - 2200

Character Child: Perfect bisque head, closed mouth; jointed composition child or toddler body; fully dressed; all in good condition.

#520, 526:

15-16in (38-41cm)	$	3100 - 3500
19-21in (48-53cm)		4000 - 4500

#536, 546, 549:

15-16in (38-41cm)	3800 - 4200
19-21in (48-53cm)	4800 - 5300

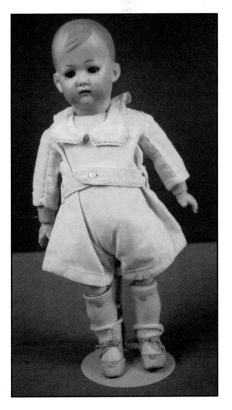

16in (41cm) 154
character toddler.
H & J Foulke, Inc.

KLEY & HAHN *continued*

#547, 18-1/2in (47cm)
at auction $ 6825
#154, 166, closed mouth, toddler or jointed
body:
16-17in (41-43cm) 2500 - 2650
19-20in (48-51cm) 3200
#154, 166, open mouth:
17-18in (43-46cm) jointed body 1400
25in (64cm) 1850 - 1950
20in (51cm) baby 1300 - 1400
#169, closed mouth:
13-14in (33-36cm) toddler 2200 - 2400
17-19in (43-48cm) toddler 3000 - 3200
#169, open mouth,
23in (58cm) baby $ 1500 - 1650**

Child Doll: Perfect bisque head; jointed
composition child body; fully dressed; all in
good condition.
#250, 282 or Walküre:
7-1/2in (19cm) $ 325 - 375
12-13in (31-33cm) 425 - 450
16-18in (41-46cm) 500 - 550*
22-24in (56-61cm) 600 - 700*
28-30in (71-76cm) 900 - 1000
35-36in (89-91cm) 1500 - 1600
Special, Dollar Princess,
23-25in (58-64cm) 525 - 575

*Allow $100-150 additional for flapper body.
**Not enough price samples to compute a
reliable range.

18in (46cm) 250 child with flapper body. *H & J Foulke, Inc.*

KLING

Bisque shoulder head: Ca. 1880. Molded hair or mohair wig, painted eyes, closed mouth; cloth body with bisque lower limbs; dressed; in all good condition. Mold numbers in **100** Series.

12-14in (31-36cm)	$	**300 - 375***
18-20in (46-51cm)		**500 - 550***
23-25in (58-64cm)		**600 - 700***

Glass eyes and molded hair,
15-16in (38-41cm)	**600 - 700***

Boy styles, such as 131:
11in (28cm)	**600 - 650**
16-18in (41-46cm)	**900 - 1000**

Girl styles, such as #186, 176.
15-17in (38-43cm)	**900 - 1000**

Lady styles with decorated bodice, such as
#135, 170, 21-23in (53-58cm)	**1500 up**
#116, lady with molded blue bonnet,	
16in (41cm) at auction	**1600**
#106, lady with molded stand-up collar,	
glass eyes. 17in (43cm) at auction	**2100**

*Allow extra for unusual or elaborate hairdo.

FACTS

Kling & Co., porcelain factory, Ohrdruf, Thüringia, Germany. 1870-on.
Mark:

Kling boy with molded hat and glass eyes. *H & J Foulke, Inc.*

6-1/2in (16cm) shoulder head child with glass eyes. *H & J Foulke, Inc.* (For information see page 134.)

KLING *continued*

China shoulder head: Ca. 1880. Black- or blonde-haired china head with bangs, sometimes with a pink tint; cloth body with china limbs; dressed; all in good condition.
#188, 189, 200 and others:

13-15in (33-38cm)	$ **275 - 325**
18-20in (46-51cm	**400 - 450**
24-25in (61- 64cm)	**525 - 575**

Bisque head: Ca. 1890. Perfect bisque head, glass eyes, appropriate body; dressed; all in good condition.

#123, closed mouth shoulder head:

6-1/2in (17cm)	$ **250 - 275**
10-12in (25-31cm)	
Original costume	**500 - 700**
Redressed	**250 - 300**

#166 or 167, closed mouth shoulder head,

16-18in (41-46cm)	**750 - 850**

#373 or 377 shoulder head, open mouth:

13-15in (33-38cm)	**375 - 425****
19-22in (48-56cm)	**475 - 525****

#370, 372, 182 socket head, open mouth:

14-16in (36-41cm)	**450 - 500**
22-24in (56-61cm)	**600 - 700**
27in (69cm)	**900 - 1000**

**Not enough price samples to compute a reliable range.

KÖNIG & WERNICKE

K & W Character: Perfect bisque head ; composition baby or toddler body; appropriate clothes; all in good condition.
#98, 99, 100, 1070:

8-1/2in (21cm)	$ **350 - 375**
10-11in (25-28cm)	**450 - 475**
14-16in (36- 41cm)	**600 - 650***
19-21in (48-53cm)	**750 - 850***
24-25in (61-64cm)	**1100 - 1250**
Toddler:	
15in (38cm)	**1200 - 1300**
20in (51cm)	**1600 - 1700**

*Allow extra for flirty eyes.

Child #4711, Mein Stolz (My Pride),

37in (94cm)	$ **1800 - 2000**

FACTS

König & Wernicke, doll factory, Waltershausen, Thüringia, Germany. Heads by Hertel, Schwab & Co. and Bähr & Pröschild. 1912-on. **Trademarks:** Mein Stolz, My Playmate
Mark: Body Mark:

16in (41cm) K&W character baby.
H & J Foulke, Inc.

KÄTHE KRUSE

Cloth Käthe Kruse: Molded muslin head, hand-painted; jointed at shoulders and hips:

Doll I (1910-1929), 16in (41cm),
Early model, wide hips:

Mint, all original	$	4000 - 5000
Very good		3000 - 3500
Fair		1800 - 2200
Jointed knees		5500 up**

Doll I (1929-on), 17in (43cm),
Later model, slim hips:

Molded hair, mint	$	3000 - 3500
Very good		2000 - 2500

Doll 1H (wigged):

Mint, all original	$	2800 - 3200
Very good		1700 - 2200

**Not enough price samples to compute a reliable average.

Doll II "Schlenkerchen" Smiling Baby (1922-1936), 13in (33cm)

at auction	$	7600 - 9400*
Very worn		2300

Doll V & VI Babies "Traumerchen" (5-pound weighted **Sand Baby**) and **Du Mein** (unweighted): (See photograph on page 136.)

Cloth head, 19-1/2–23-1/2in (50-60cm)	$	3850 - 4250
Magnesit head, 21in (53cm)		1500

Doll VII (1927-1952) and **Doll X** (1935-1952), 14in (35cm):

All original	$	1800 - 2000

With **Du Mein** head (1928-1930).
14in (36cm):

Showing wear	1800 - 2200
Mint	2900

*Due to demand in Germany.

Doll VIII "German Child" (1929-on),
20-1/2in (52cm) wigged, turning head:

Mint, all original	$	2500 - 2800

Good condition, suitably dressed
                                    1500 - 1800

FACTS

Käthe Kruse, Bad Kösen, Germany; after World War II, Donauworth. 1910-on.
Mark: On cloth: "Käthe Kruse" on sole of foot, sometimes also "Germany" and a number.

Käthe Kruse *Made in*
    81971   *Germany*
Hard plastic on back: Turtle mark and "Käthe Kruse."

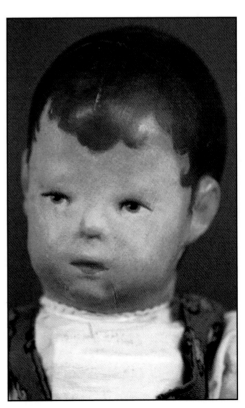

16in (41cm) *Doll I*.
H & J Foulke, Inc.

14in (36cm) *Doll IX* "Little German Child" all original with tag. *H & J Foulke, Inc.*

10in (25cm) Hanna Kruse *Daümlinchen*, all original. *H & J Foulke, Inc.*

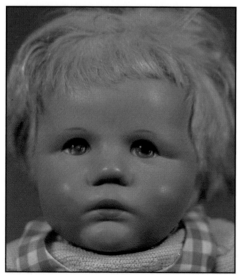

19in (48cm) 1950s *Sand Baby* Magnesit head. *H & J Foulke, Inc.* (For information see page 135.)

KÄTHE KRUSE *continued*

Doll IX "Little German Child" (1929-on), wigged, turning head, 14in (36cm):
All original, mint $ **1750 - 1950**
U.S. Zone Germany: Dolls IX or X with cloth or Magnesit heads, very thick paint finish; all original, very good condition (1945 - 1951), 14in (35cm)
Cloth head, mint	$	**1200 - 1500**
Magnesit, mint		**750 - 850**
Hard plastic, mint		**600 - 700**

17-18in (43-46cm),
Doll I, mint $ **2500 - 3000**

Hard Plastic Head: Ca. 1952-on. Hard plastic head with human hair wig, painted eyes; pink muslin body; original clothes; all in excellent condition.
Ca. 1952-1975:
14in (35cm)	$	**375 - 425**
19-21in (48-53cm)		**500 - 575**

1975-on:
14in (36cm)	**300 - 350***
19-21in (48-53cm)	**400 - 450***
20in (51cm) Du Mein	**550 - 650***

Hanna Kruse Dolls:
10in (25cm) Däumlinchen with foam rubber stuffing (1957-on)$ **200 - 225***
13in (33cm) Rumpumpel Baby or Toddler, 1959-on. **350 - 400**
10in (25cm) Doggi, (vinyl head), 1964-1967. **225 - 250****
14in (36cm) all hard plastic baby **90 - 110***

*Retail store prices may be higher.

All-Hard Plastic (Celluloid) Käthe Kruse: Wig or molded hair and sleep or painted eyes; jointed neck, shoulders and hips; original clothes; all in excellent condition. Turtle mark. 1955-1961.
16in (41cm) $ **450 - 500**

Vinyl head,16in (41cm) **350 - 450****
**Not enough price samples to compute a reliable range.

KRUSE-TYPE

Bing Art Dolls: Nurnberg, Germany. 1921-1932. Cloth head, molded face, hand-painted features; cloth body with jointed shoulders and hips (some with pinned joints), mitten hands; all original clothing; very good condition. "Bing" stamped or impressed on sole of shoe.
Cloth head, painted hair:
10-12in (25-30cm)	$	**400 - 450**
14in (35cm)		**850 - 950**
Cloth head, wigged 10in (25cm)	**250 - 300**	
Composition head, wigged		
7in (18cm)		**100 - 120**

Heine & Schneider Art Doll: Bad-Kösen, Germany. 1920-1922. All cloth or head of pressed cardboard covered with cloth, molded hair; cloth body with jointed shoulders and hips (some with cloth covered composition arms and hands.) Appropriate or original clothes; all in good condition. Mark stamped on foot.
17-19in (43-48cm) **$1300 - 1500****

Unmarked Child Dolls: Ca. 1920s.
15-17in (38-43cm) $ **300 up***

*Depending upon quality.
**Not enough price samples to compute a reliable range.

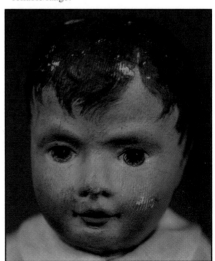

14-1/2in (37cm) cloth doll, possibly by Heine & Schneider. *H & J Foulke, Inc.*

GEBRÜDER KUHNLENZ

G. K. doll with closed mouth: Ca. 1885-on. Perfect bisque socket head (some with closed Belton-type crown), inset glass eyes, closed mouth, round cheeks; jointed composition body; dressed; all in good condition.

#32, 31:
8-10in (20-25cm)	$ 850 - 1100*
15-16in (38-41cm)	1600 - 1700*
21-23in (53-58cm)	2400 - 2600*

#34. Bru-type, French body:
12-1/2in (32cm)	1800 - 2200
18in (46cm)	3000 - 4000**

#38 shoulder head, kid body:
14-16in (36-41cm)	675 - 750*
22-23in (56-58cm)	1000 - 1100*

*Allow more for a very pretty doll.
**Not enough price samples to compute a
  reliable range.

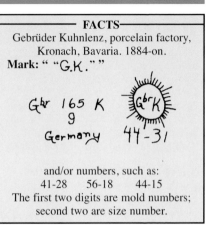

FACTS
Gebrüder Kuhnlenz, porcelain factory, Kronach, Bavaria. 1884-on.
Mark: " "G.K." "

Gʰʳ 165 K
9
Germany   44-31

and/or numbers, such as:
41-28   56-18   44-15
The first two digits are mold numbers; second two are size number.

18in (46cm) 38 shoulder head with solid dome. *H & J Foulke, Inc.*

GEBRÜDER KUHNLENZ *continued*

G.K. child doll: Ca. 1890-on. Perfect bisque socket head, sleep or paperweight-type eyes, open mouth, molded teeth; jointed composition body, sometimes French; dressed; all in good condition.

#41, 44, 56 (character-type face):
9-10in (23-25cm)	$ 700
16-19in (41-48cm)	900 - 1000
24-26in (61-66cm)	1300 - 1500

#165:
18in (46cm)	425 - 450
22-24in (56-61cm)	525 - 575
34in (86cm)	1200 - 1300

#61, 47 shoulder head,
19-22in (48-56cm)	650 - 750

G.K. Tiny Dolls: Perfect bisque socket head, wig, stationary glass eyes, open mouth with molded teeth; 5-piece composition body with molded shoes and socks; all in good condition. Usually mold #44.

7-8in (18-20cm):
Crude body	$ 185 - 210
Better body	250 - 300

All-Bisque: Swivel neck, usually mold #31, #41, or #44.
Bootines, 7-8in (18-20cm)	$ 900 - 1200

Mary Janes:
5in (13cm)	500 - 600
8in (20cm)	1000 - 1200

16in (41cm) 46 child. *H & J Foulke, Inc.*

8-1/4in (21cm) Kuhnlenz
all-bisque child.
H & J Foulke, Inc.

LANTERNIER

Marked Lanternier Child: Ca. 1915. Perfect bisque head, good or original wig, large stationary eyes, open mouth, pierced ears; papier-mâché jointed body; pretty clothes; all in good condition.

Cherie, Favorite or **La Georgienne:**
16-18in (41-46cm)	$	**675 - 775***
22-24in (56-61cm)		**900 - 1000***
28in (71cm)		**1400 - 1600***

*Allow extra for lovely face and bisque.

Lanternier Lady: Ca. 1915. Perfect bisque head with adult look, good wig, stationary glass eyes, open/closed mouth with molded teeth; composition lady body; dressed; all in good condition.

Lorraine,
16-18in (41-46cm)	$	**850 - 1250***

*Depending upon costume and quality.

Characters, "Toto" and others: Ca. 1915. Perfect bisque smiling character face, good wig, glass eyes, open/closed mouth with molded teeth, pierced ears; jointed French composition body; dressed; all in good condition.
17-19in (43-48cm)	$	**900 - 1100**

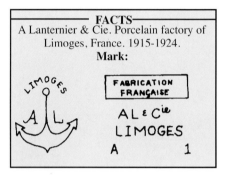

FACTS
A Lanternier & Cie. Porcelain factory of Limoges, France. 1915-1924.
Mark:

21in (53cm) child marked "Limoges". *Dr. Carole Stoessel Zvonar Collection.*

LEATHER, FRENCH

Leather Doll: Baby or child doll with molded and painted hair, painted features, jointed shoulders and hips; original clothes; excellent condition.

Baby, 5in (13cm)   **$**   **2250**
Child, 6in (15cm)   **3000****

**Not enough price samples to compute a reliable average.

FACTS

Unknown French maker. Ca. 1920. All leather.
Mark: None on doll; may have "Made in France" label.

LENCI

Lenci: All-felt (sometimes cloth torso); pressed felt head with painted features; swivel head, jointed shoulders and hips; painted features, eyes usually side-glancing; original

---
FACTS

Enrico & Elenadi Scavini, Turin, Italy. 1920-on.
Mark: "LENCI" on cloth and various paper tags; sometimes stamped on bottom of foot.

Lenci di E. SCAVINI
TURIN (Italy)
Made in ITALY
N. 159G
Pat. Sept 8, 1921, Pat N. 142453
Br& 30 DG X 97395 Brevetta 501.79

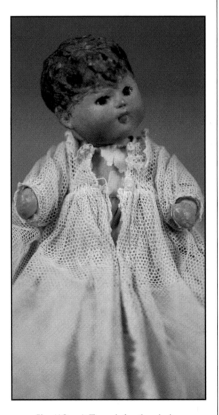

5in (13cm) French leather baby.
H & J Foulke, Inc.

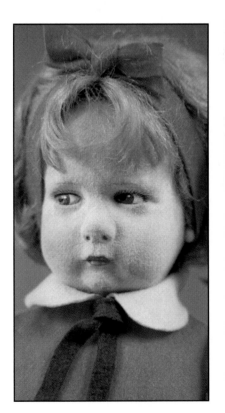

17in (43cm) 300 series face, all original.
H & J Foulke, Inc.

LENCI *continued*

clothes, often of felt or organdy; in excellent condition.

Miniatures and Mascottes:
8-9in (20-23cm) Regionals	$	300 - 350
Children or unusual costumes		400 - 600
Pan		1700-2000
Cupid, at auction		5200
Mary & Baby Jesus, 8in (20cm)		950

Children #300, 109, 149, 159, 111:
13in (33cm)	$	850 up
16-18in (41-46cm)		1000 up
20-22in (51-56cm)		1300 up

#300 children, 17in (43cm) (see photograph on page 141):
Girl in yellow organdy		
gown, boxed	$	1800
Fascist Boy		1800
Boy in coat and hat, boxed		2100

#1500, scowling face,		
17-19in (43-48cm)		$1700-2000
Baby, 18-21in (46-53cm)		2000-2500
Googly, watermelon mouth,		
22in (56cm)		1600-2000

1930s Children:
"Benedetta" face,		
19in (48cm)	$	1300 up
"Mariuccia" face,		
17in (43cm)		1100 up
"Henriette" face,		
25in (63cm)		2000 up
"Laura" face, 16in (41cm)		1000 up
"Lucia" face, 14in (36cm):		
Child clothes		800 - 1200
Regional outfits		700 - 900

9in (23cm) *Maria Theresa*, all original. *H & J Foulke, Inc*.

LENCI *continued*

Ladies and long-limbed novelty dolls,
24-28in (61-71cm) **1800 up**
40in (102cm), Faded color **1000-1250**
"Valentine," "Widow Allegra," glass
eyes, 20in (51cm) **2200 - 2600**
"Surprised Eye" (round painted eyes),
fancy clothes,
20in (51cm) **2200 - 2600**
Aladdin, 14in (36cm),
sitting, at auction **7750**
Butterfly, Japanese lady,
17in (43cm) **2000 - 2200**
Brown South Seas,
16in (41cm) **1800 - 2000**
Teenager, long legs,
17in (43cm) **1200 up**
Googly, watermelon mouth,
22in (56cm) **1600 - 2000**
Winkers,
12in (31cm) **750 - 950**
1935 Round face,
11in (28cm) **500 up**
1950 Characters **300 up**
Catalogs **900 - 1200**
Purse **300**
Wood head, 6in (15cm) **60 - 90**
Mask face, disc eyes,
23in (58cm) **600 - 700**
Hand Puppet **400 - 500**
Flocked hard plastic,
11in (28cm) **200 - 250**

21in (53cm) child with unusual face. *H & J Foulke, Inc.*

Sitting girl with knitting, all original.
H & J Foulke, Inc.

LENCI *continued*

Celluloid-type, 6in (15cm)   **60 - 75**

Collector's Note: Mint examples of rare dolls will bring higher prices. To bring the prices quoted, Lenci dolls must be clean and have good color. Faded and dirty dolls bring only about one-third to one-half these prices
.

Modern Series: 1979 on.

13in (28cm) $	110 - 135
22-21in (51-53cm) child	225 - 275
22in (56cm) surprised eyes	275 - 300
26in (66cm) lady	275 - 375
27-28in (69-71cm) long gown	325 - 425

LENCI-TYPE

Felt or Cloth Doll: Mohair wig, painted features; stuffed cloth body; original clothes or costume; excellent condition.
Child dolls, 16-18in (41-46cm) up to **$750** depending upon quality
Regional costume, very good quality:
    7-1/2–8-1/2in (19-22cm) $ **40 - 50**
    12in (31cm)   **90 - 110**
Alma, Turin, Italy,
    16in (41cm)   **400 - 500**

FACTS
Various Italian, French and English firms . 1920-1940.
Mark: Various paper labels, if any.

6in (15cm) celluloid-type, all original.
H & J Foulke, Inc.

14in (36cm) Magis Roma girl, all original.
H & J Foulke, Inc.

LENCI-TYPE *continued*

Dean's Rag Book Company,
England:
14-16in (36-41cm)	**$**	**500 - 600**

Compositiion face, 18in (46cm) **600 - 700**
Farnell's Alpha Toys, London, England,
   Alpha Imp, 10in (25cm)   **250**
Coronation Doll of
   King George VI, 1937.
   16in (41cm)   **400 - 450**

Eugenie Poir, Gre-Poir French Doll Makers,
Paris and New York.
   Cloth face, very good condition   **300 - 350**
   Felt face:
      Mint condition   **500 - 600**
      Good condition   **300 - 400**
Raynal, Venus, Marina, Clelia. Paris,
France.
   17-18in (43-46cm) mint   **550 - 750**

LIBERTY OF LONDON

British Coronation Dolls: 1939. All-cloth with painted and needle-sculpted faces; original clothes; excellent condition. The **Royal Family** and **Coronation Participants**.
   9-9-1/2in (23-24cm)   **$**   **150 - 165**
   6in (15cm), **Princess Margaret**   **400**
   7in (17cm), **Princess Elizabeth**   **400**
Other English Historical and Ceremonial Characters: All-cloth with painted and needle-sculpted faces; original clothes; excellent condition.
   9-10in (23-25cm)   **$**   **125 - 135**
Beefeater (Tower Guard)   **85**

                ┌─── **FACTS** ───┐
Liberty & Co. of London, England.
1906-on.
Mark: Cloth label or paper tag "Liberty of London."

20in (51cm) unmarked boy
H & J Foulke, Inc.

Lord Chancellor from Coronation Set.
H & J Foulke, Inc.

ARMAND MARSEILLE (A.M.)

Child Doll: 1890-on. Perfect bisque head, nice wig, sleep eyes, open mouth; composition ball-jointed body; pretty clothes; all in good condition. **#390,** (larger sizes marked only "A. [size] M."), Florodora, 1894:

9-10in (23-25cm)	$ 235 - 265*
12-14in (31-36cm)	225 - 275*
16-18in (41-46cm)	325 - 375*
20in (51cm)	400 - 425*
23-24in (58-61cm)	450 - 500*
28-29in (71-74cm)	650 - 700
30-32in (76-81cm)	750 - 850
35-36in (89-91cm)	1000 - 1200+
38in (96cm)	1500 - 1800+
40-42in (102-107cm)	2000+
23in (58cm) with outstanding clothes in original box, mint	1400

5-piece composition body, (excellent quality body):

6-7in (15-18cm)	175 - 200
9-10in (23-25cm)	235 - 265

Closed mouth,

5-5-1/2in (12-14cm)	250 - 275

Cardboard and stitck leg body:

9-10in (23-25cm)	125
12-14in (31-36cm)	135 - 165
16-18in (41-46cm)	210 - 260

#1894 (composition body; early pale bisque):

14-16in (36-41cm)	500 - 600
21-23in (53-58cm)	750 - 850
26in (66cm)	950

#370, 3200, 1894, Florodora, Anchor 2015, Rosebud Lily, Alma, Mabel, Darling, Beauty, Princess shoulder heads on kid or cloth bodies (See photograph on page 148.):

11-12in (28-31cm)	125 - 150
14-16in (36-41cm)	175 - 225
22-24in (56-61cm)	375 - 425
25-26in (64-66cm)	450 - 500

*Add $100-200 for factory original clothes;.
+Allow more for an exceptionally pretty doll.

FACTS

Armand Marseille
of Köppelsdorf,
Thüringia, Germany
(porcelain and doll
factory). 1885-on.

Marks:

A.M. - DEP
N°. 3600.
3.
Made in Germany

A0½M
Florodora
Armand Marseille
Made in Germany

1894
A M ⁴⁄₀ DEP
Germany

A M
(Baby 3¼)
DRGM

Made in Germany

25in (64cm) 390, all
original. *H & J
Foulke, Inc.*

ARMAND MARSEILLE (A.M.) *continued*

#2000: 14in (36cm)   **$ 900****
Queen Louise, Rosebud (composition body):

12in (31cm)	**340 - 365**
23-25in (58-64cm)	**550 - 600**
28-29in (71-74cm)	**700 - 800**

Baby Betty:
14-16in (36-41cm)

composition body	**525 - 575**
19-21in (48-53cm) kid body	**525 - 575**

#1894, 1892, 1896, 1897 shoulder heads (excellent quality),
19-22in (48-56cm)   **475 - 525**

Character Children: 1910-on. Perfect bisque head, molded hair or wig, glass or painted eyes, open or closed mouth; composition body; dressed; all in good condition. (For photographs of dolls not shown here, see previous *Blue Books*.)

#230 Fany (molded hair):
15-16in (38-41cm)   **$ 5500 - 6000**
#231 Fany (wigged):
14-15in (36-38cm)   **5000 - 5500**
#250, 11-13in (28-33cm)   **750**
#251/248 (open/closed mouth):

12in (31cm)	**1650**
16-18in (41-46cm)	**2600 - 3000**

#340, 13in (33cm)   **2600****
#372 Kiddiejoy shoulder head, "mama" body, 19in (48cm)   **850 - 900**
#400 (child body):

13in (33cm)	**1300 - 1500**
17in (43cm)	**2600 - 2800****

#500, 600, 13-15in (33-38cm)   **700 - 800**
#550 (glass eyes) (See photograph on page 148.):

12in (31cm)	**1600**
18-20in (46-51cm)	**2500 - 2800****

#560, 11-13in (28-33cm)   **750 - 850**
#590, (open/closed mouth),
15-16in (38-41cm)   **1300 - 1400**
#620 shoulder head, 16in (41cm)   **1250****
#640 shoulder head (same face as 550 socket), 20in (51cm)   **1500 - 1650****
#700:

11in (28cm) painted eyes	**2100****
14in (36cm) glass eyes	**3500****

A.M. (intaglio eyes),
16-17in (41-43cm)   **4500 up**

**Not enough price samples to compute a
  reliable range.

13in (33cm) *Baby Betty*, all original.
H & J Foulke, Inc.

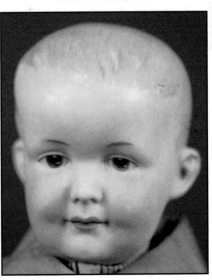

15in (38cm) 500 character boy.
H & J Foulke, Inc.

16in (41cm) 550 character child.
H & J Foulke, Inc.
(For information see page 147.)

19in (48cm) *Florodora*.
H & J Foulke, Inc.
(For information see page 146.)

12-1/2in (32cm) long 341 unusual open mouth. *H & J Foulke, Inc.* (For more information see page 151.)

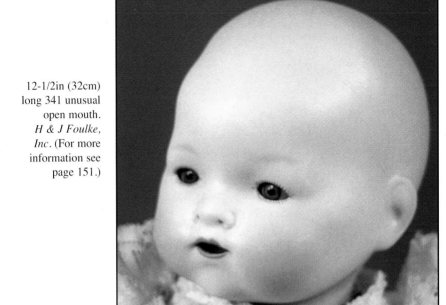

19in (48cm) 990 toddler. *H & J Foulke, Inc.* (For information see page 150.)

ARMAND MARSEILLE (A.M.) *continued*

Character Babies and Toddlers: 1910-on. Perfect bisque head, good wig, sleep eyes, open mouth some with teeth; composition bent-limb body; suitably dressed; all in nice condition. (See photograph on page 149.)

Marks:

Armand Marseille
Germany
990
A 9/0 M

Germany
326

A 11 M

Mold #990, 985, 971, 996, 1330, 326, (solid dome), 980, 991, 327, 329, 259 and others:

10-11in (25-28cm)	$	325 - 350
13-15in (33-38cm)		375 - 425
18-20in (46-51cm)		500 - 550
22in (56cm)		650 - 700
24-25in (61-64cm)		750 - 850

#233:

13-15in (33-38cm)	500 - 550
20in (51cm)	700 - 800

#250,

11in (28cm)	400

#251/248 (open/closed mouth),

11-12in (28-31cm)	800 - 900

#251/248 (open mouth),

12-14in (31-36cm)	650 - 750

#410 (two rows of teeth),

15-16in (38-41cm)	1200 - 1500**

#518:

16-18in (41-46cm)	600 - 700
25in (64cm)	1000 - 1200

#560A:

10-12in (25-31cm)	525 - 550
15-17in (38-43cm)	650 - 700

#580, 590 (open/closed mouth):

9in (23cm)	650 - 750
15-16in (38-41cm)	1200 - 1500

#590 (open mouth):

12in (31cm)	600
16-18in (41-46cm)	850 - 950

#920 shoulder head, "mama" body,

21in (53cm)	900**

Melitta, 19in (48cm) toddler   1100 - 1250

#995, painted bisque toddler,

18in (46cm)	500 - 600

**Not enough price samples to compute a reliable range.

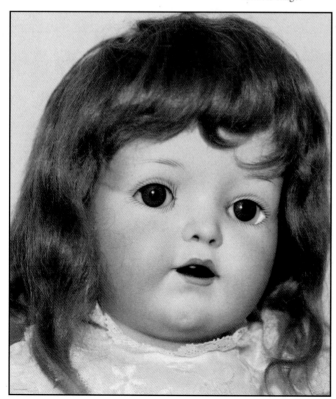

16in (41cm) *Melitta* toddler. *Mary Barnes Kelley Collection.*

ARMAND MARSEILLE (A.M.) *continued*

Infant: 1924-on. Solid-dome bisque head with molded and/or painted hair, sleep eyes; composition body or hard-stuffed jointed cloth body or soft-stuffed cloth body; dressed; all in good condition.

Mark: A. M.
Germany.
351.14K

#351, 341, Kiddiejoy and **Our Pet** (see photograph on page 149):

Head circumference:

8-9in (20-23cm)	$	225 - 250*
10in (25cm)		275 - 300*
12-13in (31-33cm)		350 - 425*
15in (38cm)		600*
6in (15cm) compo body		225 - 250
24in (61cm) wigged toddler		1000 - 1100
Hand Puppet		200 - 225

#352,

17-20in (43-51cm) long	575 - 625

#347, head circumference,

12-13in (31-33cm)	475 - 525

Baby Phyllis:

Head circumference:

9in (23cm) black	500
12-13in (31-33cm)	425 - 475

Baby Gloria, RBL, New York,

15-16in (38-41cm)	700 - 800

Kiddiejoy, open mouth
with tongue,

13-1/2in (34cm) h.c.	650

*Allow $25-75 extra for composition body.

Marked "Just Me" Character: Ca. 1925. Perfect bisque socket head, curly wig, glass eyes to side, closed mouth; composition body; dressed; all in good condition. Some of these dolls, particularly the painted bisque ones, were used by Vogue Doll Company in the 1930s and will be found with original Vogue labeled clothes.

Mark:

Just ME
Registered
Germany
A 310/5/0 M

7-1/2–8in (19-20cm)	$	1100 - 1250
9in (23cm)		1500 - 1600
11in (28cm)		1800 - 2000
13in (33cm)		2200 - 2500
9-1/2 (24cm) all original with label in original box, mint, at auction		4000

Painted bisque:

7-8in (18-20cm) all original	800 - 900
10in (25cm) all original	1100 - 1200

9in (23cm) *Just Me* 310. *H & J Foulke, Inc.*

ARMAND MARSEILLE (A.M.) *continued*

Lady: 1910-1930. Bisque head with mature face, mohair wig, sleep eyes, open or closed mouth; composition lady body with molded bust, long slender arms and legs; appropriate clothes; all in good condition.

#401 and **400** (slim body), 14in (36cm):

Open mouth	$ 1250 - 1450
Closed mouth	2000 - 2500
Painted bisque	900 - 1000

#300: (M.H.):

9in (23cm)	1400 - 1500**
All original	1650**

#400: flapper body,

16-19in (41-48cm)	2500 - 3000

**Not enough price samples to compute a reliable range.

24in (61cm) 400 on flapper jointed body, very rare. *H & J Foulke, Inc.*

153

A. MARQUE

Marked A. Marque Doll: Perfect bisque head with wistful character face (one face only), appropriate wig, paperweight eyes, closed mouth; jointed composition body of special design with bisque lower arms and hands, fixed wrists; appropriate clothes (Some original ones were made by Paris designer Margaines-Lacroix); all in excellent condition.

22in (56cm) one size only **$90,000-110,000**

FACTS
Sculptor, Albert Marque
Paris, 1916

A. Marque character boy (not perfect).
Courtesy of Richard W. Withington, Inc.

MASCOTTE

Bébé Mascotte: Bisque socket head, good wig, closed mouth, paperweight eyes, pierced ears; jointed composition and wood body; appropriate clothes; all in good condition.

11-12in (28-31cm)	$ **2250 - 2500**
17-19in (43-48cm)	**3800 - 4200**
24-26in (61-66cm)	**5300 - 5800**

FACTS
May Freres Cie, 1890-1897; Jules Nicolas Steiner, 1898-on. Paris, France. 1890-1902.
Mark:
"BÉBÉ MASCOTTE PARIS"

16in (41cm) *Bébé Mascotte. Ruth Covington West.*

METAL DOLLS
(AMERICAN)

Metal Child: All metal, body fully jointed at neck, shoulders, elbows, wrists, hips, knees and ankles; sleep eyes, open/closed mouth with painted teeth; dressed; all in good condition. (Body may be jointed composition with metal hands and feet.)

16-20in (41-51cm)	$	**325 - 425**

Babies: All metal baby.

11-13in (28-33cm)	**100 - 125**
Metal head/cloth baby,	
18-20in (46-51cm)	**165 - 185**

─────── FACTS ───────
Various U.S. companies, such as Atlas Doll & Toy Co. and Giebeler-Falk, N.Y., U.S.A. Ca. 1917-on.

METAL HEADS
(GERMAN)

Marked Metal Head Child: Metal shoulder head on cloth or kid body, bisque or composition hands; dressed; very good condition, not repainted.

Molded hair, painted eyes:

12-14in (31-36cm)	$	**125 - 150**
23in (58cm)		**210 - 235**

Molded hair, glass eyes:

12-14in (31-36cm)	**150 - 175**
20-22in (51-56cm)	**225 - 250**

Wig and glass eyes:

14-16in (36-41cm)	**225 - 250**
20-22in (51-56cm)	**275 - 325**

─────── FACTS ───────
Buschow & Beck, Germany (Minerva): Karl Standfuss, Germany (Juno); Alfred Heller, Germany (Diana). Ca. 1888-on.
Mark:

Mark may often be found on front of shoulder plate.

18in (46cm) German metal head. *H & J Foulke, Inc.*

MULTI-FACED DOLLS

Marked C.B. Doll: Carl Bergner, Sonneberg, Germany. Perfect bisque head with two or three different faces, usually sleeping, laughing and crying, papier-mâché hood hides the unwanted face(s); a ring through the top of the hood attached to a dowel turns the faces; cloth torso, composition limbs or jointed composition body; dressed; all in good condition.

13in (33cm) 2 or 3 faces **$ 1500 - 1800**
13in (33cm) two-faced black and
  white 202 dep **1800 - 2200**
13in (33cm) Red Riding Hood,
  Grandmother and Wolf **6000****
14in (31cm) two-faced, frowning and
  hint of a smile,
  Simon & Halbig-type **3500****

Character Babies: German. Ca. 1910. Perfect bisque head with two faces, usually crying, sleeping or smiling; swivel neck; composition or cloth body; dressed; all in good condition. Some have papier-mâché hoods to cover unwanted faces, while some use cloth bonnets.

17in (43cm) HvB (von Berg)
  two-faced baby **$1200 - 1400**
13in (33cm) Gebr. Heubach
  three-faced baby **1800 - 2000**
13in (33cm) Kley & Hahn
  two-faced baby **2000 - 2200**
9in (23cm) Max Schelhorn
  two-faced baby **650 - 750**

French Dolls:
Jumeau, laughing and crying character
  faces (#211 & 203),
  18in (46cm) **12,000 - 15,000**

American Composition Dolls:
Trudy. 3-in-1 Doll Corp., New York.
  Sleeping, crying, smiling, all original,
  14in (36cm) **250 - 295**
Johnny Tu-Face. Effanbee, New York.
  Crying and smiling, 16in (41cm) **400****

**Not enough price samples to compute a
  reliable average.

FACTS
Various German, French and American
companies. 1888 and perhaps earlier.

Below: 14in (36cm) three-face doll marked "C.B." *H & J Foulke, Inc.*

MUNICH ART DOLLS

Munich Art Dolls: Molded composition character heads with hand-painted features; fully-jointed composition bodies; appropriate regional or "country style" clothes; all in good condition.

13in (33cm)	$	**2400 - 3000**
18-19in (46-48cm)		**3500 - 5000**
12in (31cm) fair condition		**1100 - 1300**

————————————FACTS————————————
Marion Kaulitz. 1908-1912. All-composition, fully-jointed bodies.
Designer: Paul Vogelsanger and others.
Mark: Sometimes signed on doll's neck.

18in (46cm) Munich Art Doll. *Esther Schwartz Collection.*

OHLHAVER

Revalo Character Baby or **Toddler:** Perfect bisque socket head, good wig, sleep eyes, hair eyelashes, painted lower eyelashes, open mouth; baby bent-limb body; dressed; all in good condition.
#22:

15-17in (38-41cm)	$	**550 - 600**
22in (56cm)		**800 - 850**
Toddler,		
17-19in (41-48cm)		**1000 - 1200**

————————————FACTS————————————
Gebrüder Ohlhaver, doll factory, Sonneberg, Thüringia, Germany. Heads made by Gebrüder Heubach, Ernst Heubach and Porzellanfabrik Mengersgereuth. 1912-on.
Trademarks: Revalo.
Mark:

Revalo
Germany
3

15in (38cm) *Revalo* child. *H & J Foulke, Inc.*

OHLHAVER *continued*

Revalo Child Doll: Bisque socket head, good wig, sleep eyes, hair eyelashes, painted lower eyelashes, open mouth; ball-jointed composition body; dressed; all in good condition. Mold #150 or #10727.

14-15in (36-38cm)	$	500 - 600
18-20in (46-51cm)		700 - 750
24-25in (61-64cm)		850 - 950

Revalo Character Doll: Bisque head with molded hair, painted eyes, open/closed mouth; composition body; dressed; all in good condition.

Coquette, 12in (31cm)	750 - 850
Coquette with hairbows,	
14in (36cm)	950 - 1000

ORIENTAL DOLLS

Japanese Traditional Dolls:
Ichimatsu (play doll): 1868-on. Papier-mâché swivel head on shoulder plate, hips, lower legs and feet (early ones have jointed wrists and ankles); cloth midsection, cloth (floating) upper arms and legs; hair wig, dark glass eyes, pierced ears and nostrils; original clothes; all in very good condition.

Meiji Era (1868-1912):

3-5in (8-13cm)	$	200 - 250
12-14in (31-36cm)		350 - 400
18-20in (46-51cm)		500 - 600
Boy, 18-20in (46-51cm)		650 - 750
Early three-bend body (Mitsuore):		
14-16in (36-41cm)		1500 up
Early exceptional quality,		
24in (61cm)		1600 up
Fully jointed lady, all original and boxed with additional wigs,		
20in (51cm)		2300

15-1/2in (39cm) early **Ichimatsu** boy of exceptional quality. *Private Collection.*

ORIENTAL DOLLS *continued*

Ca. 1920s:

13-15in (33-38cm)	$	150 - 175
17-18in (43-46cm)		210 - 250
Ca. 1940s, 12-14in (31-36cm)		85 - 95

Traditional Lady (Kyoto or **Fashion Doll):**

Ca. 1900, 12in (31cm)	$	500 up
1920s:		
10-12in (25-31cm)		150 - 175
16in (41cm)		235 - 265
1940s, 12-14in (31-36cm)		85 - 95

Traditional Warrior:

1880s, 16-18in (41-46cm)	$	800 up
1920s, 11-12in (28-31cm)		250 up

Royal Personages:

Ca. 1890, 10in (25cm)	$	800 up
1920s-1930s:		
4-6in (10-15cm)		100 - 125
12in (31cm)		350 up

Baby with bent limbs:

Ca. 1910, 11in (28cm)	$	250 up

Ca. 1930s, souvenir dolls:

8-10in (20-25cm)	65 - 85

Carved Ivory, Ca. 1890:

2-3in (5-8cm) fully jointed, exquisite carving	$	350
lesser quality		225

Oriental Bisque Dolls: Ca. 1900-on. Made by French and German firms. Bisque head tinted yellow; matching ball-jointed or baby body; original or appropriate clothes; all in excellent condition. (See previous *Blue Books* for photographs of dolls not pictured here.)

B.P. #220:

16-17in (41-43cm)	$	3200 - 3500**

Belton-type:

12in (31cm) 127	1700

BSW #500:

11in (28cm)	$	1100 - 1300
14-15in (36-38cm)		1800 - 2200*

*Allow extra for elaborate original outfits.

**Not enough price samples to compute a reliable range.

12in (31cm) Empress, all original. Ca. 1850. *Betty Lunz Collection.*

ORIENTAL DOLLS *continued*

Bru Jne, 20in (51cm) $ 26,000
Tête Jumeau, closed mouth,
    19-20in (48-51cm)   48,000 - 62,000
Jumeau, open mouth, 18in (46cm) $ 4500

JDK 243:
    13-14in (33-36cm) $ 4250 - 4750
    18-20in (46-51cm)   5500 - 6000
    19in (48cm) hairline   2300

A.M. 353:
    12-14in (31-36cm) $ 1000 - 1150
    10in (25cm) cloth body   700

A.M. Girl: 8-9in (20-23cm)   650

S&H 1329 (see photograph on page 160):
    11in (28cm) $ 1200
    14-15in (36-38cm)   1800 - 2200*
    18-19in (46-48cm)   2700 - 2800*

S&H 1099, 1129, and 1199:
    8in (20cm) $ 1200
    15in (38cm)   2700 - 2800*
    19-20in (48-51cm)   3200 - 3500*

S PB H, 9in (23cm) $ 650
    19in (48cm)   2000*

#164, 16-17in (41-43cm) $ 2300 - 2500*
Unmarked:
    4-1/2in (12cm) painted eyes   175
    6in (15cm) glass eyes   500
    11-12in (28-31cm) glass eyes   850 - 950

All-Bisque Dolls:
JDK Baby,
    5-1/2in (14cm) $ 1250 - 1350**
    8in (20cm)   1650 - 1750**

Heubach Chin Chin,
    4in (10cm)   275 - 325

S&H Child,
    5-1/2in (14cm) $ 650 - 750
    7in (18cm)   850 - 950
Man with molded hat and mustache
    2-1/2in (6cm)   175 - 200

*Allow extra for elaborate original outfits.
**Not enough price samples to compute a
    reliable range.

19in (48cm) S PB H 4900.
H & J Foulke, Inc.

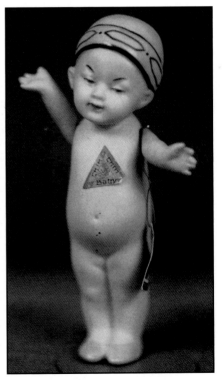

4in (10cm) *Chin Chin* with chest label and
wrist tag. *H & J Foulke, Inc.*

ORIENTAL DOLLS *continued*

Bisque Heads of Unknown Origin:
Lady with molded hair or hat, wood jointed
body. 13in (33cm) $ 750 - 850
Character man with molded mustache,
jointed body, 11in (28cm)   **1100****

#419 Papier-Mâché Man: Molded hat
and mustache, cloth body,
composition arms.   **250 - 300**

American Cloth: Oil painted stockinette in
the Chase manner. Original clothes.
16in (41cm) at auction   **850**

**Not enough price samples to compute a
reliable range.

PAPIER-MÂCHÉ
(SO-CALLED
FRENCH-TYPE)

French-type Papier-mâché: Shoulder head
with painted black pate, brush marks around
face, nailed on human hair wig (often missing), set-in glass eyes, closed or open mouth
with bamboo teeth, pierced nose; pink kid

┌─────────── **FACTS** ───────────┐
Heads by German firms such as Johann
Müller of Sonneberg and Andreas Voit
of Hildburghausen, were sold to French
and other doll makers. 1835-1850.
Mark: None.
└──────────────────────────────────┘

17-1/2in (45cm) S & H 1329 with elaborate
original costume. *Private Collection.* (For
information see page 159.)

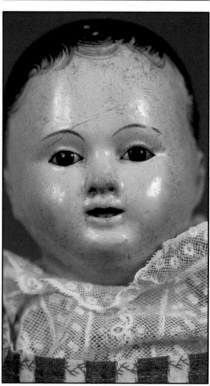

22in (56cm) French-type papier-mâché.
H & J Foulke, Inc.

PAPIER-MÂCHÉ (So-Called French-Type) *continued*

body with stiff arms and legs; appropriate old clothes; all in good condition, showing some wear.

12-14in (31-36cm)	$	1100 - 1300
18-20in (46-51cm)		1800 - 2000
24-26in (61-66cm)		2200 - 2500
32in (81cm)		2800 - 3100
Painted eyes:		
14-16in (36-41cm)		1000 - 1200
6-8in (15-20cm)		375 - 475
Wood-jointed body, 6in (15cm)		750 - 800
Shell decoration:		
4-1/2in (12cm)		500 - 600
8in (20cm) pair		1000 - 1200
18in (46cm) pair		2200
Poupard, molded bonnet and clothes,		
18in (46cm)		400 - 500

PAPIER-MÂCHÉ (GERMAN)

Papier-mâché Shoulder Head: Ca. 1840s to 1860s. Unretouched shoulder head, molded hair, painted eyes; some wear and crazing; cloth or kid body; original or appropriate old clothing; entire doll in fair condition.

16-18in (41-46cm)	$	900 - 1000*
22-24in (56-61cm)		1100 - 1300*
32in (81cm)		1900 - 2200*

*Allow extra for an unusual model.

FACTS
Various German firms of Sonneberg such as Johann Müller, Müller & Strasburger, F.M. Schilling, Heinrich Stier, A. Wislizenus, and Cuno & Otto Dressel. 1816 on.

7in (18cm) molded hair papier-mâché, all original. *H & J Foulke, Inc.* (For information see page 162).

PAPIER-MÂCHÉ (GERMAN) *continued*

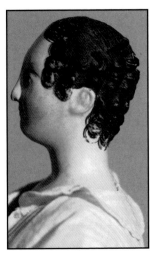

15-1/2in (39cm) papier-mâché lady with short curly hair. *Private Collection.*

Glass eyes, short hair:
19in (48cm)	$ 1650 - 1850
24in (61cm)	2400
21in (53cm) all original provincial	
costume	2600
Glass eyes, long hair,	
22in (56cm)	1700 - 2000
Flirty eyes, long hair,	
23in (58cm)	2700 - 3000
Long curls, 19in (48cm)	2300

*Allow extra for an unusual model.

Molded Hair Papier-mâché: (so-called "milliners' models") 1820s-1860s. Unretouched shoulder head, various molded hairdos, eyes blue, black or brown, painted features; original kid body, wooden arms and legs; original or very old handmade clothing; entire doll in fair condition. (See photograph on page 161.)
Long curls:
9in (23cm)	$ 550
13in (33cm)	675 - 725

23in (58cm)	1400 - 1500
13in (33cm) all original, at auction	1900
Covered wagon hairdo:	
7in (18cm)	275 - 325
11in (28cm)	450 - 500
15in (38cm)	675 - 775
Side curls with braided bun:	
9-10in (23-25cm)	750 - 850
13-15in (31-38cm)	1300 - 1500
Center part with molded bun:	
7in (18cm)	525
11in (28cm)	950 - 1000
Wood-jointed body	1200 - 1350
Side curls with high beehive (Apollo knot):	
11in (28cm)	950 - 1000
18in (46cm)	1900 - 2100
Coiled braids at ears, braided bun:	
10-11in (25-28cm)	1000 - 1100
20in (51cm)	2000 - 2200
Braided coronet,	
11in (28cm)	1250 - 1450
Molded bonnet and red snood,	
13in (33cm)	1250

PAPIER-MÂCHÉ (GERMAN) *continued*

Patent Washable Dolls: 1880-1915. Composition shoulder head with mohair or skin wig, glass eyes, closed or open mouth; cloth body with composition arms and lower legs, sometimes with molded boots; appropariately dressed; all in good condition.

Superior Quality:

12-14in (31-36cm)	$	**500 - 600**
16-18in (41-46cm)		**700 750**
22-24in (56-61cm)		**850 - 900**
30in (76cm)		**1200 - 1400**

Standard Quality:

11-12in (28-31cm)	**150 - 175**
14-16in (36-41cm)	**200 - 225**
22-24in (56-61cm)	**300 -350**
30-33in (76-84cm)	**400 - 500**
38in (97cm)	**600 - 700**
Lady, 13-16in (33-41cm)	**750 - 850**
Oriental, 12in (31cm)	**225 - 250**

12in (31cm) patent washable, superior quality. *Private collection.*

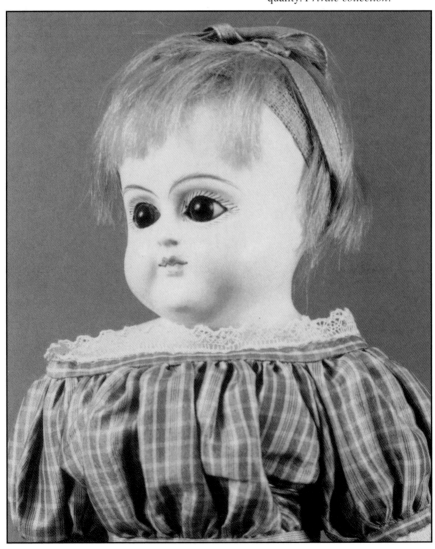

PAPIER-MÂCHÉ
(GERMAN) *continued*

Sonneberg-type Papier-mâché: Ca. 1880-1910. Shoulder head with molded and painted black or blonde hair, painted eyes, closed mouth; cloth body sometimes with leather arms; old or appropriate clothes; all in good condition, showing some wear.
Mark: Usually unmarked. Some marked:

> M & S
> Superior
> 2015

13-15in (33-38cm)	$	250 - 300*
18-19in (46-48cm)		350 - 400*
23-25in (58-64cm)		500 - 600*
Glass eyes, 13in (33cm)		475

*Allow extra for an unusual hairdo.

Papier-mâché: Ca. 1920-on. Papier-mâché head, hard stuffed body, good wig, painted features; original clothes, all in good condition.

10-12in (25-31cm)	$	90 - 110

22in (56cm) Sonneberg-type papier-mâché with glass eyes. *H & J Foulke, Inc.*

PARIAN-TYPE
(UNTINTED BISQUE)

Unmarked Parian: Pale or untinted shoulder head, sometimes with molded blouse, beautifully molded hairdo (may have ribbons, beads, comb or other decoration), painted eyes, closed mouth; cloth body; lovely clothes; entire doll in fine condition.
Common, plain style:

8-10in (20-25cm)	$	135 - 185
16in (41cm)		300 - 350*
24in (61cm)		475 - 525*

Very fancy hairdo and/or elaborately decorated blouse **800 - 2500**
Very fancy with glass eyes **1500 - 3250**
Pretty hairdo, simple ribbon or comb:

14in (36cm)	425 - 475
18-20in (46-51cm)	650 - 750

Simple hairdo with applied flowers,

20in (51cm)	850

*Allow $100 for glass eyes.

FACTS
Various German firms.
Ca. 1860s through 1870s.
Mark: Usually none,
sometimes numbers.

24in (61cm) parian lady with lustre tiara and earrings. *Private Collection.*

PARIAN-TYPE (UNTINTED BISQUE) *continued*

12in (31cm) parian lady with molded bonnet. *Private Collection.*

24in (61cm) parian lady with applied hair and shoulder plate decorations. *Richard Wright Antiques.*

16in (41cm) parian lady with green snood, lustre band and tassel. *Private Collection.*

PARIAN-TYPE (UNTINTED BISQUE) *continued*

Man, molded collar and tie,
16-17in (41-43cm) $ 750
Child, glass eyes, molded blonde curls,
14in (36cm)   1150
"Augusta Victoria,"
17in (43cm)   1200 - 1300
Molded plate, blonde curls, ribbon, glass
eyes, 14in (36cm)   1300 - 1500
Alice hairdo, 21in (53cm)   750 - 800
"Countess Dagmar," 19in (48cm)   950
"Irish Queen," Limbach 8552,
16in (41cm)   600 - 700
"Dolley Madison," glass eyes, swivel neck,
20in (51cm)   1600
Pink lustre hat or snood,
17in (43cm)   1700 - 1800
Pink lustre tiara, gold earrings,
14-16in (36-41cm)   1500

Molded straw bonnet, fancy shoulder plate,
16in (41cm)   2500
Light brown hair waving past shoulders,
applied Dresden flowers,
21in (53cm)   1700
Fancy blonde hair, molded black bow and
holes for attaching beads,
19in (48cm)   1000
Molded yellow bonnet with flowers,
10in (25cm)   1650
Molded necklace, fancy hair, glass eyes,
18in (46cm)   1800
All-Parian, pink lustre boots,
5-1/2in (14cm)   185 - 200

Head only, decorated shoulder plate, painted
eyes, 5in (13cm)   450

14in (36cm)
very rare
parian lady
with swivel
neck,
taüfling-
type body,
stout face.
*Private
Collection.*

P.D.

---FACTS---
Probably Petit & Dumontier, Paris,
France. Some heads made by Francois
Gaultier. 1878-1890.

Mark:

P.2.D

P.D. Bébé: Perfect bisque head with paper-weight eyes, closed mouth, pierced ears, good wig; jointed composition body (some have metal hands); appropriate clothes; all in good condition.

19-23in (48-58cm)   **$ 14,000 - 16,000**
23in (58cm) chip on neck, replaced
   hand, at auction   **9000**

23in (58cm) P.D.
Private Collection.

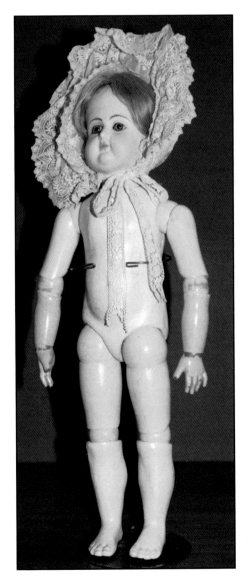

PHILADELPHIA BABY

Philadelphia Baby: All-cloth with treated shoulder-type head, lower arms and legs; painted hair, well-molded facial features, ears; stocking body; very good condition.

18-22in (46-56cm)	$	**4000**
Mint condition		**5000**
Fair, showing wear		**2500**
Very worn		**1600 - 1800**

Rare style face (See *6th Blue Book*, page 302 for exact doll.), at auction **9350**

FACTS
J.B. Sheppard & Co., Philadelphia, Pa., U.S.A. Ca. 1900. All-cloth.
Mark: None.

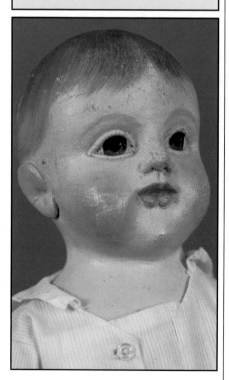

Philadelphia Baby. *Nancy A. Smith Collection.*

PRE-GREINER (SO-CALLED)

Unmarked Pre-Greiner: Papier-mâché shoulder head; molded and painted black hair, pupil-less black glass eyes; stuffed cloth body, mostly homemade, wood, leather or cloth extremities; dressed in good old or original clothes; all in good condition.

18-22in (46-56cm)	$	**1000 - 1350**
28-32in (71-81cm)		**2000 - 2300**
Fair condition, much wear,		
20-24in (51-61cm)		**700 - 800**
Flirty eye, 30in (76cm)		**3000**

FACTS
Unknown and various. Ca. 1850.
Mark: None.

27in (69cm) Pre-Greiner. *H & J Foulke, Inc.*

RABERY & DELPHIEU

Marked R.D. Bébé: Ca. 1880s. Perfect bisque head, lovely wig, paperweight eyes, closed mouth; jointed composition body; beautifully dressed; entire doll in good condition. Very good quality bisque:

12-14in (31-36cm)	$ **2200 - 2700**
18-19in (46-48cm)	**3000 - 3500**
24-25in (61-64cm)	**3700 - 4200**
28in (71cm)	**4500 - 5000**
Lesser quality bisque (uneven coloring or much speckling),	
16-18in (41-46cm)	**2250 - 2350**
Open mouth:	
19-22in (48-56cm)	**1900 - 2200**
26-28in (66-71cm)	**2800 - 3000**

FACTS

Rabery & Delphieu of Paris, France. 1856 (founded)-1899, then with S.F.B.J.

Mark:

On back of head: R 5/0 D

Body mark: BÉBÉ RABERY S.——

(Please note last two lines illegible)

12in (31cm) R. 4/0 D. *Jensens' Antique Dolls.*

RAGGEDY ANN AND ANDY

FACTS

Various makers. 1915 to present. All-cloth.

Creator: Johnny B. Gruelle.

Early Raggedy Ann or Andy: Volland. All-cloth with movable arms and legs; brown yarn hair, button eyes, painted features; legs of striped fabric for hose and black for shoes; original clothes; all in good condition.

Mark: "PATENTED SEPT. 7, 1915"

16in (41cm)	$ **1200 - 1400**
Wear, stains, not original clothes	**750 - 850**

19in (48cm) Georgene ***Raggedy Ann*** with black outlined nose. *H & J Foulke, Inc.* (For information see page 171.)

RAGGEDY ANN AND ANDY *continued*

Molly'es Raggedy Ann or **Andy:** 1935-1938, manufactured by Molly'es Doll Outfitters. Red hair and printed features; original clothes; all in good condition. (For photograph see page 9.)

Mark:
"Raggedy Ann and Raggedy Andy Dolls, Manufactured by Molly'es Doll Outfitters" (printed writing in black on front torso)
18-22in (46-56cm)　　**$　1000 - 1200**

19in (48cm) Georgene
Beloved Belindy.
Private Collection.

13in (33cm) Georgene Asleep/Awake Raggedy pair. *H & J Foulke, Inc.*

RAGGEDY ANN AND ANDY
continued

Georgene Raggedy Ann or Andy: 1938-1963, manufactured by Georgene Novelties. Red hair and button eyes; original clothes; all in good condition, some wear and fading acceptable.
Mark: Cloth label sewn in side seam of body.

15-18in (38-46cm)	$	**235 - 285**
Fair condition		**150 - 185**

Asleep/Awake,
13in (33cm)	**700 - 800 pair**

Black outlined nose (see photograph on page 169),
19in (48cm)	**650 - 750**
32in (81cm)	**1400**

Beloved Belindy,
19in (48cm)	**1500 - 1650**

Knickerbocker Toy Co. Raggedy Ann or Andy: 1963 to 1982. Excellent condition.
12-15in (28-38cm)	$	**50 - 65**
24in (61cm)		**110 - 135**
36in (91cm)		**185 - 215**
Beloved Belindy		**750 - 850**
Camel with Wrinkled Knees		**150 - 175**

RECKNAGEL

R.A. Child: Ca. 1890s-World War I. Perfect marked bisque head, jointed composition or wooden body; good wig, set or sleep eyes, open mouth; some dolls with molded painted shoes and socks; all in good condition.

1907, 1909, 1914:
8-9in (20-23cm) 5-piece body	$	**140 - 165**
16-18in (41-46cm)		**325 - 375***
24in (61cm)		**500 - 550***

*Fine quality bisque only.

20in (51cm) 1909 child.
H & J Foulke, Inc.

RECKNAGEL *continued*

R.A. Character Baby: 1909-World War I. Perfect bisque head; cloth baby body or composition bent-limb baby body; painted or glass eyes; nicely dressed; all in good condition.

#121, 126, 127, 1924 infants,		
8-9in (20-23cm) long	$	235 - 285
#23 character babies,		
7-8in (18-20cm)		300 - 350
#22, 28, and 44 bonnet babies,		
8-9in (20-23cm)		550 - 600
11in (28cm)		800
Character children:		
6-8in (15-20cm) composition		
body		300 - 350
18in (46cm) smiling face,		
at auction		1700

#31 Max and #32 Moritz,		
molded hair, painted features,		
8in (20cm)	$	650 - 700**

#45 and 46, Googlies,		
7in (18cm)		500 - 550
#43, molded hat, 7in (18cm), (for photo-		
graph, see page 8)		550 - 600

**Not enough price samples to compute a reliable average.

8-1/2in (22cm) 28 character baby with molded cap. *H & J Foulke, Inc.*

ROLLINSON DOLL

Marked Rollinson Doll: All molded cloth with painted head and limbs; painted hair or human hair wig, painted features (sometimes teeth also); dressed; all in good condition.

Chase-type with painted hair,		
18-22in (46-51cm)	$	800 - 1200
Child with wig:		
16in (41cm)		800 - 1200
26in (66cm)		1500 - 2000

---FACTS---
Utley Doll Co., Holyoke, Mass., U.S.A.
1916-on.
Designer: Gertrude F. Rollinson.
Mark: Stamp in shape of a diamond with a doll in center, around border: "Rollinson Doll Holyoke, Mass."

Chase-type Rollinson child.
Nancy A. Smith Collection.

S.F.B.J.

Child Doll: 1899-on. Perfect bisque head, good French wig, set or sleep eyes, open mouth, pierced ears; jointed composition body; nicely dressed; all in good condition.
Jumeau-type, paperweight eyes (no mold number), 1899-1910:

14-16in (36-41cm)	$	**1100- 1250**
21-23in (53-58cm)		**1700 - 1900**
25-27in (64-69cm)		**2200 - 2500**

#301 (some stampled "Tete Jumeau" on labeled Jumeau body):

12-14in (31-36cm)	**700 - 800**
20-23in (51-58cm)	**1050 - 1150**
28-30in (71-76cm)	**1500 - 1700**
37in (94cm)	**2500 - 2800**
16in (41cm) original trunk with trousseau	**2300**
22in (56cm), lady body	**1200 - 1400**

#60, end of World War I on:

12-14in (31-36cm)	**650 - 700**
19-21in (48-53cm)	**800 - 850**
28in (71cm)	**1100 - 1200**

Bleuette #301,

10-1/2–11in (27-29cm)	**825 - 925***

Walking, kissing and flirting:

22in (56cm)	**1700 - 1800**
All original	**2400**

Papier-mâché head #60, fully-jointed body:

17in (43cm)	**300 - 325**
22in (56cm)	**400 - 500**
18in (46cm) child in original sailor outfit, like new	**1400**

*Brings a much higher price in France.

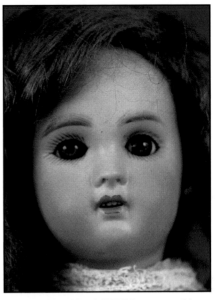

12-1/2in (32cm) SFBJ Jumeau mold, size 3. *H & J Foulke, Inc.*

┌──── FACTS ────
Société Française de Fabrication de Bébés & Jouets, Paris, France. 1899-on.
Mark:

DÉPOSÉ
S.F.B.J.

S.F.B.J
301
PARIS

22in (56cm) 230 character girl.
H & J Foulke, Inc.
(For information see page 174.)

S.F.B.J. *continued*

Character Dolls: 1910-on. Perfect bisque head, wig, molded, sometimes flocked hair on mold numbers 237, 266, 227 and 235, sleep eyes, composition body; nicely dressed; all in good condition.

Mark:

S.F.B.J. • 230 • PARIS	S.F.B.J. 236 PARIS

#226, 20in (51cm) $ 2100 - 2300

#227, 17in (43cm)	1850 - 1900
#239, 16in (41cm)	2000 - 2200

#230 (sometimes Jumeau) (See photograph on page 173.):

12-14in (30-36cm)	1200 - 1400
19-22in (48-56cm)	1900 - 2100
#233, 16in (41cm)	3000 - 3300
#234, 18in (46cm) toddler	3200
#235, 16in (41cm)	1850 - 1900

17in (43cm) 235 character boy. *H & J Foulke, Inc.*

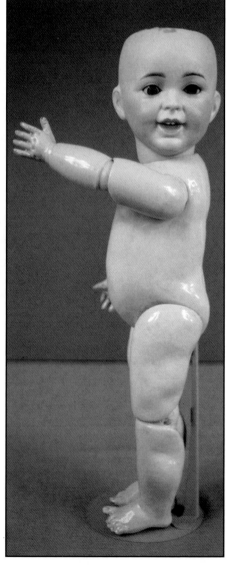

18in (46cm) 236 toddler. *H & J Foulke, Inc.*

#236 baby:	
12in (31cm)	$ 900
15-17in (38-43cm)	**1100 - 1200**
20-22in (51-56cm)	**1500 - 1700**
25in (64cm)	**2000**
Toddler:	
15-16in (38-41cm)	**1600 - 1800**
27-28in (69-71cm)	**2200 - 2500**
#237, 15-16in (38-41cm)	**2000 - 2200**
#238 child,	
15-16in (38-41cm)	**2200**
Lady, 18-19in (46-48cm)	**2400 - 2600**
#239, 13in (33cm)	
all original	**5500 - 6500**
#242 nursing baby,	
13-14in (33-35cm)	**3250**
#245 Googly. (See page 94.)	
#247 baby,	
20-22in (51-56cm)	**2300 - 2500**
Toddler:	
13-15in (33-38cm)	**2300 - 2400**
25-27in (64-69cm)	**3200 - 3700**

#248,	
10-12in (25-30cm)	**7500 - 8500**
#250, 13-15in (33-38cm)	**1500 - 1700**
#251 toddler:	
14-15in (36-38cm)	**1600 - 1700**
20in (51cm)	**2000**
27-28in (69-71cm)	**2600 - 2800**
#252 baby: 10in (25cm)	**2500 - 3000**
15in (38cm)	**4000 - 4200**
Toddler:	
10in (25cm)	**3200 - 3600**
13in (33cm)	**4800**
20in (51cm)	**6500**
24in (61cm) with hairline	**3000**

Boxed set of characters with 3 heads (#233, 235, 237) at auction   **6750**

**Not enough price samples to compute a reliable range.

17in (43cm) 251 child.
H & J Foulke, Inc.

BRUNO SCHMIDT

Marked B. S. W. Child Doll: Ca. 1898-on. Bisque head, good wig, sleep eyes, open mouth; jointed composition child body; dressed; all in good condition.

18-20in (46-51cm)	$	550 - 650
24-26in (61-66cm)		800 - 900
22in (56cm) flirty eyes		825 - 850

─────FACTS─────
Bruno Schmidt, doll factory, Waltershausen, Thüringia, Germany. Heads by Bähr & Pröschild, Ohrdruf, Thüringia, Germany. 1898-on.
Mark:

2096-4

16in (41cm) 2096
"Tommy Tucker".
H & J Foulke, Inc.

24in (61cm) 692
character baby.
*Jensens' Antique
Dolls.*

BRUNO SCHMIDT *continued*

Marked B. S. W. Character Dolls: Bisque socket head, glass eyes; jointed composition body; dressed; all in good condition.

#2048, 2094, 2096 (so-called "Tommy Tucker"), molded hair, open mouth:

13-14in (33-36cm)	$	**1100 - 1250**
19-21in (48-53cm)		**1400 - 1500**
25-26in (64-66cm)		**1900 - 2000**

#2048 (closed mouth):
16-18in (41-46cm) **2500****
#2072:
23in (58cm) toddler **4500 - 5000****
17in (43cm) **3000 - 3500****

#2033 (so-called "Wendy") (537):
12-13in (30-33cm) **12,000 - 13,000**
20in (51cm) **25,000**

#2023 (539):
24in (61cm) at auction **3000**
#2025 (529), closed mouth, wigged:
22in (56cm) **5000 - 6000****
#2026 (538), 22in (56cm) **4500 - 5000****
#2097, #692, character baby, open mouth:
13-14in (33-36cm) $ **500 - 550**
18in (46cm) **750 - 850**
24in (61cm) **1200**
#425 all-bisque baby,
5-1/2–6in (13-15cm) **250 - 300**
#426 all-bisque toddler,
9-1/2in (24cm) **1200****

**Not enough price samples to compute a reliable average.

FRANZ SCHMIDT

Marked S & C Child Doll: Ca. 1890-on. Perfect bisque socket head, good wig, sleep eyes, open mouth; jointed composition child body; dressed; all in good condition. Some are Mold #293 or 269.

6in (15cm)	$	**275 - 325**
16-18in (41-46cm)		**500 - 550**
22-24in (56-61cm)		**650 - 750**
29-30in (74-76cm)		**1050 - 1200**
42in (107cm)		**3200 - 3600**

Shoulder head, kid body,
26in (66cm) **650**
Mark:

S & C
SIMON & HALBIG
28

---FACTS---
Franz Schmidt & Co., doll factory, Georgenthal near Waltershausen, Thüringia, Germany. Heads by Simon & Halbig, Gräfenhain, Thüringia, Germany. 1890-on.

11in (28cm) S&C child.
H & J Foulke, Inc.

FRANZ SCHMIDT *continued*

Marked F.S. & Co. Character Baby: Ca. 1910. Perfect bisque character head, good wig, sleep eyes, open mouth, may have open nostrils; jointed bent-limb composition body; suitably dressed; all in good condition.

#1271, 1272, 1295, 1296, 1297, 1310:
Baby:

12-14in (31-36cm)	$	575 - 675
20-21in (51-53cm)		900 - 950
26-27in (66-69cm)		1500 - 1650

Toddler:

7in (18cm), 5-piece body	750 - 850
10in (25cm), 5-piece body	1000
13-15in (33-38cm)	1000 - 1100
19-21in (48-53cm)	1500 - 1700

#1270, 13in (33cm) baby, all original on fancy bedding with accessories **1800**
#1286, molded hair with blue ribbon, glass eyes, open smiling mouth,
16in (41cm) toddler **4000****

**Not enough price samples to compute a reliable average.

#1267 Character, open/closed mouth, painted eyes
24in (61cm) at auction **2800**
Mark:

1295
F. S. & Co.
Made in
Germany
30

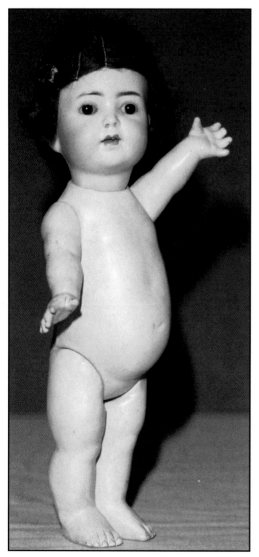

10-1/2in (26cm) 1295 toddler.
H & J Foulke, Inc.

SCHMITT

Marked Schmitt Bébé: Ca. 1879. Perfect bisque socket head with skin or good wig, large paperweight eyes, closed mouth, pierced ears; Schmitt-jointed composition body; appropriate clothes; all in good condition.

Long face:

16-18in (41-46cm)	$	**12,000 - 14,000**
23-25in (58-64cm)		**22,000 - 23,000**

Short face (parted lips) (For photograph see *12th Blue Book*, page 321.):

16-18in (41-46cm)	**16,500 - 17,500**
22in (56cm)	**20,000 - 22,000**

Oval/round face: (For photograph see *11th Blue Book*, page 321.)

11-13in (28-33cm)	**9000 - 10,000***
15-17in (38-43cm)	**12,000 - 14,000***

Cup and saucer neck,

17in (43cm) at auction	**17,050**

Open/closed mouth, two rows of teeth,

24in (61cm)	**25,000****

Papier-mâché head,

16in (41cm)	$	**2200 - 2600**

Body only, signed,

15in (38cm) at auction	**1400**

*Allow one-third less for dolls that do not have strongly molded faces.

**Not enough price samples to compute a reliable average.

FACTS

Schmitt & Fils, Paris, France.
1854-1891.
Mark: On both head and body:

27in (69cm) Schmitt with long face, size 13. *Private Collection.*

SCHOENAU & HOFFMEISTER

Child Doll: 1901-on. Perfect bisque head; original or good wig, sleep eyes, open mouth; ball-jointed body; original or good clothes; all in nice condition.

#1906, 1909, 5700, 5800:

14-16in (36-41cm)	$	350 - 400
21-23in (53-58cm)		550 - 600*
28-30in (71-76cm)		850 - 950
33in (84cm)		1200 - 1300
39in (99cm)		2400 - 2500

#4000, 4600, 5000, 5500:

15-17in (38-43cm)	450 - 500
22in (56cm)	600 - 650

Künstlerkopf,

24-26in (61-66cm)	850 - 950

*Allow $100-200 extra for a flapper body.

┌── FACTS ──┐

Schoenau & Hoffmeister, Porzellanfabrik Burggrub, Burggrub, Bavaria, Germany, porcelain factory, 1901-on. Arthur Schoenau also owned a doll factory. 1884-on.

Trademarks: Hanna, Burggrub Baby, Bébé Carmencita, Viola, Kunstlerkopf, Das Lachende Baby.

Mark:

A S   S ☆PB H
        4600
      Germany

20in (51cm) 1909, all original. *H & J Foulke, Inc.*

SCHOENAU & HOFFMEISTER *continued*

Character Baby: 1910-on. Perfect bisque socket head, good wig, sleep eyes, open mouth; composition bent-limb baby body; all in good condition. #169, 769, "Burggrub Baby" or "Porzellanfabrik Burggrub."

13-15in (33-38cm)	$	**375 - 475**
18-20in (46-51cm)		**550 - 650**
23-24in (58-61cm)		**750 - 800**
28in (71cm)		**1000 - 1100**
Painted bisque,		
14in (36cm) toddler		**250 - 300**

Princess Elizabeth, 1929. Chubby 5-piece body:

17in (43cm)	$	**1900 - 2100**
20-23in (51-58cm)		**2200 - 2500**

Pouty Baby: Ca. 1925. Perfect bisque solid dome head with painted hair, tiny sleep eyes, closed pouty mouth; cloth body with composition arms and legs; dressed; all in good condition.

11-12in (28-31cm)	$	**750 - 800****

Hanna:
Baby:

14-16in (36-41cm)	$	**750 - 800**
20-22in (51-56cm)		**1000 - 1200**
26in (66cm)		**1500**
Toddler, 14-16in (36-41cm)		**1100 - 1250**
Brown, 7-1/2in (19cm) toddler		**350 - 400**

OX: 15in (38cm) toddler **$ 1400 - 1500**

Das Lachende Baby, 1930.

23-24in (58-61cm)	**$2200 - 2500****

**Not enough price samples to compute a reliable range.

14in (36cm) 170 painted bisque toddler.
H & J Foulke, Inc.

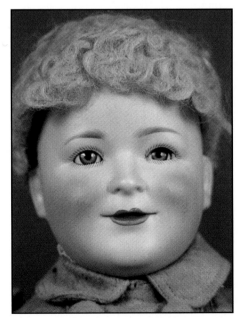

18in (46cm) *Princess Elizabeth.*
H & J Foulke, Inc.

SCHOENHUT

Salesman's Cutaway Sample:
$ 800 - 1000

Shoes, very good condition 200 - 250
Character: 1911-1930. Wooden head and
spring-jointed wooden body, marked head
and/or body; original or appropriate wig,
brown or blue intaglio eyes, open/closed
mouth with painted teeth or closed mouth;
original or suitable clothing; original paint
may have a few scuffs.
14 - 21in (36 - 53cm):
  Excellent condition $ 1500 - 1800*
  Good, some wear 900 - 1200*

*Allow extra for rare faces and exceptional original condition.

Character with carved hair: Ca. 1911-
1930. Wooden head with carved hair, comb
marks, possibly a ribbon or bow, intaglio
eyes, mouth usually closed; spring-jointed
wooden body; original or suitable clothes;
original paint may have a few scuffs.
14-21in (36-53cm):
  Excellent condition $ 2200 - 2500
  Good, some wear 1600 - 1800
  Early style 3500 - 4000
  20in (51cm) man 2200
Tootsie Wootsie,
  15in (38cm) 3000**
Snickelfritz, 15in (38cm), wear 2500**
Carved hat, restored 2500**

** Not enough price samples to compute a
   reliable average.

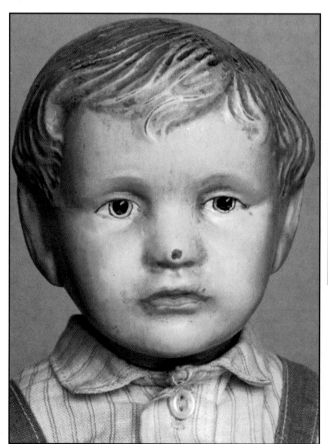

---FACTS---
Albert Schoenhut &
Co., Philadelphia,
Pa., U.S.A. 1872-on.
Wood, spring-jointed,
holes in bottom of
feet to fit metal stand.
11-21in (28-53cm).
Designer: Early:
Adolph Graziana and
Mr. Leslie;
later: Harry E.
Schoenhut.
Mark: Paper label:

Incised:

SCHOENHUT DOLL
PAT. JAN. 17, '11, U.S.A.
& FOREIGN COUNTRIES

16in (41cm)
#16/201/603 as
shown in 1911
Schoenhut catalogue.
Private Collection.
*Photograph by Carol
Corson.*

SCHOENHUT *continued*

Baby Face: Ca. 1913-1930. Wooden head and fully-jointed toddler or bent-limb baby body, marked head and/or body; painted hair or mohair wig, painted eyes, open or closed mouth; suitably dressed; original paint; all in good condition, with some wear.

Mark:

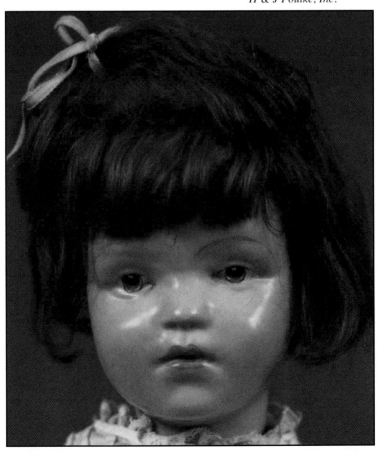

Baby:

12in (31cm)	$ **550 - 600**
15-16in (38-41cm)	**700 - 800**

Toddler:

11in (28cm)	$ **800 - 900**
14in (36cm)	**800 - 850***
16-17in (41-43cm)	**850 - 950***

*Allow more for mint condition.

Mama Doll: 1924-1927. Wood head and hands, cloth body.

14-17in (36-43cm)	**1100 - 1200****

Walker: Ca. 1919-1930. All-wood with "baby face," mohair wig, painted eyes; curved arms, straight legs with "walker" joint at hip; no holes in bottom of feet; original or appropriate clothes; all in good condition; original paint.

13in (33cm)	$ **700 - 800**
17in (43cm), excellent with original shoes	**1000 - 1100**

21in (53cm) pouty 308 girl.
H & J Foulke, Inc.

Dolly Face: Ca. 1915-1930. Wooden head and spring-jointed wooden body; original or appropriate mohair wig, decal eyes, open/closed mouth with painted teeth; original paint; original or suitable clothes.
14-21in (36-53cm):

Excellent condition	$	**750 - 850**
Good condition, some wear		**550 - 650**

Sleep Eyes: Ca. 1920-1930. Used with "baby face" or "dolly face" heads. Mouths on this type were open with teeth or barely open with carved teeth. Original paint.
14-21in (36-53cm):

Excellent condition	**$ 1100 - 1300**

Good condition	**750 - 850**

All-Composition: Ca. 1924. Molded blonde curly hair, painted eyes, tiny closed mouth; original or appropriate clothing; in good condition.
Paper label on back:

13in (33cm)	**$ 500 - 600****

**Not enough price samples to compute a reliable range.

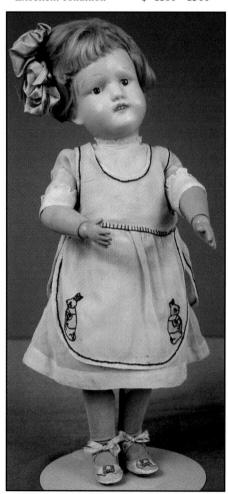

15in (38cm) dolly-face Schoenhut. *H & J Foulke, Inc.*

19in (48cm) sleep-eyed Schoenhut, all original. *H & J Foulke, Inc.*

SIMON & HALBIG

FACTS
Simon & Halbig, porcelain factory, Gräfenhain, Thüringia, Germany, purchased by Kämmer & Reinhardt in 1920. 1869-on.

Mark:

$$S\ 13\ H$$
$$949$$

$$1079-2$$
$$DEP$$
$$S\ H$$
$$Germany$$

Shoulder head with molded hair: Ca. 1870s. Perfect bisque shoulder head, painted or glass eyes, closed mouth, molded hair; cloth body, bisque lower arms; appropriately dressed; all in good condition.

Mark:

$$S\ 7\ H$$

on front shoulder plate

18-20in (46-51cm)   **$ 1500 - 2000**
9in (23cm) with painted eyes and
   swivel neck   **1250**
12in (31cm)glass eyes, swivel neck **1500**

Fashion Doll (Poupée): Ca. 1870s. Perfect bisque socket head on bisque shoulder plate, glass eyes, closed mouth, good mohair wig or molded blonde hair; gusseted kid lady body; appropriately dressed; all in good condition. No marks. (For face see *12th Blue Book* page 330.)
15-16in (38-41cm)   **$ 2800 - 3000**
Twill over wood body:
  9-10in (23-25cm)   **3300 - 3800**
  15-16in (38-41cm)   **5200 - 5700**
Cloth body, 15in (38cm)   **2100**

17in (43cm) 939 with square teeth. *H & J Foulke, Inc.* (For information see page 186.)

9in (23cm) lady with swivel neck, painted eyes. *Richard Wright Antiques.*

SIMON & HALBIG *continued*

Child doll with closed mouth: Ca. 1879.
Perfect bisque socket head on ball-jointed
wood and composition body; good wig,
glass set or sleep eyes, closed mouth,
pierced ears, dressed; all in good condition.
(See *Simon & Halbig Dolls, The Artful
Aspect* for photographs of mold numbers not
shown here.)

#719, 19-21in (48-53cm)	$ 3500 - 3800	
#749, 20-22in (51-56cm)	3500**	
#905, 908, 14-17in (36-43cm)	2500 - 3000	
#929, 18-21in (46-53cm)	3500 - 4500**	

#939 (See photograph on page 185.):

14-15in (36-38cm)	2500 - 2700
19-22in (48-56cm)	3100 - 3600
27in (69cm)	4700

#949:

15-16in (38-41cm)	2100 - 2500
22-23in (56-58cm)	2900 - 3100
27-28in (69-71cm)	3800 - 4200
#979, 15-16in (38-41cm)	3000**

All-Bisque Child: 1880-on. All-bisque
child with swivel neck, pegged shoulders
and hips; appropriate mohair wig, glass
eyes, open or closed mouth; molded stockings and shoes.

#886 and 890:
Over-the-knee black or blue stockings:

5-1/2–6in (14-15cm)	$ 750 - 850*
7-7-1/2 (18-19cm)	950 - 1100*
8-1/2in (22cm)	1500 - 1700*

Early model with 5-strap bootines, closed
mouth:

7in (18cm)	1600 - 1800*
9in (23cm)	2200 - 2500*

Open mouth with square cut teeth:

6in (15cm)	1250 - 1400*
8in (20cm)	1800 - 2000*

Kid or **Cloth Body**:
#720, 740, 940, 950:

9-10in (23-25cm)	$ 550 - 650
16-18in (41-46cm)	1200 - 1400
22in (56cm)	1600 - 1800
#949, 18-21in (46-53cm)	1800 - 2200
#920, 16-20in (41-51cm)	2000 - 2500
#905, 12in (31cm)	1200 - 1300
20in (51cm)	2000 - 2200

*Allow extra for original clothes.
**Not enough price samples to compute a
reliable range.

21in (53cm) shoulder head.
H & J Foulke, Inc.

SIMON & HALBIG *continued*

Child doll with open mouth and composition body: Ca. 1889 to 1930s. Perfect bisque head, good wig, sleep or paperweight eyes, open mouth, pierced ears; original ball-jointed composition body; very pretty clothes; all in nice condition. (See *Simon & Halbig Dolls, The Artful Aspect* for photographs of mold numbers not shown here.)

#719, 739, 749, 759, 769, 939, 949, 979:

12-14in (31-36cm)	**$ 1150 - 1450***
19-22in (48-56cm)	**2000 - 2300***
29-30in (74-76cm)	**2800 - 3000***
23in (58cm) Edison, operating	**4800**

*Allow $200-300 extra for square cut teeth.

#929, 23in (58cm) at auction	**3800**
#939, 40in (102cm)	**4000 - 4400**
#905, 908, 12-14in (31-36cm)	**1500 - 1800**
#1009:	
15-16in (38-41cm)	**900 - 1000**
19-21in (48-53cm)	**1300 - 1600**
24-25in (61-64cm)	**1800 - 2000**
#1039:	
16-18in (41-46cm)	**800 - 1000**
23-25in (58-64cm)	**1150 - 1350**

#1139, 13in (33cm)	**1100 - 1200**
#1039, key-wind walking body,	
16-17in (41-43cm)	**1700 - 1800**
#1039, walking, kissing,	
20-22in (51-56cm)	**1050 - 1250**
#1078, 1079:	
7-8in (18-20cm) 5-piece body	**425 - 475**
8in (20cm)	**500 - 550**
10-12in (25-31cm)	**500 - 600**
14-15in (36-38cm)	**650 - 675**
17-19in (43-48cm)	**775 - 850**
22-24in (56-61cm)	**900 - 1000**
28-30in (71-76cm)	**1200 - 1400**
34-35in (86-89cm)	**2000 - 2200**
42in (107cm)	**3800 - 4200**
#1248, 1249, Santa:	
13-15in (33-38cm)	**900 - 1000**
21-24in (53-61cm)	**1300 - 1500**
26-28in (66-71cm)	**1700 - 1900**
32in (81cm)	**2200 - 2300**
38in (96cm)	**3200**
#540, 550, 570, Baby Blanche:	
22-24in (56-61cm)	**750 - 850**
#176, (A. Hülss):	
Flapper, 18in (46cm)	**850**

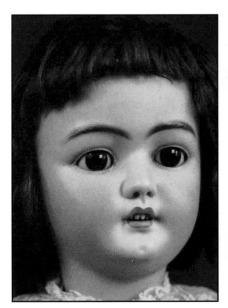

28in (71cm) 1079 child. *H & J Foulke, Inc.*

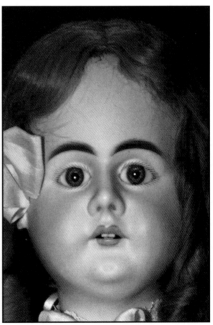

33in (84cm) 979 child.
Jensens' Antique Dolls.

19in (48cm) 1299 character girl. *H & J Foulke, Inc.* (For information see page 190.)

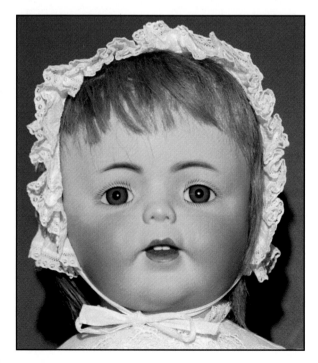

27in (69cm) *Erika* #1489. *Jensens' Antique Dolls.* (For information see page 191.)

Next Page: 22in (56cm) 174 character child. *H & J Foulke, Inc.* (For information see page 190.)

SIMON & HALBIG *continued*

SIMON & HALBIG *continued*

Child doll with open mouth and kid body: Ca. 1889 to 1930s. Perfect bisque swivel head on shoulder plate or shoulder head with stationary neck, sleep eyes; well costumed; all in good condition.

#1010, 1040, 1080, 1260:

14-16in (36-41cm)	$ 500 - 600
21-23in (53-58cm)	700 - 800
#1009, 17-19in (43-48cm)	850 - 950

#1250 with pink kid body and composition arms:

14-16in (36-41cm)	550 - 650
22-24in (56-61cm)	800 - 900
29in (74cm)	1000 - 1100
#949, 19-21in (48-53cm)	1200 - 1400

So-called "Little Women" type: Ca. 1900. Mold number 1160. Shoulder head with fancy mohair wig, glass set eyes, closed mouth; cloth body with bisque limbs, molded boots; dressed; all in good condition.

5-1/2–7in (14-18cm)	$ 350 - 400
10-11in (25-28cm)	425 - 475
14in (36cm)	650 - 750

Character Child: Ca. 1909. Perfect bisque socket head with wig or molded hair, painted or glass eyes, open or closed mouth, character face, jointed composition body; dressed; all in good condition. (See photographs on pages 188 and 189 and see *Simon & Halbig Dolls, The Artful Aspect* for photographs of mold numbers not shown here.)

#120, 21in (53cm)	$ 3500 - 4000**	
#150:		
14in (36cm)		12,000**
20in (51cm)		23,000**
#151:		
14-15in (36-38cm)		4000 - 4500
24in (61cm)		8500
#153:		
14in (36cm)		18,000
17in (43cm)		30,000
#174, 22in (56cm)		1650**
#600, 19in (48cm) toddler		1650
#1279:		
14-17in (36-43cm)		2000 - 2400
19-21in (48-53cm)		2700 - 3200
27in (69cm)		5500 - 6000
#1299, 14-17in (36-43cm)		1200 - 1600
#1339:		
18in (46cm)		1000 - 1100**
28-32in (71-81cm)		1900 - 2100**
#1388, 23in (58cm)		30,000**
Large chip and 2 hairlines in neck socket	$	16,500
#1398, 23in (58cm)		20,000**
IV, #1448:		
13-14in (33-36cm)	16,000 - 18,000**	
17-18in (43-46cm)		24,000**

**Not enough price samples to compute a reliable range.

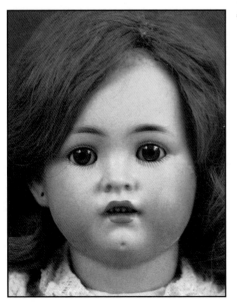

19in (48cm) 600 toddler.
H & J Foulke, Inc.

SIMON & HALBIG *continued*

Character Baby: Ca. 1909 to 1930s. Perfect bisque head, molded hair or wig, sleep or painted eyes, open or open/closed mouth; composition bent-limb baby or toddler body; nicely dressed; all in good condition. (See *Simon & Halbig Dolls, The Artful Aspect* for photographs of mold numbers not shown here.)

#156 (A. Hülss):
Baby, 15-17in (38-43cm)	$	650 - 750
23in (58cm)		1250 - 1350
Toddler, 10-11in (25-28cm)		850 - 950
18-20in (46-51cm)		1300 - 1500

#1294:
Baby, 17-19in (43-48cm)	750 - 850
23-25in (58-64cm)	1100 - 1300
Toddler, 20in (51cm)	1500 - 1600
28in (71cm) with clockwork eyes	2500**

#1428:
Baby, 13-14in (33-36cm)	1500 - 1800
21in (53cm)	2700 - 3000
Toddler, 15-18in (38-46cm)	2400 - 2600
24in (61cm)	3750

#1488:
Baby, 20in (51cm)	5500
Toddler, 16-18in (41-46cm)	4500 - 5000

#1489 Erika, baby:
21-22in (53-56cm)	3700 - 4200**

#1498:
Baby, 16in (41cm)	2500**
Toddler, 22in (56cm)	4600**
#172, baby:	3500

Lady doll: Ca. 1910. Perfect bisque socket head, good wig, sleep eyes, pierced ears; lady body, molded bust, slim arms and legs; dressed; all in good condition.

#1159 (may have an H. Handwerck body):
12in (31cm)	$	1100 - 1200
16-18in (41-46cm)		1800 - 2000
24in (61cm)		2500 - 2700
20in (51cm) with trunk and trousseau		5200

#1468, 1469:
13-15in (33-38cm)	
naked	2000 - 2300
Original clothes	3000 - 4200

#1303 lady,
20in (51cm)	18,000 - 20,000

#152 lady:
18in (46cm)	15,000 up**
25in (64cm)	25,000**

#1308 man,
13in (33cm)	13,000**
#1307, 21in (53cm)	12,500

#1303 Indian,
21in (53cm)	17,000**
#1305, 18in (46cm)	12,500

Mary Pickford,
40in (102cm) at auction	34,000

**Not enough price samples to compute a reliable range.

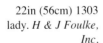

22in (56cm) 1303 lady. *H & J Foulke, Inc.*

SNOW BABIES AND SANTAS

Snow Babies: All-bisque with snowsuits and caps of pebbly-textured bisque; painted features; various standing, lying or sitting positions.

1-1/2in (4cm)	$	**50 - 60**
2-1/2in (6cm)		**125 - 140**
3in (9cm) huskies pulling sled with snow baby		**300**
2-1/2in (6cm) snowman		**95 - 110**
3in (8cm) baby riding snow bear		**250 - 300**
2-1/2in (6cm) tumbling snow baby		**165 - 175**
2in (5cm) musical snow baby		**85 - 95**
2in (5cm) baby on sled		**125**
3in (8cm) baby on sled		**175 - 200**
2in (5cm) reindeer pulling snow baby		**250**
2-1/2in (6cm) snow baby riding reindeer		**300**
2in (5cm) twins		**110 - 125**
2in (5cm) early fine quality babies with high hoods		**165 - 175**

Three small babies on sled	**175 - 195**
Santa on snow bear	**350 - 400**
3-1/2in (9cm) jointed snow baby	**350**
1-1/2in (4cm) seated dressed snow girl	**125**
2-1/2in (6cm) babies sliding on cellar door	**250 - 300**
2in (5cm) snow dog and snowman on sled	**250 - 300**
2-1/2in (6cm) Santa going down chimney	**350**
Snow bears	**50 - 75**
Snow boy or girl on sled	**150 - 165**
Shoulder head, cloth body:	
4-1/2in (11cm)	**185**
10in (25cm)	**250 - 300**
Train engine with coal car and Santa	**400**

"No Snows":

Boy and girl on sled, 2in (5cm)	**165**
Skiing boy, 2-1/2in (6cm)	**95**

FACTS

Various German firms including Hertwig & Co. and Bähr & Pröschild after 1910. **Mark:** Sometimes "Germany."

1-1/4-1-1/2 (3-4cm) snow babies. *H & J Foulke, Inc.*

2in (5cm) children on sleds. *H & J Foulke, Inc.*

SONNEBERG TÄUFLING
(SO-CALLED MOTSCHMANN BABY)

Sonneberg Täufling: Papier-mâché or wax-over-composition head with painted hair, dark pupil-less glass eyes; composition lower torso; composition and wood arms and legs jointed at ankles and wrists, cloth covered midsection with voice box, upper arms and legs cloth covered, called floating joints; dressed in shift and bonnet. (For body photograph see *11th Blue Book*, page 336.)

Very good condition:

6in (15cm)	$	600
12-14in (31-36cm)		1000 - 1200
18-20in (46-51cm)		1600 - 2000
24in (61cm)		2200 - 2500

Fair condition, with wear:

12-14in (31-36cm)	500 - 600
18-20in (46-51cm)	800 - 900

Note: For many years it was thought that these dolls were made by Ch. Motschmann because some were found stamped with his name; hence, they were called Motschmann Babies by collectors. However, research has shown that they were made by various factories and that Motschmann was the holder of the patent for the voice boxes, not the manufacturer of the dolls.

FACTS
Various Sonneberg factories such as Heinrich Stier; many handled by exporter Louis Lindner & Söhn, Sonneberg, Thüringia, Germany. 1851-1880s.
Mark: None.

23in (58cm) Sonneberg Täufling.
H & J Foulke, Inc.

STEIFF

Steiff Doll: Felt, plush or velvet, jointed; seam down middle of face, button eyes, painted features; original clothes; most are character dolls, many have large shoes to enable them to stand; all in excellent condition.

Children (Character Dolls):

11-12in (28-31cm)	$	900 - 1250
16-17in (41-43cm)		1500 - 1650
Black child, 17in (43cm)		2100
Adults,*		2000 - 4000
Gnome, 12in (31cm)		700 - 900

*Fewer women are available than men.

U.S. Zone Germany:
12in (31cm) child with glass eyes   500 - 600

Collector's Note: To bring the prices quoted, Steiff dolls must be clean and have good color. Faded and dirty dolls bring only one-third to one-half of these prices.

FACTS
Fräulein Margarete Steiff, Würtemberg, Germany. 1894-on.
Mark: Metal button in ear.

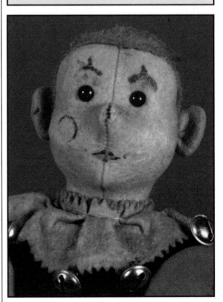

Steiff clown. *Nancy A. Smith Collection.*

JULES STEINER

Round face: Ca. 1870s. Perfect very pale bisque socket head, appropriate wig, bulgy paperweight eyes, round face, pierced ears; jointed composition body; dressed; all in good condition.
Mark: None, but sometimes body has a label.

Two rows of pointed teeth,
  16-19in (41-48cm) $ **6000 - 7000**
    Closed mouth,
    18-22in (46-56cm)   **7500 - 8500**

Gigoteur: Kicking, crying bébé, mechanical key-wind body with composition arms and lower legs.
  17-18in (43-46cm) $ **2100 - 2300**
  23in (58cm)   **2600 - 2750**
Täufling-type body: Bisque shoulders, hips and lower arms and legs.
  18-21in (46-53cm) $ **6500**
  Swivel neck   **7500**

```
┌─────────── FACTS ───────────┐
│  Jules Nicolas Steiner and successors,  │
│       Paris, France. 1855-1908.         │
└─────────────────────────────┘
```

23in (58cm) *Bébé Gigoteur*. *H & J Foulke, Inc.*

17in (43cm) Series C, all original. *Private Collection.* (For more information see page 196.)

9in (23cm) Figure A, size 2, all original swaddled *Bébé. H & J Foulke, Inc.* (For more information see page 196.)

23in (58cm) Figure A-15. *Kay & Wayne Jensen Collection.* (For more information see page 196.)

JULES STEINER *continued*

Marked C or A Series Steiner Bébé: 1880s. Perfect socket head, cardboard pate, appropriate wig, sleep eyes with wire mechanism or bulgy paperweight eyes with tinting on upper eyelids, closed mouth, round face, pierced ears with tinted tips; jointed composition body with straight wrists and stubby fingers (sometimes with bisque hands); appropriately dressed; all in good condition. Sizes 4/0 (8in) to 8 (38in). Series "C" more easily found than "A."

Mark: (incised)

$S^{IE} A O$

(red script)

J. Steiner Bte Sg Dg J Bourgoin Sze

(incised)

$S^{IE} C 4$

(red stamp)

J. STEINER B.S. G.D.G.

8-10in (20-25cm)	$ 3500 - 4500
15-16in (38-41cm)	5000 - 6000
21-24in (53-61cm)	6900 - 7500
28in (71cm)	8500 - 9500
32in (81cm) wire eyes and bisque hands, at auction	15,400

Wax plate with inset hair, 15-1/2in (39cm)	25,000**

Series G:

18in (46cm)	21,000
28in (71cm)	32,000

Figure A Steiner Bébé: Ca. 1887-on. Perfect bisque socket head, cardboard pate, appropriate wig, paperweight eyes, closed mouth, pierced ears; jointed composition body; appropriately dressed; all in good condition. Figure "A" more easily found than "C."

Mark: (incised)

J. STEINER

B^{TE} S.G.D.G.

PARIS

F^{RE} A 15

Body and/or head may be stamped:
"Le Petit Parisien
BEBE STEINER
MEDAILLE d'OR
PARIS 1889"
or paper label of doll carrying flag

8-10in (20-25cm)		
5-piece body	$	2600 - 3000
8-10in (20-25cm)		
fully jointed		3000 - 3500
15-16in (38-41cm)		4400 - 5000
22-24in (56-61cm)		5500 - 6500
28-30in (71-76cm)		7000 - 7500

Open mouth:	
17in (43cm)	2500
22in (56cm)	2900
33in (84cm) with wire eyes	4500

Figure B: Open mouth with two rows of teeth.

23-25in (58-64cm)	5000 - 6000
32in (81cm) at auction	7000
Figure C: closed mouth,	
19-23in (48-58cm)	6000 - 7500
Figure D: closed mouth,	
25in (64cm) at auction	38,000

Bébé Le Parisien: 1892-on. Perfect bisque socket head, cardboard pate, appropriate wig, paperweight eyes, closed mouth, pierced ears; jointed composition body; appropriately dressed; all in good condition.

Mark: head (incised):

A -19
PARIS

(red stamp):

"LE PARISIEN"
body (purple stamp):
"BEBE 'LE PARISIEN'
MEDAILLE D'OR
PARIS"

8-10in (20-25cm) fully jointed body	$	2800 - 3200
13-15in (33-38cm)		3500 - 4000
18-20in (46-51cm)		4500 - 5000
23-25in (58-64cm)		5500 - 6000
30in (76cm)		7000 - 8000
5-piece body:		
8in (20cm)		2000 - 2200
10-12in (25-31cm)		2200 - 2500

Open mouth,	
20-22in (51-56cm)	2600 - 2800

SWAINE & CO.

Swaine Character Babies: Ca. 1910-on. Perfect bisque head; composition baby body with bent limbs; dressed; all in good condition. (See previous *Blue Books* for photographs of specific models.)
Incised Lori, molded hair, glass eyes, open/closed mouth,

22-24in (56-61cm)	$ **2700 - 3000**

#232, (open-mouth Lori):

8-1/2in (21cm)	**750 - 800**
12-14in (31-36cm)	**1000 - 1100**
20-22in (51-56cm)	**1700 - 1800**

DIP (wig, glass eyes, closed mouth):

8-1/2–9-1/2in (21-24cm)	**750 - 800**
11in (28cm)	**900 - 950**
14-16in (36-41cm)	**1300 - 1400**
14in (36cm) toddler	**1800**

DV (molded hair, glass eyes, open/closed mouth):

13in (33cm)	**1450**
16in (41cm)	**1650**

DI (molded hair, intaglio eyes, open/closed mouth):

12-13in (31-33cm)	**850 - 900**

B.P., B.O. (smiling character):

16-18in (41-46cm)	**5000****

F.P.,

8-9in (20-23cm)	**900 - 1250****

**Not enough price samples to compute a reliable range.

FACTS

Swaine & Co., porcelain factory, Hüttensteinach, Sonneberg, Thüringia, Germany. Ca. 1910-on for doll heads.
Mark: Stamped in green:

8-1/2in (22cm)
DIP. *H & J Foulke, Inc.*

THUILLIER

Marked A.T. Child: Perfect bisque head, cork pate, good wig, paperweight eyes, pierced ears, closed mouth; body of wood, kid or composition; appropriate old wig and clothes, excellent quality; in good condition.

12-13in (31-33cm)	$	25,000 - 30,000
16-18in (41-46cm)		35,000 - 43,000
22-24in (56-61cm)		47,000 - 52,000

Open mouth, two rows of teeth:

20-22in (51-56cm)	9000 - 12,000
36in (91cm)	25,000

Approximate size chart:
1 = 9in (23cm)
3 = 12in (31cm)
7 = 15-1/2in (39cm)
9 = 18in (46cm)
12 = 22-23in (56-58cm)
15 = 36-37in (91-93cm)

---FACTS---
A. Thuillier, Paris, France. Some heads by F. Gaultier. 1875-1893.
Mark:
A. 8 . T.

21in (53cm) open mouth A.9T. *Kay & Wayne Jensen Collection.*

UNIS

Unis Child Doll: Perfect bisque head, wood and composition jointed body; good wig, sleep eyes, open mouth; pretty clothes; all in nice condition.

#301 or 60 (fully-jointed body):

8-10in (20-25cm)	$	425 - 475
15-17in (38-43cm)		650 - 700
23-25in (58-64cm)		900 - 1000
28in (71cm)		1200

5-piece body:

5in (13cm) painted eyes	150 - 175
6-1/2in (17cm) glass eyes	240 - 265
11-13in (28-33cm)	325 - 350

Black or brown bisque,

11-13in (28-33cm)	375 - 425

Bleuette,

11in (28cm)	800 - 850*

Princess (See page 111.)

#251 character toddler:

14-15in (36-38cm)	1400 - 1500
28in (71cm)	2200 - 2400

Composition head 301 or 60:

11-13in (28-33cm)	150 - 175
20in (51cm)	350 - 400

Composition head #251 or #247 toddler,

22in (56cm)	650 - 750

*Brings a much higher price in France.

FACTS

Société Française de Fabrication de Bébés et Jouets. (S.F.B.J.) of Paris and Montreuil-sous-Bois, France. 1922 on.

Mark:

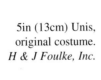

5in (13cm) Unis, original costume. *H & J Foulke, Inc.*

IZANNAH WALKER

Izannah Walker Doll: Stockinette, pressed head, features and hair painted with oils, applied ears, treated limbs; muslin body; appropriate clothes; in good condition.

Pre-patent dolls:

17-19in (43-48cm)	$	**16,000 - 18,000**
Fair condition		**8500 - 9500**
Very worn		**3000 - 4000**
1873 patent dolls, molded ears,		
18in (46cm)		**4000 - 6000**

---FACTS---

Izannah Walker, Central Falls, R.I., U.S.A. 1873, but probably made as early as 1840s.

Mark: Later dolls are marked:

Patented Nov. 4ᵗʰ 1873

17in (43cm) Izannah Walker (restoration). *Pearl D. Morley Collection.*

WAX DOLL, POURED

WAX (REINFORCED)

Poured Wax Doll: Head, lower arms and legs of wax; cloth body; set-in hair, glass eyes; lovely elaborate original clothes or very well dressed; all in good condition.

Baby:

17-19in (43-48cm)	**$ 1500 - 1750***
23-24in (58-61cm)	**1900 - 2200***
Child, 17-18in (43-46cm)	**1500 - 1800***

Baby or child, lackluster ordinary face,

20-22in (51-56cm)	**800 - 1000**
Lady, 22-24in (56-61cm)	**2500 - 3500**

*Varies greatly depending upon appeal of face.

FACTS

Various firms in London, England, such as Montanari, Pierotti, Peck, Meech, Marsh, Morrell, Cremer and Edwards. 1850s through the early 1900s.
Mark: Sometimes stamped on body with maker or store.

Reinforced Poured Wax Doll: Poured wax shoulder head lined on the inside with plaster composition, glass eyes (may sleep), closed mouth, open crown, pate, curly mohair or human hair wig nailed on (may be partially inset into the wax around the face); muslin body with wax-over-composition lower limbs (feet may have molded boots); appropriate clothes; all in good condition, but showing some nicks and scrapes.

11in (28cm)	$	**225 - 250**
14-16in (36-41cm)		**325 - 375**
19-21in (48-53cm)		**500 - 550**
Lady, 23in (58cm)		**800 - 1000**
with molded shoulder plate		**2500****
with molded gloves, all original		**2500****

Socket head on ball-jointed composition body (Kestner-type):

13in (33cm)	**700 - 800**
19in (48cm)	**1200 - 1300**

**Not enough price samples to compute a reliable average.

FACTS

Various firms in Germany. 1860-1890.
Mark: None.

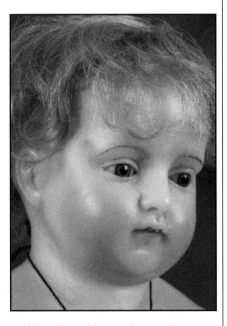

24in (61cm) Montanari, poured wax.
Private Collection.

WAX-OVER-COMPOSITION

English Slit-head Wax: Ca. 1830-1860. Round face, human hair wig, glass eyes (may open and close by a wire), faintly smiling; all in fair condition, showing wear.

18-22in (46-56cm)	$	900 - 1100
26-28in (66-71cm)		1300 - 1500

Molded Hair Doll: Ca. 1860-on. German wax-over-composition shoulder head; nice old clothes; all in good condition, good quality.

14-16in (36-41cm)	$	275 - 325
22-25in (56-64cm)		450 - 550

Alice hairdo, 16in (41cm), early model, squeaker torso   **550 - 650**

Wax-over Doll with Wig: Ca. 1860s to 1900. German. Original clothing or suitably dressed; entire doll in nice condition.

Standard quality:

16-18in (41-46cm)	$	250 - 300
22-24in (56-61cm)		350 - 400

Superior quality (heavily waxed):

16-18in (41-46cm)		375 - 425
22-24in (56-61cm)		550 - 650

30in (76cm)		750

"Blinking" eye doll, eyes open and close with bellows in torso,

16in (41cm) all original	**1000**

Molded Bonnet Wax-over Doll: Ca. 1860-1880. Nice old clothes; all in good condition.

16-17in (41-43cm),		
common model	$	350
20in (51cm) boy with cap		550 - 600
20-24in (51-61cm) lady with		
unusual hat		2000 - 3000

Double-Faced Doll: 1880-on. Fritz Bartenstein. One face crying, one laughing, rotating on a vertical axis by pulling a string, one face hidden by a hood. Body stamped "Bartenstein."

15-16in (38-41cm)	$	850

FACTS

Numerous firms in England, Germany or France. During the 1800s.
Mark: None.

20in (51cm) wax-over with wig, all original. *H & J Foulke, Inc.*

NORAH WELLINGS

Wellings Doll: All-fabric, stitch-jointed shoulders and hips; molded fabric face (also of papier-mâché, sometimes stockinette covered), painted features; all in excellent condition. Most commonly found are sailors, Canadian Mounties, Scots and Black Islanders.

Characters (floppy limbs):
8-10in (20-25cm)	$	75 - 100
13-14in (33-36cm)		150 - 200
Glass eyes, 14in (36cm) black		250

Children:
12-13in (31-33cm)	400 - 500
16-18in (41-46cm)	600 - 700
23in (58cm)	900 - 1000
11-1/2in (29cm) chubby toddler	350
Glass eyes, 16-18in (41-46cm)	700 - 800

Boudoir Doll, 22-24in (56-61cm)	300 - 400
Old Couple,	
26in (66cm)	1200 - 1500 pair
Bobby, 16in (41cm) glass eyes	800 - 1000
Harry the Hawk, 10in (25cm)	200
Nightdress Case	400
Baby, 11in (28cm)	350 - 400
Rabbit, 9in (23cm)	350

FACTS
Victoria Toy Works, Wellington, Shropshire, England, for Norah Wellings. 1926-Ca. 1960.
Designer: Norah Wellings
Mark: On tag on foot: "Made in England by Norah Wellings."

9in (23cm) rabbit.
H & J Foulke, Inc.

9-1/2in (24cm) pixie.
H & J Foulke, Inc.

WOOD, ENGLISH

William & Mary Period: Ca. 1690. Carved wooden face, painted eyes, tiny lines comprising eyebrows and eyelashes, rouged cheeks, flax or hair wig; wood body, cloth arms, carved wood hands (fork shaped), wood-jointed legs. Appropriate clothes; all in fair condition.

12-17in (31-43cm)	**$ 40,000**

Queen Anne Period: Ca. early 1700s. Carved wooden face, dark glass eyes (sometimes painted), dotted eyebrows and eyelashes; jointed wood body, cloth upper arms; appropriate clothes; all in fair condition.

24in (61cm)	**$ 25,000 up**

Georgian Period: Mid to late 1700s. Round wooden head with gesso covering, inset glass eyes (later sometimes blue), dotted eyelashes and eyebrows, flax or hair wig; jointed wood body with pointed torso; appropriate clothes; all in fair condition.

12-13in (31-33cm)	**$ 2500 - 3200**
16-18in (41-46cm)	**4500**
24in (61cm)	**6000**

Early 19th Century: Wooden head, gessoed, painted eyes, pointed torso, flax or hair wig; old clothes (dress usually longer than legs); all in fair condition.

13in (33cm)	**$ 1300 - 1600**
16-21in (41-53cm)	**2000 - 3000**

FACTS

English craftsmen. Late 17th to mid 19th century.
Mark: None.

26in (66cm) Queen Anne Period wood. *Private Collection.*

WOOD, GERMAN (PEG WOODENS)

Early to Mid 19th Century: Delicately carved head, varnished, carved and painted hair and features, with a yellow tuck comb in hair, painted spit curls, sometimes earrings; mortise and tenon peg joints; old clothes; all in fair condition.

4in (10cm)	$	450 - 550
6-7in (15-18cm)		650 - 750
12-13in (31-33cm)		1350 - 1450
17-18in (43-46cm)		1800 - 2000
28in (71cm) exceptional carving,		
naked, at auction		16,200
Fortune tellers,		
17-20in (43-51cm)		2500 - 3000
Shell dolls,		
8-1/2in (28cm)		1200 - 1300 pair
Peddler with lovely old wares,		
8in (20cm)		2400

Late 19th Century: Wooden head with painted hair, carving not so elaborate as previously, sometimes earrings, spit curls; dressed; all in good condition.

4in (10cm)	$	125 - 135
7-8in (18-20cm)		175 - 225

12in (31cm)	350 - 400
Turned red torso,	
10in (25cm)	150 - 200

Wood shoulder head, carved bun hairdo, cloth body, wood limbs:

9in (23cm) all original	350 - 400
17in (43cm)	500 - 550
24in (61cm)	800 - 900

Early 20th Century: Turned wood head, carved nose, painted hair, peg-jointed, painted white lower legs, painted black shoes.

11-12in (28-31cm)		
	$	60 - 80

FACTS

Craftsmen of the Grodner Tal, Austria, and Sonneberg, Germany, such as Insam & Prinoth (1820-1830) Gorden Tirol and Nürnberg verlagers of pegwood dolls and wood doll heads. Late 18th to 20th century.
Mark: None.

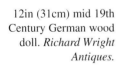

12in (31cm) mid 19th Century German wood doll. *Richard Wright Antiques.*

WOOD, GERMAN (20TH CENTURY)

"Bébé Tout en Bois" (Doll All of Wood): All of wood, fully jointed; wig, inset glass eyes, open mouth with teeth; appropriate clothes; all in fair to good condition.

Child:

13in (33cm)	$	425 - 475
17-19in (43-48cm)		650 - 750
22-24in (56-61cm)		950
18in (46cm) mint, all original		1100
Baby, 16-1/2in (42cm)	$	400 - 500

---FACTS---
Various companies, such as Rudolf Schneider and Schilling, Sonneberg, Thüringia, Germany. 1901-1914.
For French trade.
Mark: Usually none; sometimes Schilling "winged angel" trademark.

17-/12in (45cm) *Tout en Bois* child.
H & J Foulke, Inc.

WOOD, SWISS

Swiss Linden Wood Doll: Wooden head with hand-carved features and hair with good detail (males sometimes have carved hats); all carved wood jointed body; original, regional attire; excellent condition.

9-10in (23-25cm)	$	275 - 375
12in (31cm)		450 - 550
17-18in (43-46cm)		900 - 1000
12in (31cm) boy with carved hat		600 - 650
13in (33cm) wood and cloth babies		450
14in (36cm) wood, cloth papier-mâché lady		400 - 450

---FACTS---
Various craftsmen, Brienz, Switzerland.
20th century.
Mark: Usually a paper label on wrist or clothes.

14in (36cm) Swiss wood, cloth and papier-mâché lady, all original. *H & J Foulke, Inc.*

MODERN & COLLECITBLE DOLLS

Unless otherwise indicated, values gven in this section are retail prices for clean dolls in excellent overall condition, with good complexion color on the doll, perfect hair in original set, and original unfaded clothing including underwear, shoes and socks. Dirty and faded dolls that have been heavily played with are worth 10-30% of these values.

14in (36cm) hard plastic Mary Hoyer, all original. *H & J Foulke, Inc.*
(For more information see page 279.)

MADAME ALEXANDER

Cloth Dolls. Original tagged clothing.
Characters: Ca. 1933-1940. All-cloth with molded felt or flocked mask face, painted eyes to the side. **Little Women, David Copperfield, Oliver Twist, Edith, Babbie,** and others.
16in (41cm) only:

Fair	$	200 - 300
Good		350 - 450
Excellent		650 - 750

Alice (See photograph on page 210.), 19-20in (48-51cm)

Fair	200 - 300
Good	350 - 450
Excellent	650 - 750

Playmates, 1940s. 28in (71cm)

Fair to good	400

Bunny Belle,
13in (33cm) mint, at auction $ 600 - 700
Cloth Baby: Ca. 1936.

13in (33cm) very good	$	300 - 350
17in (43cm) very good		475 - 525
24in (61cm)		625

Cloth Dionne Quintuplet: Ca. 1935.

17in (43cm) very good	$	850 - 900**
24in (61cm) very good		1200 - 1300**

Susie Q. & Bobby Q.: Ca. 1938.
12-16in (31-41cm) excellent with purse or book strap $ 900 - 1050
Little Shaver: 1942. Yarn hair. Very good condition. (See photograph on page 210.)

7in (18cm)	$	450 - 475
10-12in (25-31cm)	$	400 - 425
20in (51cm)		550 - 650

Kamkins-type (hard felt face). Very good condition.

20in (51cm)	$	650 - 750**

Funny, 18in (46cm) 1963-1977. 65
Muffin, 14in (36cm) 1963-1977. 95

**Not enough samples to compute a reliable average.

FACTS

Alexander Doll Co. Inc., New York, N.Y., U.S.A. 1923 - on, but as early as 1912 the Alexander sisters were designing doll clothes and dressing dolls commercially. **Mark:** Dolls themselves marked in various ways, usually "ALEXANDER." Clothing has a white cloth label with blue lettering sewn into a seam which says "MADAME ALEXANDER" and usually the name of the specific doll. Cloth and other early dolls are unmarked and identifiable only by the clothing label.

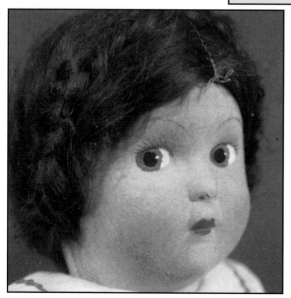

16in (41cm) All-cloth *Jo* from Little Women, all original. *H & J Foulke, Inc.*

MADAME ALEXANDER *continued* ~~Betsy Ross~~

COMPOSITION DOLLS. All in original tagged clothing; excellent condition, with bright color and perfect hair, faint crazing acceptable.

Dionne Quintuplets: 1935.

7-8in (18 - 20cm)	$ 250 - 275
Matched set	1500
in basket with extra outfits	2200
10in (25cm) baby	325 - 350
11-12in (28 - 31cm) toddler	375 - 425
14in (36cm) toddler	475 - 525
16in (41cm) baby with cloth body	450
20in (51cm) toddler	650 - 700
23-24in (58 - 61cm) baby with cloth body	550 - 650
Pins, each	90 - 100

Each Quint has her own color for clothing: Yvonne - pink; Annette - yellow; Cecile - green; Emelie - lavender; Marie - blue.

Small dolls, 1935-1945. 7-9in (18-23cm).
Foreign Countries $ 175 - 225

Storybook Characters	200 - 300
Special Outfits	400 - 500
Birthday Dolls	325 - 375
Bride and Bridesmaids	225 - 250 each
Little Women	275 each
Little Colonel: 1935.	
13in (33cm)	600 - 650
Unnamed Girl: Dimples, sleep eyes. Ca. 1935. 13in (33cm)	375 - 425
Nurse: Ca. 1935. 13in (33cm)	750 - 850
Betty: Ca. 1935. Painted or sleep eyes, wigged or molded hair.	
13in (33cm)	375 - 425
19in (48cm)	700 - 750
Baby Jane, 1935.	
16in (41cm)	900 - 1000
Topsy Turvy: Ca. 1936.	
7-1/2in (19cm)	185 - 210
Dr. DaFoe, 1936.	
14in (36cm)	1400 - 1600

8in (20cm) *Dionne Quintuplets* in original wicker suitcase with extra outfits. *H & J Foulke, Inc.*

7in (18cm) composition *Scotch*, all original. *Rhoda Shoemaker Collection.*

Top Left: 19in (48cm) All-cloth *Alice-in-Wonderland*, all original. *H & J Foulke, Inc.* (For further information see page 208.) *Top Right:* 10in (25cm) All-cloth *Little Shaver*, all original. *H & J Foulke, Inc.* (For further information see page 208.) *Left:* 21in (53cm) Composition *Alice-in-Wonderland*, all original. *H & J Foulke, Inc.*

Next Page: Top Left: 13in (33cm) *McGuffey Ana*, all original. *H & J Foulke, Inc.* (For further information see page 212.) *Top Right:* 16in (41cm) *Flora McFlimsey*, all original. *Rhoda Shoemaker Collection.* (For further information see page 212.) *Bottom Left:* 14in (36cm) *Scarlett O'Hara*, rare outfit, all original. *H & J Foulke, Inc. Bottom Right:* 20in (51cm) *Kate Greenaway*, all original. *H & J Foulke, Inc.* (For further information see page 212.)

MADAME ALEXANDER COMPOSITION *continued*

Marionettes: 1935. Character faces.
10-12in (25-30cm)

Tony Sarg	$ 250 - 275
Disney	350 - 400

Babies: 1936-on. "Little Genius", "Baby McGuffey," "Precious," "Butch," "Bitsey." Composition head, hands and legs, cloth bodies.

11-12in (28-31cm)	$ 250 - 300
16-18in (41-46cm)	400 - 450
24in (61cm)	550
Pinky, 16-18in (41-46cm)	450 - 550

Princess Elizabeth Face: Original tagged clothes; all in excellent condition.

Princess Elizabeth, 1937.

13in (33cm) closed mouth	$ 400 - 500
16-18in (41-46cm)	550 - 650
22-24in (56-61cm)	750 - 850
27in (69cm)	950 - 1000

McGuffey Ana, 1937, braids. (See photograph on page 211.)

9in (23cm) painted eyes	$ 350 - 400
11in (28cm) closed mouth	425 - 475
15-16in (38-41cm)	525 - 625
20-22in (51-56cm)	750 - 850
23in (58cm) boxed, at auction	2100

Snow White, 1937, closed mouth, black hair.

13in (33cm)	$ 425 - 475
16-18in (41-46cm)	625 - 675
17in (43cm)	1400

Flora McFlimsey, 1938. (See photograph on page 211.)

15in (38cm)	$ 700 - 800

Kate Greenaway, 1938. (See photograph on page 211.)

16-18in (41-46cm)	$ 675 - 775

Wendy Ann Face. Original tagged clothes; all in excellent condition.

Wendy Ann, 1936. (See photograph on page 214.)

9in (23cm) painted eyes	$ 325 - 350
14in (36cm) swivel waist	450 - 550
21in (53cm)	650 - 750

Scarlett O'Hara, 1937, black hair, blue or green eyes. (See photograph on page 211.)

11in (28cm)	$ 600 - 700
11in (28cm) boxed	1000
14in (36cm)	725 - 850
18in (46cm)	1100 - 1250
21in (53cm)	1500 - 1650

Bride & Bridesmaids, 1940.

14in (36cm)	$ 325 - 375
18in (46cm)	450 - 525

Portraits, 1940s.

21in (53cm)	$ 2000 up
Judy, boxed at auction	4000

Carmen (Miranda), 1942 (black hair).

9in (23cm) painted eyes	$ 275 - 325
14-15in (36-38cm)	425 - 475

Fairy Princess or **Fairy Queen,** 1942.

18in (46cm)	$ 650 - 750

Armed Forces Dolls, 1942.
WAAC, WAVE, WAAF, Soldier, Marine

14in (36cm)	$ 750 - 850

Miss America, 1939.

14in (36cm)	$ 850**

Sleeping Beauty, Cinderella. Ca. 1941.

14in (36cm)	$ 450 - 500

Madelaine du Bain, 1938.

14in (36cm)	$ 500 - 600

**Not enough price samples to compute a reliable average.

Special Faces. Original tagged clothes; all in excellent condition.

Jane Withers, 1937.

13in (33cm) closed mouth	$ 1000 - 1100
15-16in (38-41cm)	1100 - 1250
21in (53cm)	1500 - 1650

Sonja Henie, 1939.

14in (36cm), swivel waist	$ 500 - 600
15in (38cm), gift set, boxed	3200
17in (43cm) boxed	1250
18in (46cm)	800 - 850
21in (53cm)	1000 - 1100

Jeannie Walker, 1941.

13in (33cm) boxed	$ 1200 - 1400
13 - 14in (33 - 36cm)	500 - 600
18in (46cm)	750 - 850

Special Girl, 1942, cloth body.

22in (56cm)	$ 550 - 650

Margaret Face: Original tagged clothes; all in excellent condition with perfect hair and pretty coloring.

Margaret O'Brien, 1946.
with dark braided wig:

14in (36cm)	$ 700 - 800
14in (36cm) boxed	1200
18in (46cm)	950 - 1000

Karen Ballerina, 1946. (See photograph on page 214.)
with blonde wig in coiled braids:

14in (36cm)	$ 750 - 800
18in (46cm)	1000 up

Alice-in-Wonderland, 1947.

14in (36cm)	$ 425 - 475
18in (46cm)	550 - 650

14in (36cm)
Sonja Henie, all
original. *H & J
Foulke, Inc.*

Top Left: 14-1/2in (37cm) *Karen Ballerina*, all original. *H & J Foulke, Inc.* (For further information see page 213.)
Top Right: 14in (36cm) *Wendy Ann*, all original. *H & J Foulke, Inc.* (For further information see page 212.)

Left: 14in (36cm) *Cinderella*, all original. *Rhoda Shoemaker Collection.* (For further information see page 216.)

Top Left: 14in (36cm) *Margot Ballerina*
#1541, 1955, all original. *H & J Foulke,
Inc.* (For further information see page 217.)
Top Right: 14in (36cm) *Amy* from Little
Women, all original. *H & J Foulke, Inc.*
(For further information see page 216.)

14in (36cm) *Jo* from Little Women, all
original. *H & J Foulke, Inc.* (For further
information see page 217.)

216

MADAME ALEXANDER HARD PLASTIC

HARD PLASTIC DOLLS. 1948-on. Original tagged clothes; excellent condition with bright color and perfect hair.

Margaret face: 1948 - 1956.
Babs, 1948 - 1949.
| 14in (36cm) | $ | 675 |
| 18in (46cm) | | 900 |

Bride, Pink, 1950.
| 14in (36cm) | 750 |
| 18in (46cm) | 950 |

Cinderella*, 1950. (See photograph on page 214.)
| 14in (36cm) | 750 |
| 18in (46cm) | 950 |

Cynthia (black), 1952 - 1953.
| 14in (36cm) | 850 |
| 18in (46cm) | 1150 |

Fairy Queen, 1947 - 1948.
| 14in (36cm) | 600 |
| 18in (46cm) | 750 |

Fashions of the Century, 1954.
| 18in (46cm) at auction | 3400 |

Glamour Girls, 1953.
| 18in (46cm) | 1250 - 1650 |

Godey Ladies, 1950.
| 14in (36cm) | 1200 - 1600 |

Margaret O'Brien, 1948. (See photograph on page 218.)
| 14in (36cm) | 800 - 900 |

Margaret Rose, 1948-1953.
| 14in (36cm) | 600 |
| 18in (46cm) | 750 |

Mary Martin, 1950. Sailor suit,
| 14in (36cm) | 850 |
| 18in (46cm) | 1000 |

McGuffey Ana, 1949.
14in (36cm)	750
17in (43cm)	950
21in (53cm) at auction	2300

Nina Ballerina, 1949-1951, blonde:
14in (36cm)	650
18in (46cm)	950
21in (53cm)	1200

Peggy Bride, Ca. 1950.
| 20in (51cm) at auction | 2200 |

Poor Cinderella, 1950.
| 14in (36cm) | 550 |

Princess Margaret, 1953. Beaux Arts Series, 18in (46cm) | 1600 |

Prince Charming, 1950.
| 14in (36cm) | 775 |

| 18in (46cm) | 875 |

Prince Philip, Ca. 1950.
| 18in (46cm) | 800 - 850 |

Queen Elizabeth, 1953.
| 18in (46cm) with cape | 1600 |
| no cape | 800 - 1000 |

Snow White, 1952.
| 14in (36cm) | 725 |
| 18in (46cm) | 950 |

Story Princess, 1954-1956.
| 14in (36cm) | 650 |
| 18in (46cm) | 750 |

Wendy-Ann, 1947-1948.
| 14in (36cm) | 725 |
| 18in (46cm) | 850 |

Wendy Bride, 1950.
| 14in (36cm) | 550 |
| 18in (46cm) | 750 |

Wendy (from **Peter Pan** set), 1953.
| 14in (36cm) | 500 - 600 |

Maggie Face: 1948-1956.
Alice in Wonderland, 1950-1951.
| 14in (36cm) | 600 |
| 18in (46cm) | 750 |

Annabelle, 1952.
| 15in (38cm) | 550 |
| 18in (46cm) | 700 |

Glamour Girls, 1953.
| 18in (46cm) | 1250 - 1650 |

Godey Man, 1950.
| 14in (36cm) | 1000 - 1100 |

John Powers Models,
| 14in (36cm) | 1500 - 1600 |

Kathy, 1951.
| 14in (36cm) | 725 |
| 18in (46cm) | 875 |

Margot Ballerina, 1953. (See photograph on page 215.)
| 14in (36cm) | 600 |
| 18in (46cm) | 700 |

Maggie, 1948 - 1953.
| 14in (36cm) | 525 |
| 17in (43cm) | 650 |

Me and My Shadow, 1954.
| 18in (46cm) | 1600 - 2000 |

Peter Pan, 1953.
| 15in (38cm) | 700 - 800 |

Polly Pigtails, 1949. (See photograph on page 218.)
| 14in (36cm) | 525 |
| 17in (43cm) | 700 |

Rosamund Bridesmaid, 1953.
15in (38cm) $ 525
Little Women: 1948-1956. (See photographs on page 215.)
Floss hair, 1948 - 1950.
  14-15in (36-38cm)   425 - 475 each
    Amy, loop curls   525
    Dynel hair   350 - 400 each
  Little Men, 1952.   900 - 1100
  (Nat, Stuffy, Tommy Bangs.)
Portraits, 1951. Elaborate gowns,
  21in (53cm) $ 9000 - 10,000

Babies: 1948-1951. Cloth body, hard plastic or vinyl limbs. Baby Genius, Bitsey, Butch.
  12in (31cm) $250 - 275
  16-18in (41-46cm)   325 - 375
  Lovey, Dovey, 15in (38cm) boxed   325
  Slumbermate, 1951. Closed eyes,
    13in (33cm)   150

Winnie and Binnie: 1953-1955.
  15in (38cm) $ 325 - 375
  18in (46cm)   500 - 550
  25in (64cm)   650
  Mary Ellen, 31in (79cm)   550 - 600
  Sweet Violet, fully jointed body,
    18in (46cm)   1000 up
  Victoria, black, green-and-white dress,
    15in (38cm) at auction   3200
  Flower Girl, 15in (38cm)   450

Cissy: 1955-1959. (See photograph on page 13.)
  21in (53cm) street clothes $ 375 - 425
    Evening gowns   475 up
    Elaborate fashion gowns   700 up
    Queen   950
    Bride   475 - 575

Alexander-Kins: 1953-to present. All hard plastic; original tagged clothes; all in excellent condition with perfect hair and rosy cheeks. A played-with doll having partial or faded costume will bring 25% of quoted prices.

Wendy: 7 1/2-8in (19-20cm).
  1953. Straight-leg nonwalker $ 450 up
    nude   300

1954-55. Straight-leg walker   400 up
  nude   275
1956-1964. Bent-knee walker   350 up
  nude   185
1965-1972. Bent-knee nonwalker   275
  nude   90
Wendy, basic (panties, shoes and socks)
  boxed   275 - 375
Quizkin, 1953.   450 - 550
Wendy in Special Outfits:
  Billy or Bobby, 1955-1963.   450 - 500
  Prince Charles, 1957.   800
  Princess Ann, 1957.   800
  My Shadow, 1954.   1000
  Cherry Twin, 1957.   900 each
  Little Minister, 1957.   1500
  Groom, 1956-1972.   450
  Bride, 1955-1960.   350
  Baby Clown, 1955.   1200
  Nurse, 1956-1965.   450 - 500
  Parlour Maid, 1956.   1000
  Scarlett, 1965-1972.   400
  McGuffey Ana, 1964-1965.   350
  Little Victoria, 1954.   1300
  Maypole Dance, 1954, boxed.   650
  Little Southern Girl, 1953.   850
  Wendy Does Highland Fling, 1955. 400
  Wendy Loves to Waltz, 1955.   625
  Wendy Dude Ranch, 1955.   600
  Wendy in Riding Habit, 1965.
    Boxed   550
  Wendy Can Read, 1957. Boxed   950
  Priscilla or Colonial Girl,
    1962-1970.   350
  Amish Boy or Amish Girl,
    1966-1969.   350
  Davy Crockett Boy or Girl, 1955. 600
  Hiawatha, 1967-1969.   350
  Pocahontas, 1967-1969.   350
  Southern Belle, 1963.   450
  Miss USA, 1966-1968. Boxed.   425
  American Girl, 1962-1963.   350
  Guardian Angel, 1954. (See photograph on page 218.)
                              550
  Wendy Ice Skater, 1956.   450
  Easter Wendy, 1953.   1000
  Cousin Marie, 1963.   475
  Cousin Grace, 1957. Boxed   1600
  Aunt Pitty Pat, 1957.   1600

MADAME ALEXANDER HARD PLASTIC

Top Left: 14in (36cm) *Polly Pigtails*, all original. *H & J Foulke, Inc.* (For further information see page 216.) *Top Right:* 14in (36cm) *Margaret O'Brien*, all original. *Rhoda Shoemaker Collection.* (For further information see page 216.)

Left: 8in (20cm) *Alexander-Kin Guardian Angel*, nonwalker, no harp, all original. *Rhoda Shoemaker Collection.* (For further information see page 217.)

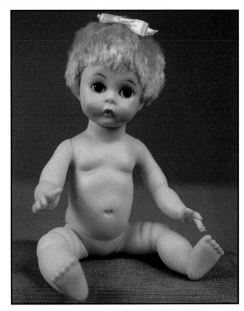

Left: 8in (20cm) *Maggie Mixup*, all original. *Rhoda Shoemaker Collection.* (For further information see page 220.) *Right:* 8in (20cm) *Little Genius.* *H & J Foulke, Inc.*

International Costumes:

Bent-knee walker	$	150 - 200
Bent-knee nonwalker, 1965-1972.		75 - 100
Korea, Africa, Hawaii, Vietnam,		
Eskimo, Morocco, Ecuador,		
Bolivia		300 - 400
Straight-leg, rosy cheeks, 1973-1976.		60
Straight-leg, pinched lips, 1982-1987.		35 - 40
Current face, 1988-on.		40 - 50

Storybook, Ballerinas & Brides:

Bent-knee nonwalker	$	75 - 100
Straight-leg, rosy cheeks, 1973-1976.		60 - 70
Straight-leg, pinched lips, 1982-1987.		40 - 45
Current face, 1988-on.		45 - 55

Little Women: Set of 5.

Straight-leg walker, 1955.	$	1500
Bent-knee walker, 1956-1964.		1200
Bent-knee		750

Exclusive and Special Editions:

Enchanted Doll House,		
1980-1981.	$	250 - 275
Wendy, 1989. Mme Alex.		
Doll Club		200
Bobbie Sox, 1990. Disney		125
David & Diana, 1989. FAO Schwarz,		
Set		175
Mouseketeer, 1991. Disney		100
Little Women, 1994. FAO Schwarz,		
Set of 5		500
Little Miss Magnin, 1992. I. Magnin		
with tea set and teddy bear		110
Tippi Ballerina, 1988. CU Gathering		350
Little Emperor, 1992.		
UFDC Luncheon		500

Little Genius: 1956-1962. Baby with short curly wig, 8in (20cm).

Basic or simple outfit	$	175 - 200
Fancy outfit		225 - 250

Lissy Face: 1956-1958.

12in (31cm) **Lissy**	$ **300 - 400**
Boxed with trousseau	**1200 - 1500**
Bridesmaid	**600**
Kelly, 1959.	**400 - 500**
Little Women, 1957-1959.	**250**
Southern Belle, 1963.	**1200**
McGuffey Ana, 1963.	**1600**
Katie, 1962.	**1200**
Tommy, 1962.	**1000**
Cinderella, 1966.	**850**
Boxed Set	**1250**
Laurie, 1967.	**400**
Pamela, 1962-1963.	
Boxed with wigs	**1000**
Suitcase gift set	**1500**

Elise: 1957-1964.

16-1/2in (42cm) street clothes	$ **300 - 350**
Gowns	**450 up**
Bride, Ballerina	**350 - 375**
Elaborate gowns	**500 up**
Sleeping Beauty	**550 - 600**

Vinyl head, 1964. (Kelly Face) **275 - 325**
Gown #1775 **375**

Cissette Face: 1957-1973.

10in (25cm) **Cissette,** 1957-1963.	
Basic doll, mint-in-box	$ **275 - 325**
Day dresses	**275**
Evening gowns	**375**
Queen	**350**
Gold Ballerina, 1959.	**450 - 500**
Jacqueline, 1962.	**600 - 650**
Margot, 1961.	**400 - 450**
Sleeping Beauty, 1959-1960.	**350**
Portrettes: 1968-1973.	
Gody, 1968-1970.	**300**
Scarlett, 1968-1973.	**300**
Renoir, 1968-1970.	**325**
Agatha, 1968.	**350**
Southern Belle, 1968-1973.	**300**
Melinda, 1968-1970.	**300**
Jenny Lind, 1969.	**550**
Melanie, 1969-1970.	**375**
Queen, 1972-1973.	**250**

Shari Lewis: 1959.

14in (36cm)	$ **400 - 500**
21in (53cm)	**700 - 800**

Maggie Mixup: 1960-1961.
(See photograph on page 219.)

16-1/2in (42cm)	$ **400 - 450**
8in (20cm)	**450 - 550**
8in (20cm) angel	**800 - 1000**
Little Lady	**350**
Little Lady Gift Set	**1000**

21in (53cm) *Madame Pompadour*, 1970, all original. *H & J Foulke, Inc.*

MADAME ALEXANDER VINYL

Vinyl Dolls. Original tagged clothing; excellent never-played-with condition, bright color.

Kelly Face: 1958-1965. 15in (38cm).

Kelly	$	**225 - 250**
Pollyana		**225 - 250**
Marybel		**275 - 325**
Edith		**225 - 250**
Elise		**275 - 325**

Jacqueline: 1961-1962.

21in (53cm) suit	$	**550 - 650**
Riding habit		**525 - 575**
Brocade gown		**700 - 750**
10in (25cm)		**600 - 650**

Portraits: 1962-current. 21in (53cm).

Scarlett, 1968. Cotton print	$	**700**
1975-1982. Green velvet or taffeta		**350**
1978. Satin print		**500**
Melanie, 1967-74.		**400 - 500**
Queen, 1968.		**700**
Godey, 1969.		**500**
Bride, 1969.		**550**
Madame Pompadour, 1970.		**900**
Mimi, 1971.		**450**
Gainsborough, 1973.		**350**
Madame Alexander, 1984-1990.		**200 - 300**
Sarah Bernhardt, 1987.		**300**

Caroline: 1961-1962.

15in (38cm)	$	**250 - 300**
Riding habit		**350**

Melinda: 1963. 14in (36cm) $ **250 - 350**

Janie Face: 1964-1990. 12in (31cm).

Janie, 1964-1966.	$	**225 - 250**
Lucinda, 1969-1970		**250 - 275**
Rozy, 1969.		**275 - 300**
Suzy, 1970.		**275 - 300**
Muffin, 1989-1990.		**50 - 60**

Brenda Starr: 1964.

12in (31cm)	$	**225**
Yolanda, 1965.		**225**

Betty: 1960. Smiling face, walker,

30in (76cm)	$	**350**

Patty: 1965.(See photograph on page 222.)

18in (46cm)	$	**250 - 275**

Chatterbox: 1961. Battery-operated talker,

24in (61cm)	$	**250 - 275**

Smarty Face: 1962-1965. 12in (31cm).

Smarty, 1962-1963.	$	**200 - 250**
with baby		**300 - 350**
Brother.		**225 - 275**
Katie (black), 1965.		**350 - 400**

Polly Face: 1965-1971. 17in (43cm).

Polly, 1965.	$	**225 - 275**
Mary Ellen Playmate		**275**
Leslie (black), 1965-1971.		**300 - 325**

12in (31cm)
Smarty, all original.
H & J Foulke, Inc.

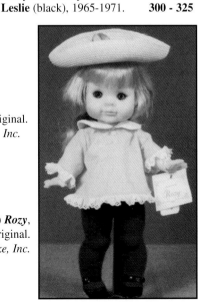

12in (31cm) *Rozy*,
all original.
H & J Foulke, Inc.

MADAME ALEXANDER VINYL

18in (46cm) *Patty*, all original. *H & J Foulke, Inc.* (For further information see page 221.)

Mary Ann Face: 1965-current. 14in (36cm).

Mary Ann, 1965. $	**225**
Orphant Annie, 1965-1966.	**300**
Gidget, 1966.	**275**
Little Granny, 1966.	**150**
Riley's Little Annie, 1967.	**175**
Renoir Girl, 1967-1971	**175**
Disney Snow White, 1967-1977.	**400 - 450**
Easter Girl, 1968.	**750 - 850**
Scarlett, flowered gown, 1968. (See photograph on page 223.)	**450 - 500**
Madame, 1969.	**150 - 175**
Jenny Lind & Cat, 1969-1971.	**225**
Gone with the Wind, 1969-1986.	**75**
Jenny Lind, 1970.	**275**
Grandma Jane, 1970.	**150 - 175**
Goldilocks, 1978-1982.	**75**
Bonnie Blue, 1989.	**80**
Discontinued dolls, 1982-1995.	**50 - 90**

Babies: 1963-present. (See photographs on page 224.)

Littlest Kitten, 1963. 8in (20cm).	
Basic or simple outfit $	**200 - 225**
Fancy outfit	**250 - 275**
Sugar Tears, 1964. 14in (36cm)	**75 - 100**
Sweet Tears, 1965-1982.	
14in (36cm)	**55 - 65**
Layette sets	**125 up**
Baby Ellen (black), 1965-1972.	
14in (36cm)	**100**
Pussy Cat (black) 20in (51cm)	**100**
Mary Cassatt Baby, 1969-1970.	
20in (51cm)	**200 - 250**
Happy, 1970. 20in (51cm)	**200 - 250**
Smiley, 1971. 20in (51cm)	**200 - 250**
Baby Lynn, 1973-1976.	
20in (51cm)	**100 - 125**
Baby Brother, 1977-1979.	
20in (51cm)	**75 - 100**

Sound of Music: Small set, 1965-1970.

Friedrich, 8in (20cm) $	**150**
Gretl, 8in (20cm)	**150**
Marta, 8in (20cm)	**150**
Brigitta, 10in (25cm)	**200**
Louisa, 10in (25cm)	**200**
Liesl, 10in (25cm)	**200**
Maria, 12in (31cm)	**225**

14in (36cm) *Grandma Jane*, 1970-1972 all original. *H & J Foulke, Inc.*

MADAME ALEXANDER VINYL

14in (36cm) *Scarlett* with print
dress, 1968, all original.
(For further information
see page 222.)

8in (20cm) *Littlest
Kitten*, all original.
H & J Foulke, Inc.

Sound of Music: Large set. 1971-1973.
Allow 100% more for sailor outfits.

Friedrich, 11in (28cm) $	**175 - 200**
Gretl, 11in (28cm)	**150 - 165**
Marta, 11in (28cm)	**150 - 165**
Brigitta, 14in (36cm)	**125 - 150**
Louisa, 14in (36cm)	**125 - 150**
Liesl, 14in (36cm)	**125 - 150**
Maria, 17in (43cm)	**275**
Kurt, 11in (28cm) sailor suit	**350**

Coco: 1966. Right leg bent slightly at knee.

21in (53cm) $	**1800 - 2000**
1966 Portrait Dolls	**2200 up**

Elise Face: 1966-1991. Redesigned vinyl face. 17in (43cm).

Elise Portrait Doll, 1972-1973. $	**125 - 150**
Ballerinas	**75 - 85**
Brides	**65 - 75**
Formals	**65 - 75**

Marlo, 1967.	**550 - 650**
Maggie, 1972-1973.	**175 - 200**

Peter Pan Set: 1969.

Peter Pan, 14in (36cm) $	**200 - 225**
Wendy, 14in (36cm)	**200 - 225**
Michael, 11in (28cm)	**250**
Tinker Bell, 10in (25cm)	**300**

Nancy Drew Face: 1967-1994. 12in (31cm).

Nancy Drew, 1967. $	**200 - 225**
Renoir Child, 1967.	**125 - 150**
Pamela with wigs, late 1960s.	**400 - 500**
Poor Cinderella, 1967.	**125 - 150**
Little Women, 1969-1989.	**60 - 65**
Romantic Couples, pair	**75**
Discontinued dolls	**30 - 35**

First Ladies: 1976-1989.

14in (36cm) each $	**50 - 75**

20in (53cm) *Smiley*, 1971; 14in (36cm) *Sugar Tears*, 1964; 14in (36cm) black *Baby Ellen*; all original. *Barbara Crescenze Collection.* (For further information see page 222.)

Marked Petite or American Character Mama Dolls: 1923-on. Composition/cloth; original clothes; all in good condition.

    16-18in (41-46cm)   **$ 225 - 265**
    24in (61cm)   **325 - 375**

Baby Petite, 12in (31cm) **$ 200**

Puggy: 1928. All-composition, frowning face; original clothes; all in good condition.

    12in (31cm)   **$ 525 - 575**

Marked Petite Girl Dolls: 1930s. All-composition; original clothes; all in good condition with nice coloring and perfect hair.

    16-18in (41-46cm)   **$ 265 - 295**
    24in (61cm)   **325 - 375**

Sally: 1930. All-composition. Painted eyes and molded hair or wigged with sleeping eyes; original clothes; all in good condition with nice coloring.

    12in (31cm)   **$ 225 - 250**
    16in (41cm)   **250 - 275**

Saly-Joy: 1930. Composition/cloth.

    18in (46cm)   **$ 300-325**
    21in (53cm)   **350**

FACTS

American Character Doll Co., New York, N.Y. 1919-on.
Trademark: Petite.

21in (53cm) *Sally-Joy*, all original and tagged. *H & J Foulke, Inc.*

12in (31cm) *Puggy*, all original. *H & J Foulke, Inc.*

16-1/2in (42cm) *Carol Ann Beery*. *H & J Foulke, Inc.*

12in (31cm) *Tiny Tears*, original dress. *H & J Foulke, Inc.*

21in (53cm) *Sweet Sue*, all original. *H & J Foulke, Inc.*

Carol Ann Beery, 1935. All-composition."Two-Some Doll" with special crown braid, matching playsuit and dress.

13in (33cm)	$	450 - 500
16-1/2in (42cm)		600 - 650

Toodles: 1956. Hard rubber baby, drinks and wets; original clothes; excellent condition.

18-1/2in (47cm)	$	225 - 250

Toodles Toddler: 1960. Vinyl and hard plastic, "Peek-a-Boo" eyes.

24in (61cm)	$	250 - 275
30in (76cm)		350 - 375

Tiny Tears: 1950s. Hard plastic head with tear ducts; drinks and wets; original clothes; excellent condition.

Rubber body,		
12in (31cm)	$	150 - 165
18in (46cm)		200 - 225
Original box and accesories		350
All vinyl, 1963.		
12in (31cm)	$	65
15in (38cm)		85
Boxed with accessories		150 - 175

Sweet Sue: 1953. All-hard plastic or hard plastic and vinyl, some with walking mechanism, some fully-jointed including elbows, knees and ankles; original clothes; all in excellent condition, with perfect hair and pretty coloring. (See photograph on page 13.)

14in (36cm)	$	225 - 250
18-20in (46-51cm)		275 - 300
24in (61cm)		325 - 375

Annie Oakley, 1955.

14in (36cm)	$	450

Sweet Sue Sophisticate, vinyl head,

20in (51cm)	$	225 - 250

Toni, vinyl head:

10-1/2in (26cm)	$	150 - 200
20in (51cm)		225 - 250

Ricky, Jr., 1955. All vinyl:

14in (36cm)	$	95
21in (53cm)		150

Eloise: Ca. 1955. All-cloth, yellow yarn hair; original clothing; in excellent condition. Designed by Bette Gould from the fictional little girl "Eloise" who lived at the Plaza Hotel in New York City.

21in (53cm)	$	375- 425
Mint-in-box, at auction		775

Whimsies: 1960. Characters, original clothing; excellent condition. **Hedda Get Bedds** (3 faces), **Wheeler the Dealer, Lena the Cleaner, Polly the Lady, Bessie the Bashful Bride, Dixie the Pixie,** and others.

19-21in (48-53cm)	$	90-110
Mint-in-box with tag		225

Little Miss Echo: 1962. Recorded voice; original clothing, excellent condition.

Boxed, 30in (76cm)	$	250 - 300
Out of box		150

Tressy: 1963-1965. Growing hair:

12-1/2in (32cm) boxed	$	60 - 70
Doll only		25
Pre-teen Tressy, 1963. Growing hair.		
14in (36cm) boxed		50 - 55
Cricket, 1965. Boxed		30 - 40
Mary Make-up: 1965. Boxed		50 - 60

19in (48cm) ***Whimsey "Hedda Get Bedda"***. *Private Collection.*

ARRANBEE

My Dream Baby: 1924. Bisque head/cloth body. See Armand Marseille infant on page 151 for description and prices.

Storybook Dolls: 1930s. All-composition; original storybook costumes; all in excellent condition, with perfect hair and pretty coloring.

9-10in (23-25cm)	$	**175 - 195**
Boxed		**275**

Bottletot: 1926. All-composition; molded celluloid bottle in hand; appropriate clothes; all in good condition.

13in (33cm)	$	**195**

┌─────── FACTS ───────┐
Arranbee Doll Co., New York, N.Y.,
U.S.A. 1922-1960.
Mark: "ARRANBEE" or
"R & B."
└──────────────────────┘

13in (33cm) *Bottletot*. *H & J Foulke, Inc.*

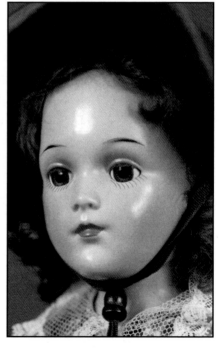

17in (43cm) *Debu'teen,* all original. *H & J Foulke, Inc.*

Nancy: 1930. All-composition; original clothes; all in good condition, with pretty coloring.

12in (31cm) molded hair, painted eyes	$	240 - 265
16in (41cm) sleep eyes, wig, open mouth		350 - 375
12in (31cm) with trousseau in wardrobe trunk		550

Debu'Teen and Nancy Lee: 1938- on. All-composition; original clothes; all in good condition with perfect hair and pretty coloring.

11in (28cm)	$	195 - 210
14in (36cm)		270 - 295
21in (53cm)		375 - 425

Skating Doll, 18in (46cm)	$	350 - 400
Brother, 14in (36cm)		325 - 350
WAC, 18in (46cm)		500

Little Angel Baby: 1940s. Composition/ cloth; original clothes; all in good condition.

16-18in (41-46cm)	$	275 - 300
Hard plastic, 18in (46cm)		325

Nanette and Nancy Lee: 1950s. All-hard plastic; original clothes; all in excellent condition, with rosy cheeks.

14in (36cm)	$	250 - 275
17in (43cm)		325 - 375
Mint-in-box, 20in (51cm)		725 - 825

Cinderella, 14in (36cm)	500
Floss wig, evening gown, 14in (36cm)	400 - 450

Littlest Angel: 1956. All-hard plastic jointed knee, walker; original clothes; all in excellent condition.

10-11in (25-28cm)	$	100 - 125

Little Angel: 1950s.

12in (31cm)	100 - 125

Coty Girl: 1958. All-vinyl, fashion body, high-heeled feet.

10-1/2in (27cm) boxed	$	150 - 175

12in (31cm) *Little Angel,* all original.
H & J Foulke, Inc.

12in (31cm) *Nancy,* all original and tagged. *H & J Foulke, Inc.*

ARTIST DOLLS

Traditional Artists: Many members of NIADA or ODACA. All dolls original and excellent.

Armstrong-Hand, Martha, porcelain babies and children.   **$ 1200 up**

Barrie, Mirren, cloth historical children   **95**

Beckett, Bob & June, carved wood children.   **300 - 375**

Blakeley, Halle, high-fired clay lady dolls.
550 - 750

Brandon, Elizabeth, porcelain children. Theola, Joshua, Joi Lin, Jael   **300 - 500**

Bringloe, Frances, carved wood.
American Pioneer Children,
6-1/4in (16cm) pair   **600**

Bullard, Helen, carved wood.
Holly   **100 - 125**
Hitty   **300 - 350**
American Family Series
(16 dolls)   **225 - 250 each**

Campbell, Astry, porcelain.
Ricky & Becky   **750 pair**

Clear, Emma, porcelain, china and bisque shoulder head dolls.   **350 - 500**
Danny   **450**
George & Martha Washington
500 - 600 pair

DeNunez, Marianne,
10in (25cm) Bru Jne.   **300**

Florian, Gertrude, ceramic composition dressed ladies.   **300**

Goodnow, June, bisque Indians,
16-17in (41-43cm)   **550 - 650**

Heiser, Dorothy, cloth sculpture.
Fashion Pair of 1770s   **2800**
Queens 10-13in (25-33cm)   **1100 - 1500**

Hale, Patti, carved wood heads.   **200 - 300**
Hitty, all wood   **300**

Johnson, Sharon, porcelain children.
Elizabeth, Lil Jewel   **125**

Kane, Maggie Head, porcelain.
Gypsy Mother   **400 - 450**

Oldenburg, Mary Ann,
porcelain children.   **200 - 250**

Park, Irma, wax-over-porcelain miniatures, depending upon detail.   **150 up**

Parker, Ann,
historical characters.   **200 - 250**

Redmond, Kathy, elaborately modeled porcelain children. (See page 12 for photo.)   **400 - 450**
Historical characters   **600 - 1000**

Singer, Jeanne, porcelain children.   **85**

Smith, Sherman, carved wood,
5-6in (13-15cm).   **250**
Pinocchio, 7-1/2in (19cm)   **350**
Hitty   **300**

Sorensen, Lewis, wax.
Father Christmas   **1200**
Toymaker   **800**
Gibson Girls   **350**

Sweet, Elizabeth, 18in (46cm).
Amy, 1970.   **250**

Alice In Wonderland, by Ann Parker. *H & J Foulke, Inc.*

Thompson, Martha, porcelain.

Princess Caroline, Prince Charles, Princess Ann	**$800 - 900 each**
Little Women	**600 - 700**
Betsy	**800 - 900**
McKim Child (not bisque)	**800**
Princess Margaret Rose, Princess Grace	**1500 - 2000**
Young Victoria	**2300**
Queen Anne	**2300**

Thorp, Ellery, porcelain

children.	**300 - 500**

Tuttle, Eunice, miniature porcelain

children.	**600 - 800**
Angel Baby	**400 - 425**

Walters, Beverly, porcelain, miniature

fashions.	**500 up**

Wyffels, Berdine, porcelain.

6in (15cm) girl, glass eyes	**195**

Zeller, Fawn, porcelain.

One-of-a-kind Dolls	**2000 up**
Angela	**800 - 900**
Jeanie	**600 - 800**
Jackie Kennedy	**800**
Polly Piedmont, 1965.	**600 - 800**
Holly, U.S. Historical Society	**500 - 600**
Polly II, U.S. Historical Society	**200 - 225**

Candy, by Eunice Tuttle. *H & J Foulke, Inc.*

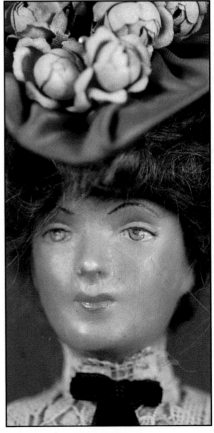

14-1/2in (37cm) *Gibson Girl,* by Lewis Sorensen. *H & J Foulke, Inc.*

ARTIST DOLLS *continued*

U.F.D.C. National & Regional Souvenir Dolls: Created by doll artists in limited editions and distributed to convention attendees as souvenirs. Before 1982, most dolls were given as kits; after 1982, most dolls were fully made up and dressed. Except as noted, dolls have porcelain heads, arms and legs; cloth bodies. A few are all porcelain.

Alice in Wonderland: Yolanda Bello, 1990 Region 10. Complete doll. **$ 165**
Alice Roosevelt: Kathy Redmond, 1990 National. Complete doll.   **100 - 125**
Crystal Faerie: Kazue Moroi and Lita Wilson, 1983 Midwest Regional. Complete.   **85**
Father Christmas: (Kit) Beverly Walters, 1980 National. Fully made up.   **400 - 500**
Janette: Fawn Zeller, 1991 National. Complete doll and pattern portfolio.   **350**
Kate: All cloth by Anili, 1986 National. With original box.   **165 - 185**
Li'l Apple: Faith Wick, 1979 National. Fully made up with romper suit.   **40 - 50**
Ken-Tuck: (Kit) Janet Masteller, 1972 Regional. Fully made up.   **65 - 75**

Little Miss Sunshine: (Kit) 1974 Florida Regional. Fully made up.   **65 - 75**
Mary: Linda Steele, 1987 National. Fully made up.   **90 - 100**
Miami Miss: (Kit) Fawn Zeller, 1961 National.
    Fully made up.   **200 - 250**
    Dressed.   **300 - 350**
PuPitt: X. Kontis, composition, 1958 National   **100 - 125**
Bo-Peep: carved wood, Fred Laughton, 1989 Region 15. with staff and sheep.   **85**
Precious Lady: Maori Kazue, 1972 National. Fully made up.   **95**
Laurel: Lita Wilson and Muriel Kramer. 1985 Regional. Fully made up.   **65**
Gibson Girl Bathing Beauty:
    Phyllis Wright. 1993 Regional, with bathing costume and beach chair.   **85**
Nellie Bly: Muriel Kramer, 1985 Pittsburgh Regional. Complete doll.   **85 - 95**
Pinky: Linda Cheek, California Regional. Complete doll.   **300**
Portrait of a Young Girl: Jeanne Singer, 1986 Rochester Regional.
    Complete doll.   **300**
Princess Kimimi: (Kit) 1977 Ohio Regional. Fully made up.   **85 - 95**
Rose O'Neill: Lita Wilson, 1982 National. Complete doll.   **165 - 200**
Sunshine: Lucille Gerrard, 1983 National. Complete doll.   **75 - 85**
Tammy: Jeanne Singer. 1989 Western N.Y. Doll Club. Complete doll.   **85**
Emma: Rappahannock Rags. Cloth. 1993 National.   **95**
Scarlett: Beverly Walters, 1976 Regional. Half doll, fully made up.   **135**
Scarlett: Lita Wilson and Muriel Kramer, 1989 Florida Regional. Half doll, fully made up.   **125 - 135**
Osceola: X. Kontis, compsoition. Early convention doll.   **$ 100 - 125**

12in (31cm) ***Osceola,*** by X. Kontis, all original. *H & J Foulke, Inc.*

ARTIST DOLLS *continued*

Commercial Doll Artists: Prices are for a factory perfect doll, never played with; including all accessories, wrist tag and box if any.

Bello, Yolanda. (See also **Ashton-Drake.**)
  Jill, porcelain $ 350
Dolls by Jerri, porcelain.
  Laura Lee   250
  Obediah   300
  Blossom   350
  Goldilocks   195
Good-Krueger, Julie, vinyl.
  Puppet Show, Puddle Jumper, Hug Bug Baby, High Spirits   175-200
Gunzel, Hildegard, wax-over-porcelain.
  Zaida, 43in (109cm)
    edition of 5 $ 1600
    Atholwin, 32in (81cm)   1950
  Vinyl **Zak**   95
  For Alexander
    Melody and Friend   500
    Courtney and Friends   600
Hartmann, Sonja, porcelain and vinyl.
  Rainbow Sailor and other
    children   295
Heller, Karin, all-cloth.
  Children   250-300
Iacono, Maggie, cloth.
  Children   400-450
Roche, Lynne & Michael, porcelain (See photograph on page 234.).
  17-20in (43-51cm) children **1200-1500**
  Small Emily, Small Hannah,
    fully jointed porcelain   600-700
Sandreuter, Regina, carved wood.
  17in (43cm) children   700-800
Scattolini, Laura, cernit, one-of-a-kind.
  22-24in (56-61cm)   350-450
Schrott, Rotrout for Gadco.
  Martina, porcelain   600
         vinyl   375
  Marlene   400
Spanos, FayZah, vinyl (see photograph on page 234).
  Babies   200-250
Thompson, Pat, for Vlasta, porcelain.
  Ladies in fancy period one-of-a-kind
    costumes, 31in (79cm)   **1000-1400**
Treffeisen, Ruth, porcelain.
  25-30in (64-76cm) children **1700-2000**

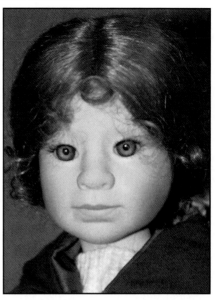

High Spirits by Julie Good-Krueger, 1994. *Rae-Ellen Koenig, The Doll Express.*

Martina by Rotrout Schrott, 30in (76cm) vinyl. *McMasters Doll Auctions.*

Small Emily by the Roches, 1993, all porcelain, fully jointed. *Rae-Ellen Koenig, The Doll Express*. (For further information see page 233.)

Baby Bubbles by FayZah Spanos, 1996. Limited Edition of 1000. *Rae-Ellen Koenig, The Doll Express*. (For further information see page 233.)

ASHTON DRAKE

Designed by **Yolanda Bello** for Ashton-Drake:

Picture Perfect Babies, porcelain/cloth.

Jason (1st)	$	**450-500**
Heather (2nd)		**175-200**
Jennifer (3rd)		**150-175**
Matthew (4th)		**100-125**
Jessica (1989)		75
Lisa (1990)		75
Emily (1991)		75
Danielle (1991)		75
Amanda		75
Michael		85
Sarah		85

Designed by **Mel Odom** for Ashton-Drake:
Gene, Premiere, 1996, blonde hair in
   black tulle gown $ **250-300**
1996 Christmas **Holiday Magic**
   outfit only   **100-150**

Jennifer from "Picture Perfect Babies", series by Yolanda Bello. *Rae-Ellen Koenig, The Doll Express*.

BARBIE®

FACTS

Mattel, Inc., Hawthorne, Calif., U.S.A. 1959 to present. Hard plastic and vinyl.
11-1/2–12in (29-31cm).
Mark: 1959-1962: BARBIE TM/Pats. Pend./© MCMLVIII/by/Mattel, Inc.
1963-1968: Midge TM/© 1962/BARBIE®/© 1958/by/Mattel, Inc.
1964-1966: © 1958/Mattel, Inc./U.S. Patented/U.S. Pat. Pend.
1966-1969: © 1966/Mattel, Inc./U.S. Patented/U.S. Pat.
Pend./Made in Japan.

Pricing Note: Condition is extremely important in pricing BARBIE® dolls. Mint condition means the doll has never been played with, coloring is beautiful, hair is perfect, all accessories are present. Rule of thumb dictates that to price out-of-original-box dolls and accessories, deduct 50%; for lightly played with items, deduct an additional 25%.

#3 Ponytail BARBIE®.
Courtesy of McMasters Doll Auctions.

#4 Ponytail BARBIE®.
Courtesy of McMasters Doll Auctions.

BARBIE® *continued*

First BARBIE®: 1959. Vinyl, solid body; very light complexion, white irises, pointed eyebrows, ponytail, black and white striped bathing suit, holes in feet to fit stand, gold hoop earrings; mint condition.

11-1/2in (29cm) boxed	**$ 4500 - 5500**

Doll only, no box or accessories

Mint	**3000**
Very good	**2500**
Stand	**1200**
Shoes	**50**
Hoop earrings	**65**
Dressed display boxed doll	
#878 Let's Dance	**5500**

Second BARBIE®: 1959-1960. Vinyl, solid body; very light complexion, same as above, but no holes in feet, some wore pearl earrings; mint condition. Made 3 months only.

11-1/2in (29cm) boxed	**$3500 - 4000***
Doll only, no box or accessories, very good	**2600**

*Brunette harder to find than blonde.

Third BARBIE®: 1960. Vinyl, solid body; very light complexion, same as above, but with blue irises and curved eyebrows; no holes in feet; mint condition. (See photograph on page 235.)

11-1/2in (29cm) boxed	**$ 900 - 1000**
Doll only, mint	**500 - 600**
Dressed display boxed doll	
#861 Evening Splendor	**2500**

Fourth BARBIE®: 1960. Vinyl; same as #3; but with solid body of flesh-toned vinyl; mint condition. (See photograph on page 235.)

11-1/2in (29cm) boxed	**$ 550 - 600**
Doll only, mint	**350**
Dressed display boxed doll	
#881 Busy Gal	**2800**

Fifth BARBIE®: 1961. Vinyl; same as #4; ponytail hairdo of firm Saran; mint condition.

11-1/2in (29cm) boxed	**$ 450 - 500**
Doll only, mint	**275 - 325**
Bubble Cut BARBIE®, 1961 on.	
Mint-in-box	**$ 300 - 325**
Doll only, mint	**135 - 160**
Fashion Queen BARBIE®, 1963.	
Mint-in-box	**500**
Doll only with 3 wigs	**125 - 135**
Miss BARBIE®, 1964.	
Mint-in-box	**1300**
Swirl Ponytail BARBIE®, 1964.	
Mint-in-box	**475 - 500**
Doll only, mint	**250**

Miss BARBIE®.
Courtesy of McMasters Doll Auctions.

Bubble Cut BARBIE®.
Courtesy of McMasters Doll Auctions.

BARBIE® is a registered trademark of Mattel, Inc.

BARBIE® *continued*

Bendable Leg BARBIE®, 1965 and 1966.
American Girl, center part,

mint-in-box	**1200 - 1500**
Side part, mint-in-box	**3500 - 4500**

Color Magic BARBIE®, 1966.

Mint-in-box, brunette	**1700**
blonde	**1100**
Doll only, mint, brunette	**1300**
blonde	**850**

Twist & Turn BARBIE®, 1967.

Mint-in-box	**350**

Talking BARBIE®, 1970.

Mint-in-box	**225 - 250**

Living BARBIE®, 1970.

Mint-in-box	**200**

Hair Happenin's BARBIE®, 1971.

Mint-in-box	**850**

Montgomery Ward BARBIE®, 1972.

Mint doll	**225 - 275**

Gift Sets:

Fashion Queen BARBIE® & Ken, 1964.	$ **1200**
Wedding Party, 1964.	**1200**
On Parade (*Barbie®, Ken* and *Midge*), 1964.	**1100**
Skipper Party Time, 1964.	**500**

Outfits: All never removed from package. Deduct 50% for *complete* but out-of-package outfits.

Roman Holiday	$	**3000 up**
Gay Parisienne		**2000 up**
Easter Parade		**2500 up**
Shimmering Magic		**1500 up**
Here Comes the Bride		**950 up**
Pan Am Stewardess		**2000 up**
BARBIE® Baby Sits		**300 up**
Dogs & Duds		**300 up**
Enchanted Evening		**400 up**
1600 Series and Jacqueline Kennedy-style outfits		**295 up**
Dinner at 8		**250**
Commuter Set		**1500**
Picnic Set		**295**
Sorority Meeting		**150**
Silken Flame		**135 up**
Midnight Blue		**500 up**
Miss Astronaut		**750 up**

Accessories: Mint in package.

BARBIE® doll's First Car	$	**250**
BARBIE® doll's First Dreamhouse		**150**
Fashion Shop		**300**
Little Theatre		**500**
Cases		**25 up**
BARBIE® doll's Bed		**100**

American Girl BARBIE®, center part.
Courtesy of McMasters Doll Auctions.

Living BARBIE®.
Courtesy of McMasters Doll Auctions.

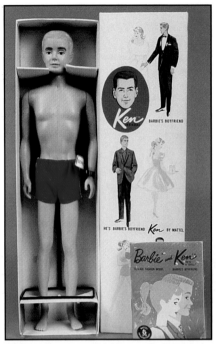

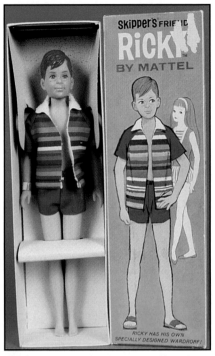

#1 Ken. Courtesy of McMasters Doll Auctions.
  (For further information see page 240.)

Ricky. Courtesy of McMasters Doll Auctions.
  (For further information see page 240.)

Skipper. Courtesy of McMasters Doll Auctions. (For further information see page 240.)

Francie "No Bangs", wearing a pink square neck pak sweater. *Courtesy of McMasters Doll Auctions.* (For further information see page 240.)

Blue Rhapsody, first in Porcelain Collection, 1986. *Courtesy of McMasters Doll Auctions.* (For further information see page 241.)

1994 Happy Holidays. Courtesy of McMasters Doll Auctions. (For further information see page 241.)

BARBIE® *continued*

Other Dolls:

Ken #1 (see photograph on page 238),
1961. Mint-in-box $ **200**
   Bendable legs, mint-in-box   **300 - 325**
   Dressed boxed doll   **275 up**

Midge, 1963. Mint-in-box   **180**
   1966. Bendable legs, mint-in-box   **500**

Allen, 1964-1966.
   Mint-in-box, bendable legs   **350**
         straight legs   **175**

Skipper (see photograph on page 238),
1964. Straight legs, mint-in-box   **175**

Ricky, 1965. Mint-in-box   **200**

Scooter, 1965. Straight legs,
   mint-in-box   **200**

Francie, 1966-1967.
   Doll only, mint bendable leg   **185**
         straight legs   **200**
         Twist 'n Turn   **235**

Black, 1967. Mint-in-package.
   Doll only, mint   **700**
"No Bangs" (See photograph on page
239.), 1970.
   Mint-in-box   **1200**
   Doll only, mint   **700 up**
Hair Happenin's, 1970. Mint-in-box   **275**

Casey, 1967. Mint-in-box   **250**

Twiggy, 1967.
   Mint-in-box   **325**

Christie, 1968-1972. (Black) Twist 'n Turn
   Mint-in-box   **225**

Stacey, 1968-1971. Twist 'n Turn
   Mint-in-box   **250**

P.J., 1969-1971. Twist 'n Turn
   Mint-in-box   **175**

Truly Scrumptious, 1969.
   Mint-in-box   **525**
   Doll only, mint   **300**

Julia, 1969.
   Mint-in-box, one-piece
     uniform   **125**
   Mint-in-box, two-piece uniform   **165**
   Talking, mint-in-box   **135**

Tutti, 1967-1970. Mint-in-box   **150**

Chris, 1967-1970. Mint-in-box   **210**

Todd, 1967-1970. Mint-in-box   **200**

Tutti. *Courtesy of
McMasters Doll
Auctions.*

BARBIE® *continued*

Bob Mackie BARBIES Dolls

1990 Gold	$	775 up
1991 Platinum		650 up
1991 Starlight Splendor (black)		600 up
1992 Empress Bride		900 up
1992 Neptune Fantasy		850 up
1993 Masquerade Ball		350
1994 Queen of Hearts		225
1995 Goddess of the Sun		200

Christmas BARBIES:

1988, English language box	$	795 up
1989		235
1990		175
1991		175
1992		125
1993		120
1994		145
1995		50
1996		50

Exclusive Store Specials:

1990 Winter Fantasy		
(FAO Schwarz)	$	250
1993 Little Debbie		65
1994 Nicole Miller (Bloomingdales)		125
1994 Theatre Elegance (Spiegel)		175
1994 Victorian Elegance (Hallmark)		125
1994 Silver Screen (FAO Schwarz)		200
1994 Tooth Fairy (WalMart)		25
1995 Shopping Chic (Speigel)		85
1995 Jeweled Splendor		
(FAO Schwarz)		225
1995 Circus Star (FAO Schwarz)		125
1995 International Traveller		
(Duty Free Shops)		75
1995 Donna Karan (Bloomingdales)		135

Timeless Creations (now BARBIE®
Collectibles)

Stars and Stripes Collection:

1990 Air Force BARBIE®	$	55
1991 Navy BARBIE®		50
1992 Marine BARBIE®		40
1992 Marine Gift Set		80
1993 Army Gift Set		60
1994 Air Force Gift Set		60

Classique Collection:

1992 Benefit Ball	$	200
1993 Opening Night		125
1993 City Style		110
1994 Uptown Chic		90
1994 Evening Extravaganza		90
1994 Evening Extravaganza		
(black)		110
1995 Midnight Gala		85

Nostalgia Series:

1994 35th Anniversary		
(blonde)	$	40
(brunette)		55
1994 Gift Set		150
1994 Solo in the Spotlight		40
1995 Busy Gal		80
1996 Enchanted Evening		35

Scarlett Series, 1994 & 1995.

Green Velvet	$	85
Red Velvet		85
Barbecue		75
Honeymoon		85
Ken as **Rhett Butler**		75

Great Eras:

1993 Gibson Girl	$	110
1993 1920s Flapper		145
1994 Egyptian Queen		110
1994 Southern Belle		90
1995 Grecian Goddess		60

Other BARBIE® Dolls:

1986 Blue Rhapsody (porcelain) (See		
photograph on page 239.)	$	800
1988 Mardi Gras		100
1989 Pink Jubilee		1500 up
1990 Wedding Fantasy		50
1992 My Size		140
1994 Snow Princess		125
1994 Gold Jubilee		900
1994 Evergreen Princess		125
1994 Evergreen Princess		
(red hair)		500
1995 Peppermint Princess		85
1995 Starlight Waltz		100
1995 Dior		140
1995 50th Anniversary		
(porcelain)		500
1996 Pink Splendor		675

BETSY McCALL

American Character Doll Co.: 1957. All hard plastic, molded eyelashes, jointed knees, rooted Saran hair on wig cap; original clothes, excellent with rosy cheeks.

8in (20cm) basic, (undergarment, shoes and socks)	$	**150**
mint-in-box		**275**
in dresses		**175-200**
in gowns		**250-275**
Clothes, clean and in very good condition:		
dresses		**25-45**
shoes and socks		**25**

American Character, 1960. All vinyl, lashed sleep eyes, slender limbs; original clothes; excellent condition.

14in (36cm)	$	**285-310**
20in (51cm)		**350**
30in (76cm)		**500-550**
36in (91cm)		**650-750**

Jointed at wrists, waist, knees and ankles:

22in (56cm)	**400**
30in (76cm)	**625**

Ideal Novelty & Toy Co., 1948. Vinyl head, hard plastic body; original clothes; excellent condition

14in (36cm)	$	**300**
mint-in-box		**500**

Ideal Novelty & Toy Co., 1959. All vinyl; original clothes; excellent condition.

36in (91cm) **Betsy McCall**	$	**550-650**
38in (96cm) **Sandy McCall**		**500-600**

Uneeda, 1959-1961.

All vinyl, 11-1/2in (29cm)	$	**95**

20in (51cm) *Betsy McCall*, all original with label. *H & J Foulke, Inc.*

8in (20cm) *Betsy McCall*, boxed. *Rosemary Kanizer.*

BOUDOIR DOLLS

BUDDY LEE

Boudoir Doll: Head of composition, cloth or other material, painted features, mohair wig, composition or cloth stuffed body, unusually long extremities, usually high-heeled shoes; original clothes elaborately designed and trimmed; all in excellent condition.

1920s Art Doll, exceptional quality, silk
  hair, 28-30in (71-76cm) $ **400 - 500**

Standard quality, dressed,
  28-30in (71-76cm) **175 - 225**
  undressed **90 - 110**
1940s composition head,
  dressed **125**

Lenci, 24-28in (61-71cm) **1800 up**
  faded color **1000 - 1250**

Smoking Doll, 25in (64cm) **450 - 500**

Poured Wax, 22in (56cm) **600**

FACTS
Various French, U.S. and Italian firms.
Early 1920s into the 1940s.

Italian felt boudoir doll by Lenci.
Jensen's Antique Dolls.

Marked Buddy Lee: Molded hair, painted eyes to side; jointed at shoulders, stiff hips, legs apart; dressed in original Lee clothes; all in very good condition.
  Composition, 1920-1948.
    13in (33cm) $ **400-450**
  Hard Plastic, 1949-1962.
    13in (33cm) **400-450**

FACTS
H.D. Lee Co., Inc. garment manufacturers
of Kansas City, MO.
1920-1962.
Mark: "Buddy Lee" embossed on back

13in (33cm) **Buddy Lee**, all original in Lee Overall outfit. *Wayne Jensen Collection.*

BURGARELLA

Burgarella Doll: Excellent quality all-composition, jointed at neck, shoulders, elbows, hips and knees; semi-spherical joints make the doll very posable; human hair or mohair wig; distinctive short face with chubby cheeks; dramatic painted eyes, small mouth; lovely original clothes; all in excellent condition.

16-18in (41-46cm) all original	**$ 500-600**
21-22in (53-56cm) all original	**600-700**
Sexed boy, all original	**650-750**

FACTS
Gaspare Burgarella, Flaminia Street, Rome, Italy.1925-1940. Designer: Ferdinando Stracuzzi **Mark:** Cloth label BURGARELLA Made in Italy

Pair of 16in (41cm) Burgarella dolls, all original.
Gracia Caiani Collection.

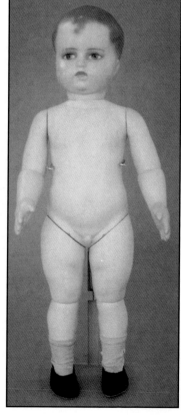

Sexed boy, probably by Burgarella; original tagged clothes are marked only "Made in Italy."
Lesley Hurford Collection.

CAMEO DOLL COMPANY

Baby Bo Kaye: 1925. (See page 39.)
Kewpie: 1913. (See page 127.)
Scootles: 1925. Designed by Rose O'Neill. All-composition; appropriate clothes; all in very good condition.

7in-8in (18-20cm)	$	**400 - 450**
12-13in (31-33cm)		**500 - 550**
15-16in (38-41cm)		**675 - 725**
20in (51cm)		**900 - 1000**
Sleep eyes:		
12in (31cm)		**700 - 750**
20in (51cm)		**1250 - 1500**
Black,		
13-14in (33-36cm)		**750 - 850**
All-bisque, marked on feet:		
5-6in (13-15cm), Germany		**650 - 750**
6-7in (15-18cm), Japan		**500 - 550**
Vinyl, 14in (36cm), 1973 Maxine's Ltd. Ed.		**125 - 150**

Wood Segmented Characters: Designed by Joseph L. Kallus. Composition head, segmented wood body; undressed; all in very good condition.

Margie, 1929. 10in (25cm)	$	**225 - 250**
15in (38cm)		**400 - 450**
Pinkie, 1930. 10in (25cm)		**275 - 325**
Joy, 1932. 10in (5cm)		**275 - 325**
15in (38cm)		**400 - 450**
Betty Boop, 1932.		
12in (31cm)		**550 - 650**

With molded bathing suit and composition legs; wearing a cotton print dress

	650 - 700
Pop-Eye, 1935.	**300****
Hotpoint Man, 16in (41cm)	**800****
RCA Radiotron, 16in (41cm)	**800****

Giggles: 1946. Designed by Rose O'Neill. All-composition; original romper; all in very good condition.

14in (36cm)	$	**650 - 750****

**Not enough price samples to compute a reliable range.

┌─ **FACTS** ─┐
Cameo Doll Company, New York, N.Y., later Port Allegany, Pa. Original owner: Joseph L. Kallus.
1922-on.

16in (41cm) *Scootles,* all original. *H & J Foulke, Inc.*

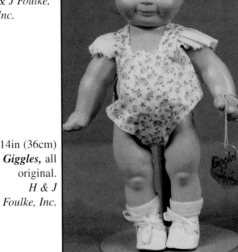

14in (36cm) *Giggles,* all original. *H & J Foulke, Inc.*

CAMEO DOLL COMPANY *continued*

Little Annie Rooney: 1925. Designed by
Jack Collins. Composition, painted eyes,
yarn wig, all original.
16in (41cm)   **$ 700****

Baby Blossom: 1927. Composition and
cloth, 19-20in (48-51cm) **$ 550 - 650****

Champ: 1942. Composition, molded hair,
freckles, all original.
16in (41cm)   **$ 500 - 600****

Vinyl Dolls:
Miss Peep, 1957. All original,
16-18in (41-46cm) boxed **$ 195**
Black   **135**

Baby Mine, 1961. All original,
20in (51cm) boxed   **175**

Margie, 1958. All original,
17in (43cm) boxed   **175 - 225****

Scootles, 1964. All original,
14in (36cm)   **165 - 185**

Scootles, 1980s. (Jesco), all original,
12in (31cm)   **40 - 60**

**Not enough price samples to compute a
reliable range.

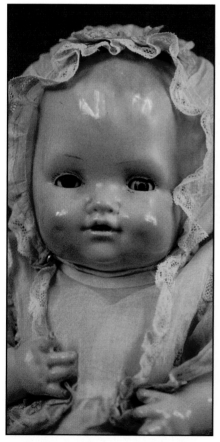

15in (38cm) ***Baby Blossom,*** all original.
H & J Foulke, Inc.

Large ***Joy,*** redressed.
Rhoda Shoemaker Collection.

CAMPBELL KIDS

E.I. Horsman Co., 1910-1914. Designed by Grace Drayton. Composition head, molded and painted bobbed hair; original cloth body; appropriate or original clothes; all in good condition.

Mark: On head:

E.I.H.© 1910

Cloth label on sleeve:

> The Campbell Kids
> Trademark by
> Joseph Campbell.
> Mfg. by E.I. HORSMAN Co

10-13in (25-33cm)	$	250 - 300
16in (41cm)		375 - 425

American Character & E.I. Horsman Co., 1923. Designed by Grace Drayton, sometimes called *Dolly Dingle*. All composition, molded bobbed hair, painted eyes to side; original clothes; all in good condition.

12in (31cm)	$	550 - 650

E. I. Horsman Co., 1948. All composition, molded bobbed hair, painted eyes to side, watermelon mouth; original clothes; all in good condition.

12in (31cm)	$	400 - 450
With Campbell Soup outfit and label		600

All Vinyl, 1971. Original clothes, bright color, unplayed with condition.

8in (20cm)	$	25
11in (28cm)		40

All Cloth, 1980s. Perfect, unplayed with condition | $ | 15-18

13in (33cm) 1920s *Campbell Kid*, all original with Horsman tag. *H & J Foulke, Inc.*

12in (31cm) 1948 *Campbell Kid*, all original. *H & J Foulke, Inc.*

DEWEES COCHRAN

Dewees Cochran Doll: Latex with jointed neck, shoulders and hips; human hair wig, painted eyes, character face; dressed; all in good condition.

15-16in (38-41cm) Cindy,
1947-1948.   **$ 800 - 900**
Grow-up Dolls: Stormy, Angel, Bunnie,
J.J. and Peter Ponsett each at ages 5, 7, 11,
16 and 20, 1952-1958.   **$ 1800 - 2200**
Look-Alike Dolls
(6 different faces)   **$ 1800 - 2200**
Individual Portrait
Children   **$ 2000 - 2200**
Composition American Children (see Effanbee, page 264).

FACTS
Dewees Cochran, Fenton, Calif.,
1940-on.
Mark: Signed under arm or behind
right ear.

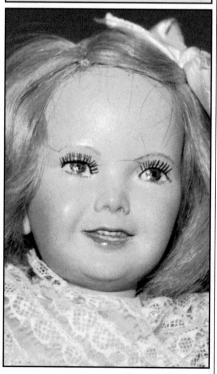

12in (31cm) Look-Alike Portrait doll.
Ruth Covington West.

COMPOSITION
(AMERICAN)

Condition: Unless otherwise noted, all dolls should be all original with perfect hair, good coloring, original clothes; light crazing acceptable.

All-Composition Child Doll: 1912-1920. Various firms, such as Bester Doll Co., New Era Novelty Co., New Toy Mfg. Co., Superior Doll Mfg. Co., Artcraft Toy Product Co., Colonial Toy Mfg. Co. Ball-jointed composition body; appropriate clothes; all in good condition. These are patterned after German bisque head dolls.
22-24in (56-61cm)   **$ 300 - 350**
Character baby, all-composition
19in (48cm)   **275 - 300**

Early Composition Character Doll: Ca. 1912. Composition head with molded hair and painted features; appropriate clothes. (See photograph on page 250.)
12-15in (31-38cm)   **$ 150 - 200**
18-20in (46-51cm)   **250 - 300**
24-26in (61-66cm)   **350 - 450**
Two-face toddler,
14in (36cm)   **275 - 300**

Molded Loop Dolls: Ca. 1930s. Composition head with molded bobbed hair and loop for tying on a ribbon; quality is generally mediocre.
12-15in (31-38cm)   **$ 150 - 175**

Patsy-type Girl: Ca. 1930s. All-composition with molded bobbed hair; of good quality.
9-10in (23-25cm)   **$ 165 - 185**
14-16in (36-41cm)   **250 - 275**
20in (51cm)   **325 - 350**

Mama Dolls: Ca. 1920-on. Composition head with hair wig; composition lower limbs; cloth body. (See photograph on page 250.)
16-18in (41-46cm)   **$ 225 - 250**
20-22in (51-56cm)   **300 - 350**
24-26in (61-66cm)   **400 - 450**

COMPOSITION (AMERICAN) *continued*

Babies: Ca. 1930. All-composition or composition head, arms and legs, cloth torso, of good quality. (See photograph on page 250.)

12-14in (31-36cm)	$	**165 - 225**
18-20in (46-51cm)		**250 - 300**
24in (61cm)		**375 - 425**

19in (48cm) mama doll, ***Happy Ann,*** all original. *H & J Foulke, Inc.*

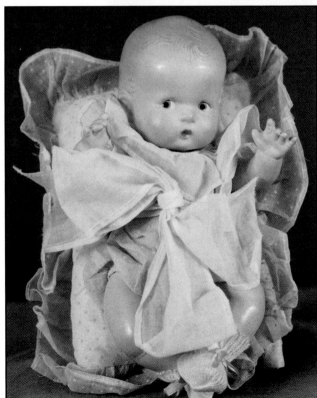

12in (31cm) all-composition baby. *H & J Foulke, Inc.*

COMPOSITION (AMERICAN) *continued*

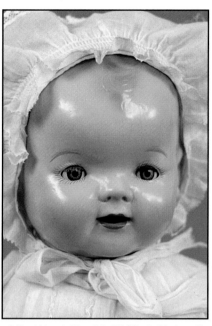

25in (64cm) *Hug Me Kiddie Pal* baby, all original. *H & J Foulke, Inc.* (For further information see page 249.)

14in (36cm) early composition character girl. *H & J Foulke, Inc.* (For further information see page 248.)

18in (46cm) mama doll, all original. *H & J Foulke, Inc.* (For further information see page 248.)

COMPOSITION (AMERICAN) *continued*

Top Left: 18in (46cm) Shirley Temple-type girl, all original. *H & J Foulke, Inc.* (For further information see page 252.) ***Right:*** 11in (28cm) costume doll, all original. *H & J Foulke, Inc.* (For further information see page 252.)

13in (33cm) ***Jackie Robinson,*** all original. *H & J Foulke, Inc.* (For further information see page 252.)

COMPOSITION (AMERICAN) *continued*

Dionne-type Doll: Ca. 1935. All-composition with molded hair or wig; of good quality.

7-8in (18-20cm) baby	$	125 - 135
13in (33cm) toddler		225 - 250
18-20in (46-51cm) toddler		300 - 350

Alexander-type Girl: Ca. 1935. All-composition; of good quality.

13in (33cm)	$	200 - 225
16-18in (41-46cm)		275 - 325
22in (56cm)		350 - 400

Shirley Temple-type Girl: Ca. 1935-on. All-composition; of good quality. (See photograph on page 251.)

16-18in (41-46cm)	$	400 - 500

Little Miss Movie, (See photograph on page 254.)

27in (69cm)	700 - 800

Costume Doll: Ca. 1940. All-composition. (See photograph on page 251.)

11in (28cm)

Excellent quality	$	150 - 175
Standard quality		65 - 75

Miscellaneous Specific Dolls:

Royal "Spirit of America,"

15in (38cm) with original box and outfits	$	300 - 350

Jackie Robinson (see photograph on page 251),

13-1/2in (34cm)	700**

Trudy 3 faces, 1946. (See photograph on page 254.)

14in (36cm)	250 - 295

Lone Ranger,

16in (41cm)	500 - 600

Kewpie-type characters,

12in (31cm)	80 - 90

Miss Curity,

18in (46cm)	450 - 500

P.D. Smith,

22in (56cm)	2600**

G.G. Drayton,

14in (36cm)	450 - 500**

Madame Louise,

20in (51cm) mint-in-box	550

**Not enough price samples to compute a reliable average.

16in (41cm) Alexander-type girl, all original. *H & J Foulke, Inc.*

Hedwig/DiAngeli
   Elin, (See photograph on page 254.),
   Hannah,
   Lydia, Suzanne,
   14in (36cm) $ 450 - 500
3 Pigs and Wolf boxed set,
   all original   800 - 1000
Sterling Doll Co. Sports Dolls,
   29in (74cm) all original   300 - 350
Paris Doll Co. Peggy,
   28in (71cm) walker   350 - 400
Monica, 1941-1951.
   18in (46cm)   550
Famlee, 1921. Boxed with 6 heads and 6
   costumes   1000
Cat, Rabbit or Pig head, naked,
   10-11in (25-28cm)   200 - 250
Santa Claus,
   19in (48cm)   450 - 500
Pinocchio, Crown Toy, 1939.
   12in (31cm)   250 - 300
Puzzy, 1948. H. of P.,
   15in (38cm)   350 - 400
Sizzy, 1948. H. of P.,
   14in (36cm)   250 - 300

Black Composition Doll: Ca.
1930. Original or appropriate
clothes; some have three yarn
tufts of hair on either side and
one top of the head; all in good
condition. (See photograph on
page 254.)
   "Topsy" Baby:
      10-12in (25-31cm) **150 - 165**
      16in (41cm)   **225 - 250**

Toddler,
   15-16in (38-41cm)   300 - 350
   Girl, 17in (43cm) $ 350 - 400
   1910 character,
   13-1/2in (34cm)   300 - 350
Patsy-type,
   13-14in (33-36cm)   300 - 350

Tony Sarg Mammy with Baby,
   17in (43cm)   900 - 1000

Ming Ming Baby: Quan-Quan Co., Los
Angeles and San Francisco, Calif. Ca. 1930.
All-composition baby; original Oriental costume of colorful taffeta with braid trim; feet
painted black or white for shoes.
   10-12in (25-31cm) $ 175 - 200

12-1/2in (32cm)
Rabbit head doll, all
original. *H & J
Foulke, Inc.*

27in (69cm) Goldberger *Little Miss Movie*, all original. *H & J Foulke, Inc.* (For further information see page 252.)

18in (46cm) Black composition girl, all original. *H & J Foulke, Inc.* (For further information see page 253.)

14in (36cm) Helwig/DiAngeli *Elin* (replaced vest). *H & J Foulke, Inc.* (For further information see page 253.)

14in (36cm) *Trudy* with 3 faces, all original. *H & J Foulke, Inc.* (For further information see page 252.)

COMPOSITION (GERMAN)

All-Composition Child Doll: Socket head with good wig, sleep (sometimes flirty) eyes, open mouth with teeth; jointed composition body; appropriate clothes; all in good condition, of excellent quality.

12-14in (31-36cm)	**$ 225 - 275**
18-20in (46-51cm)	**375 - 425**
22in (56cm)	**450 - 500**

Character face,

18-20in (46-51cm)	**$ 425 - 525**

Black Composition Doll: All composition; molded hair or wig, glass eyes (sometimes flirty); appropriate clothes; all in good condition.

11in (28cm)	**$ 350**
16-18in (41-46cm)	**650 - 750***
Patsy-type, 11in (28cm)	
all original	**$ 650**

Dora Petzoldt Child: 1919 on. Molded

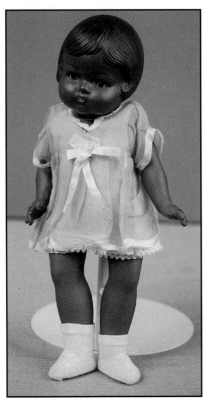

composition (sometimes cloth) head, closed mouth, pensive character face, painted eyes, mohair wig; cloth body, sometimes with long arms and legs; original clothing; all in very good condition.

19-22in (48-56cm)	**$ 850 - 950**
Moderate wear, redressed	**400 - 450**

Character Baby: Composition head with good wig, sleep eyes, open mouth with teeth; bent-limb composition baby body or hard-stuffed cloth body; appropriate clothes; all in good condition, of excellent quality.

All-composition baby,

16-18in (41-46cm)	**$ 375 - 425**
Cloth body,	
18-20in (46-51cm)	**300 - 350**
All composition toddler,	
16-18in (41-46cm)	**450 - 500**

FACTS

Various German firms such as König & Wernicke, Kämmer & Reinhardt and others. Ca. 1920s on.

11in (28cm) Two views of a Patsy-type German composition #1227, all original. *H & J Foulke, Inc.*

COMPOSITION
(JAPANESE)

Japanese Composition Doll: All-composition with molded hair, painted features; dressed (may have original rayon panties with "Japan" stamp) or undressed; all in excellent condition.

Dionne Quintuplets:

Baby, 7in (18cm)	$	**165-185**
Baby, 9in (23cm)		**250-300****
Toddler, 7-1/2in (19cm)		**165-185**

Choir Boy, with book molded in hands,
10in (25cm) **135-150**
Toddler, 8in (20cm), all original **125-135**
Shirley Temple. See page 300.

FACTS

Unidentified Japanese Companies,
1920-1940
Mark: "JAPAN" incised or stamped
on back torso.

7-1/2in (19cm) *Dionne Quintuplet*
toddlers. *H & J Foulke, Inc.*

COSMOPOLITAN

Ginger. 1954 on. All-hard plastic walker, sleep eyes; original clothes; excellent condition with good color and perfect hair.
Unmarked. 8in (20cm) $ **90-125**

Mint-in-box	**175**
Roundup, Mouseketeer, or Davy Crockett	**225**
Disneyland Costumes	**200-300**
Girl Scout or Brownie	**150**
Boxed outfits	**30-60**
Vinyl head, all original	**40-50**

Miss Ginger: 1957 on. Vinyl head, hard plastic body with adult figure, high-heeled feet; original clothes; excellent condition.
Mark: "GINGER" on head.
10-1/2in (27cm) $ **125**

Little Miss Ginger: 1958 on. Vinyl head, rigid vinyl body, adult figure with high-heeled feet; original clothes; excellent condition, eyes not askew.
Mark: "GINGER" on head.
8in (20cm) $ **75**

FACTS

Cosmopolitan Doll & Toy Corp.,
Jackson Heights, NY.

Ginger in Official Roundup Costume.
Terri & Kathy's Dolls.

EFFANBEE

Early Characters: Composition character face, molded painted hair; cloth stuffed body; appropriate clothes; in good condition. Some marked "Deco."
12-16in (30-41cm).

Baby Grumpy, 1912. Molds 172, 174 or 176	$ 325 - 350**
Miss Coquette Naughty Marietta, 1912.	325 - 350**
Pouting Bess, 1915, 162 or 166	325 - 350**
Billy Boy, 1915.	325 - 350
Whistling Jim, 1916.	325 - 350
Harmonica Joe, 1924.	325 - 350
Katie Kroose, 1918.	325 - 375
Buds, 1915-1918.	175 - 195
Black	200 - 225
Aunt Dinah, 1915. (See page 12 for photograph.) 16in (41cm)	600

**Not enough price samples to compute a reliable average.

Johnny Tu-Face, 1912.	**400**
Betty Bounce, 1913.	**325 - 350**
Baby Huggins, 1915.	**300**

Metal Heart Bracelet and chain $ **45 - 50**

---FACTS---
EFFanBEE Doll Co., New York, N.Y., 1912-on.
Marks: Various, but nearly always marked "EFFanBEE" on torso or head, sometimes with doll's name. Wore a metal heart-shaped bracelet; later a gold paper heart label.

Effanbee   EFFANBEE DURABLE DOLLS   EFFANBEE DOLLS WALK-TALK-SLEEP

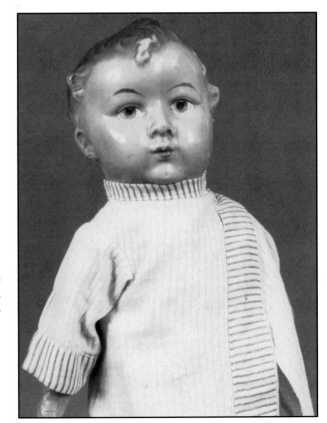

16in (41cm) Effanbee
Billy Boy, all original.
H & J Foulke, Inc.

Top Left: 17in (43cm) mama doll, all original. *H & J Foulke, Inc.* (For further information see page 260.) **Right:** 11in (28cm) Amish man, all original. *H & J Foulke, Inc.* (For further information see page 260.)

30in (76cm) **Mae Starr**, all original. *H & J Foulke, Inc.* (For further information see page 260.)

EFFᴀɴBEE *continued*

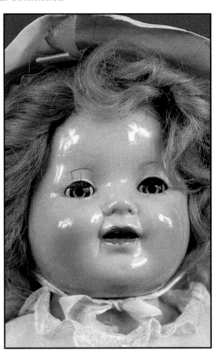

Top Left: 18in (46cm) ***Baby Bright Eyes***, all original. *H & J Foulke, Inc.* (For further information see page 260.) ***Right:*** 17in (43cm) ***Lovums***, all original. *H & J Foulke, Inc.* (For further information see page 260.)

11in (28cm) ***Patsy Baby***, all original. *H & J Foulke, Inc.* (For further information see page 261.)

Shoulder Head Dolls: Composition shoulder head; cloth torso, composition arms and legs; original clothes; all in good condition.

Baby Grumpy, 1925-1939.
12in (31cm) white	$	**275 - 300**
Black		**350 - 375**

Pennsylvania Dutch Dolls, 1936-1940. All original and excellent. (See photograph on page 258.) **225**

Baby Dainty, 1912-1922.
15in (38cm)	**225 - 250**
Patsy, 1925. 15in (38cm)	**300 - 350**

Rosemary, 1925. Marilee, 1924.
14in (36cm)	**275 - 300**
17in (43cm)	**325 - 375**
25in (64cm)	**450 - 550**
30in (76cm)	**600 - 625**

Mary Ann, 1928.
19-20in (48-51cm)	**375 - 425**
All-composition	**450 - 500**

Mary Lee, 1928.
16-17in (41-43cm)	**325 - 375**
All-composition	**375 - 425**

Early Mama Dolls, 1920s. (See photograph on page 258.)
20-22in (51-56cm)	**400 - 450**
26-28in (66-71cm)	**550 - 600**

Mae Starr, 1928. (See photograph on page 258.)
30in (76cm) phonograph doll	**550 - 650**

Babies: Composition head; cloth body, original clothes; all in good condition, with perfect hair and good coloring, light crazing acceptable.

Bubbles, 1924.

Mark:

19 © 24
EFFANBEE
DOLLS
WALK-TALK-SLEEP
MADE IN U S A

EFFANBEE
BUBBLES
COPYR 1924
MADE IN U.S.A.

16-18in (41-46cm)	$	**375 - 425**

22-24in (56- 61cm)	**475 - 525**
26in (66cm) mint, all original with tag	**700 - 800**

Baby Evelyn, 18in (46cm) **250 - 275**
Lovums, 1928. (See photogrpah on page 259.)
Mark:

EFFAN BEE
LOVUMS
©
PAT Nº. 1,283,558

16-18in (41-46cm)	$	**325 - 375**
22-24in (56-61cm)		**425 - 475**

Mickey, Baby Bright Eyes (See photograph on page 259.), Tommy Tucker, 1939-1949.
16-18in (41-46cm)	**350 - 385**
22-24in (56-61cm)	**450 - 500**

Sweetie Pie, 1942.
16-18in (41-46cm)	**350 - 385**
22-24in (56-61cm)	**450 - 500**

Baby Effanbee, 1925.
12in (31cm)	**160 - 180**

Lambkin, 1930s.
16in (41cm)	**375 - 425**

Sugar Baby, 1936. Caracul wig,
16-18in (41-46cm)	**300 - 350**

Babyette, eyes closed,
13in (33cm) boxed with pillow
550 - 600

Pat-O-Pat, (clap hands), 1925.
13in (33cm)	**150 - 165**

Patsy Family: 1928-on. All-composition; original or appropriate old clothes; may have some light crazing.

Mark:

EFFANBEE
PATSY JR.
DOLL

EFFANBEE
PATSY
DOLL

Bra, cler

EFFANBEE
PATSY
BABY KIN

Wee Patsy, 6in (15cm)	$	375 - 425
boxed with extra outfits		600 - 650
Sewing set, boxed set		650
Storybook Doll, all original		600
Baby Tinyette, 7in (18cm)		300 - 325
Quintuplets, set of 5, boxed, all original		2000
Tinyette Toddler, 8in (20cm)		300 - 325
Patsy Babyette, 9in (23cm)		325 - 350
Patsyette, 9in (23cm)		375 - 425
Brown		500 - 550
Hawaiian		450 - 500
Patsy Baby (See photograph on page 259.),		
11in (28cm)		350 - 375
Brown		500 - 550

Patsy Jr. (See photograph on page 262.),	
Patsy Kins, Patricia Kin,	
11in (28cm)	400 - 450
Patsy, 14in (36cm)	450 - 525
1946, unmarked	400
Patricia, 15in (38cm)	500 - 525
Patsy Joan, 16in (41cm)	500 - 525
Brown	700
1946 (different mold)	400-425
Patsy Ann, 19in (48cm)	525 - 575
Brown (See photograph on page 262.)	950
Patsy Lou, 22in (56cm)	550 - 600
Patsy Ruth, 26in (66cm)	1000 - 1100
Patsy Mae (See photograph on page 262.)	
30in (76cm)	1300 - 1500

Skippy: 1929. (See photograph on page 263.)	
14in (36cm) all original	500 - 600
cowboy, at auction	1050
redressed	350 - 400
Brown	900

9in (23cm) *Patsyette*,
all original.
H & J Foulke, Inc.

EFFANBEE *continued*

Top: Left: 11in (28cm) *Patsy Jr.*, all original. *H & J Foulke, Inc.* (For further information see page 261.) *Right:* 30in (76cm) *Patsy Mae. H & J Foulke, Inc.* (For further information see page 261.)

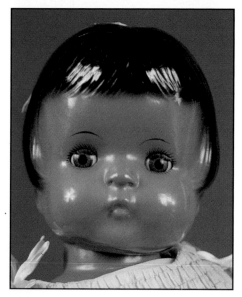

19in (48cm) brown *Patsy Ann. H & J Foulke, Inc.* (For further information see page 261.)

EFFANBEE *continued*

14in (36cm) *Skippy*, all original. *H & J Foulke, Inc.* (For further information see page 261.)

17in (43cm) *Anne Shirley*. *Joanna Ott Collection*. (For further information see page 264.)

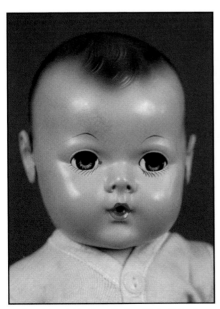

16in (41cm) *Dy-Dee Baby*. *H & J Foulke, Inc.* (For further information see page 264.)

20in (51cm) *American Child*. *H & J Foulke, Inc.* (For further information see page 264.)

EFFanBEE *continued*

Dy-Dee Baby: 1933-on. Hard rubber head with soft rubber body; appropriate old clothes; good condition. (See photograph on page 263.)
Mark:

> *"EFF-AN-BEE*
> *DY-DEE BABY*
> *US PAT.-1-857-485*
> *ENGLAND-880-060*
> *FRANCE-723-980*
> *GERMANY-585-647*
> *OTHER PAT PENDING"*

9in (23cm)	$	250 - 300
14-16in (36-41cm)		225 - 275
24in (61cm)		400 - 450
14in (36cm) boxed with layette and accessories		475 - 500
Carded 5-piece nursery set with **Dy-Dee** booklet		100 - 110
Dy-Dee pajamas		20 - 25
Bottle		12 - 15

All-Composition Children: 1933-on. Original clothes; all in very good condition, with nice coloring and perfect hair.

Anne Shirley, 1935-1940. (See photograph on page 263.)

14-15in (36-38cm)	$	275 - 300
17-18in (43-46cm)		300 - 325

21in (53cm)		400 - 450
27in (69cm)		450 - 500

American Children, 1936-1939. (See photograph on page 263.) Open mouth, unmarked.

Barbara Joan, 15in (38cm)	$	550 - 650
Ice Queen (skater)		650
Barbara Ann, 17in (43cm)		650 - 750
Barbara Lou, 21in (53cm)		750 - 850

Closed mouth. 19-21in (48-53cm) marked head on Anne Shirley body,

painted eyes	$	1600 - 1800
sleep eyes	$	1500 - 1600

17in (43cm) boy, unmarked, painted eyes	$	1600 - 1800

Suzette, 1939. Painted eyes, 11-1/2in (29cm)	$	250 - 300
Suzanne, 1940. 14in (36cm)	$	300 - 350

Little Lady, 1940-1949. Same prices as Anne Shirley

Portrait Dolls, 1940. Ballerina, **Bo-Peep**, Gibson Girl, bride, groom, dancing couple, colonial.

11in (28cm)	$	275 - 325

EFFANBEE *continued*

Candy Kid, 1946. (See photograph on page 266.) Toddler, molded hair.

12in (31cm)	$	350 - 400

Betty Brite, 1933. Caracul wig.

16-1/2in (42cm)	325 - 375

Butin-Nose, 1939.

9in (23cm)	250 - 275

Brother and Sister, 1943. (See photograph on page 266.) Yarn hair, 16in (41cm) and 12in (31cm) each **250-300**

Charlie McCarthy: 1937. Strings at back of head to operate mouth; original clothes; all in very good condition.

17-20in (43-51cm)	$	650 - 750
Mint-in-box with button		850 - 950

Historical Dolls: 1939. All-composition. Three each of 30 dolls portraying the history of American fashion, 1492-1939. "American Children" heads with elaborate human hair wigs and painted eyes; elaborate original costumes using velvets, satins, silks, and brocades; all in excellent condition. (See photographs on page 266.)

Mark: On Head:
"EFFanBEE AMERICAN
CHILDREN"

21in (53cm)	$1500 - 1800

Historical Doll Replicas: 1939.

14in (36cm)	$500 - 600

Howdy Doody: 1949-1950. Hard plastic head and hands, molded hair, sleep eyes; cloth body; original clothes; all in excellent condition.

19-23in (48-58cm)	$	300 - 400
Mint-in-box		525 - 575

Honey: 1949-1955. All-hard plastic; original clothes; all in excellent condition.

Mark: EFFANBEE

14in (36cm)	$	275 - 300
18in (46cm)		325 - 375
24in (61cm)		450 - 500
Prince Charming		400 - 500
Cinderella		400 - 500
Alice		350 - 400

Tintair Honey,

14in (36cm)	400 - 450
In original box with accessories	600 - 650

16in (41cm) **Brother**, all original. *H & J Foulke, Inc.* (For further information see page 265.)

12-1/2in (32cm) **Candy Kid**. *H & J Foulke, Inc.* (For further information see page 265.)

21in (53cm) Historical Doll, **Massachusetts Bay, 1666**, all original. *H & J Foulke, Inc.* (For further information see page 265.)

14in (36cm) Historical Doll Replica **Industrial South, 1873**, all original. *H & J Foulke, Inc.* (For further information see page 265.)

Vinyl Dolls: All original and excellent condition.

Mickey, 1956.
    10-11in (25-28cm) $ **125 - 135**
Champagne Lady, 1959.
    19in (48cm)   **250 - 300****
Fluffy, 1957 on. 11in (28cm)   **35 - 40**
    Girl Scout   **60 - 70**
Patsy Ann, 1960 on.
    15in (38cm)   **100 - 125**
    Girl Scout   **175 - 195**
Mary Jane, 1959 on.
    32in (81cm)   **225 - 275**
    Nurse   **275 - 325**
Little Lady, 1958. (See photograph on page 268.)
    19in (48cm)   **125 - 150**

Fashion Lady, Ca. 1958.
    19in (48cm)   **250**
Most Happy Family, 1958. (Mother, Sister, Brother, Baby.)
    Boxed 8-21in (20-53cm)   **250 - 300**
Alyssa, Ca. 1960. 23in (58cm)   **200 - 225**
Disney Alice in Wonderland, 1977. (See photograph on page 268.)
    14in (36cm)   **150 - 175**
Happy Boy, 1961.
    10-1/2in (27cm)   **50 - 60**
Half Pint, 1982 on.
    11in (28cm) toddler   **25 - 35**

1979 *Skippy*, all original
H & J Foulke, Inc. (For further
information see page 268.)

15in (38cm) *Patsy Ann*
Girl Scout, all original.
H & J Foulke, Inc.

Effanbee Club Limited Edition Dolls:

1975 Precious Baby	$	200 - 300
1976 Patsy		200 - 225
1977 Dewees Cochran		75 - 100
1978 Crowning Glory		50 - 60
1979 Skippy		200 - 225
1980 Susan B. Anthony		50 - 60
1981 Girl with Watering Can		65 - 75
1982 Princess Diana		50 - 60
1983 Sherlock Holmes		75 - 85
1984 Bubbles		55 - 65
1985 Red Boy		40
1986 China Head		25 - 35

Legend Series: Mint-in-box.

W.C. Fields, 1980.	$	200
John Wayne, (cowboy),1981.		250
John Wayne, (cavalry),1982.		250
Mae West, 1982.		95
Groucho Marx, 1983.		95
Judy Garland, 1984.		125
Lucille Ball, 1985.		125
Liberace, 1986.		135
James Gagney, 1987.		65

Presidents: Mint-in-box.

Abraham Lincolns, 1983.	75
George Washington, 1983.	75
Teddy Roosevelt	95
Franklin D. Roosevelt	75

Personalities: Mint-in-box.

Mark Twain, 1984.	60
Louis Armstrong, 1984-5.	85
Sir Winston Churchill, 1984.	75
Eleanor Roosevelt	75
Babe Ruth	200

Pride of the South: 1981-1983.
13in (33cm) mint-in-box. **50 - 60**

Grande Dames: 1976-1983.
15in (38cm) mint-in-box. **50 - 60**

Gigi: 1979-1980.
11in (28cm) mint-in-box. **40**

International & Storybook: 1976 on.
11in (28cm) mint-in-box. **15 - 25**

**Not enough price samples to compute a reliable average.

14in (36cm) Walt Disney's *Alice in Wonderland*. *H & J Foulke, Inc.* (For further information see page 267.)

19in (48cm) vinyl *Little Lady*, all original. *H & J Foulke, Inc.* (For further information see page 267.)

FREUNDLICH

General Douglas MacArthur: Ca. 1942. All-composition portrait doll, molded hat, original khaki uniform; all in good condition. (See photograph on page 13.)
Mark: Cardboard tag: "General MacArthur"

18in (46cm)	$	**325 - 350**

Military Dolls: Ca. 1942. All-composition with molded hats; original clothes. Soldier, Sailor, WAAC, and WAVE, all in good condition.

15in (38cm)	$	**225 - 250**

Baby Sandy: 1939-1942. All-composition; appropriate clothes; all in good condition.

8in (20cm)	$	**185 - 195**
12in (31cm)		**275 - 300**
14-15in (36-38cm)		**350 - 400**

Other Composition Dolls:
Orphan Annie & Sandy,

12in (30cm)	$	**275 - 325**

Red Ridinghood, Wolf & Grandmother Set, all original

9in (23cm)	**500 - 600**

Dionne Quints and
Nurse Set, all original **500 - 600**
Dummy Dan,

15in (38cm)	$	**125**

Goo Goo Eva and others,

20in (51cm)	**90 - 110**

Goo Goo Topsy (black),

20in (51cm)	**110 - 135**
Wolf, naked	**200 - 250**

FACTS

Freundlich Novelty Corp., New York, N.Y., U.S.A. 1923-on.

15in (38cm) soldier, all original.
H & J Foulke, Inc.

12in (31cm) *Baby Sandy,* all original.
H & J Foulke, Inc.

G. I. JOE®

Marked G.I. Joe: Molded and painted hair and features, scar* on right cheek; fully-jointed body; complete original outfit; all in perfect condition. Dolls less than perfect sell for considerably less.

*All G.I. Joe dolls have a scar on the right cheek except Foreign dolls and the Nurse.

Action Soldier, all original, boxed
$ 285 - 300
Action Sailor (painted hair), boxed   450
Action Marine, boxed   350
Action Pilot, boxed   600
Action Soldier Black
   (painted hair), boxed   1300
Naked Dolls:
   Action Soldier (painted hair)   85
   Adventure Team (flocked hair*)   55 - 60
   Adventure Team (flocked hair and
      beard*)   50 - 55
   Black Action Soldier
      (painted hair)   300 - 350

*Hair must be in excellent condition.

Action Soldiers of the World (painted hair, no scars):
   German Soldier,
      boxed, large box $ 1200
      boxed, small box   600
      dressed doll only, no accessories 200 - 225
   Russian Infantry Man:
      boxed, large box   1200
      boxed, small box   600
      dressed doll only, no accessories 200 - 225

   British Commando:
      boxed, large box   1250
      boxed, small box   225
      dressed doll only, no accessories 200 - 225

FACTS
Hasbro (Hassenfeld Brothers, Inc.)
Pawtucket, RI, U.S.A. 1964 - 1979.
Hard plastic and vinyl. 12in (31cm)
fully-jointed.
Mark: G.I. Joe   After 1967 added:
Copyright 1964   Pat. No. 3,277,602
By Hasbro
Patent Pending
Made in U.S.A.

Left, *G.I. Joe Sea Adventurer*; right *Talking G.I. Joe*.
Courtesy of McMasters Doll Auctions.

G. I. JOE® *continued*

French Resistance Fighter:
boxed, large box $	900
boxed, small box	500
dressed doll only, no accessories	200 - 225

Australian Jungle Fighter:
boxed, large box	700
boxed, small box	400
dressed doll only, no accessories	150 - 175

Japanese Imperial Soldier (unique model used only for this type):
boxed, large box $	1300
boxed, small box	800
dressed doll only, no accessories	275 - 300

Talking Action Soldier, boxed	$	400
Talking Action Sailor, boxed		575
Talking Action Marine, boxed		475
Talking Action Pilot, boxed		800

Nurse Action Girl, boxed	1800
dressed doll only	800
naked doll	250
Adventurer (lifelike hair) Black, boxed	300
Man of Action (lifelike hair), boxed	200 - 225
Man of Action with Kung-Fu Grip (lifelike hair), boxed	200 - 225
Talking Man of Action (lifelike hair), boxed	225 - 250
Land Adventurer (lifelike hair and beard), boxed	185 - 200
Air Adventurer (lifelike hair and beard), boxed	240 - 265
Sea Adventurer (lifelike hair and beard), boxed	225 - 250
Talking Astronaut (lifelike hair), boxed	400 - 425
dressed doll	275 - 300

Accessories:
Footlocker, green	$	40

Space Capsule, boxed	325
Five Star Jeep, boxed	350
Desert Patrol Jeep, boxed	1500
Motorcycle, boxed	200

Outfits in unopened packages:
#7532 Green Beret Special Forces	$	500
#7521 Military Police (brown)		400
#7521 Military Police (aqua)		1250
#7531 Ski Patrol		250
#7620 Deep Sea Diver		300
#7710 Dress Parade Set		225
#7824 Astronaut Suit		250
#7537 West Point Cadet		1200
#7624 Annapolis Cadet		1200
#7822 Air Cadet		1200
#7612 Shore Patrol		300
#7807 Scramble Set		275

Japanese Imperial Soldier, Action Soldiers of the World. *Courtesy of McMasters Doll Auctions.*

Left, *G.I. Joe Land Adventurer*; right *Talking G.I. Joe Action Soldier*. *Courtesy of McMasters Doll Auctions.*

GODEY'S LITTLE LADY DOLLS

Ruth Gibbs Doll: Pink or white china head; cloth body with china limbs and painted slippers; original clothes.

7in (18cm)	$ 85 - 95
7in (18cm) boxed	135 - 150
Black, boxed	300 - 350**
10in (25cm) skin wig	295
12in (31cm) original underclothes	165 - 185
12in (31cm) boxed	215 - 235
Little Women, set of 5	750 - 850
Trousseau, boxed set (4 outfits)	575
Fairy Tale, boxed	575

**Not enough price samples to compute a reliable average.

FACTS
Ruth Gibbs, Flemington, N.J., U.S.A. 1946.
Designer: Herbert Johnson.
Mark: Paper label inside skirt "Godey's Little Lady Dolls;" "R.G." incised on back plate.

HALLMARK

Tagged Hallmark Cloth Doll: Printed on cloth with an article of separate clothing, usually a coat or skirt, stitch-jointed shoulders, hips and knees, shaped shoes and hats. All original and excellent.
6-1/2-7-1/2in (17-19cm)
1976 Bicentennial Commemorative Series: George Washington, Martha Washington, Betsy Ross, Benjamin Franklin, boxed $ 45-50 each
1979 Series I: Amelia Earhart, Annie Oakley, G. W. Carver, Chief Joseph, Babe Ruth, Susan B. Anthony, boxed   12-13
Holiday Dolls: Little Drummer Boy, Santa Claus, Winifred Witch, Indian Maiden, boxed   16-18
Series II: Davy Crockett, Molly Pitcher, Mark Twain, P. T. Barnum, Clara Barton, never had boxes   6-8
Juliette Low (founder of the Girl Scouts)   65

FACTS
Hallmark Cards, Inc., Kansas City, MO. 1976-1979.
Mark: Cloth label on each doll

7in (18cm) Ruth Gibbs *Godey's Little Lady Doll*, all original. *H & J Foulke, Inc.*

Annie Oakley. H & J Foulke, Inc.

HARD PLASTIC DOLLS

Marked "Made in U.S.A." or with various letters: All hard plastic; sleep eyes; perfect wig; original clothes; all in excellent condition with very good coloring.

14in (36cm)	$	**225-250**
18in (46cm)		**275-300**
24in (61cm)		**300-325**

Miscellaneous Specific Dolls: All original clothes including underwear, shoes and socks; excellent condition with lovely complexion and perfect hair; unmarked except as indicated.

Answer Doll, 1951. Block Doll Corp.; toddler with yes/no button,
10in (25cm) $ **55-65**

Baby Walker, 1950s. Block Doll Corp.;
toddler, 10in (25cm) **55-65**

Duchess Doll Corp., 1950s. Slender storybook and fashion dolls in various costumes. Marked on back, 7-8in (18-20cm) **8-10**

Walt Disney's Peter Pan and Tinkerbelle $ **20-25 each**
boxed **95-100**

Gigi, 1955. A & H Doll Mfg Corp; Ginny-type walker, 7-1/2in (19cm) **40-50**
boxed **65-75**

Gigi Perreau, 1952. Goldberger Doll Mfg Co.; portrait doll of the movie star with smiling mouth and teeth, dynel hair, hard plastic body, vinyl head, excellent face color,
20in (51cm) $ **600 up** **

Haleloke, 1950s. Roberta Doll Co. 18in (46cm), with accessories and additional clothing **450**

Heddi Stroller, 1952. Belle Doll & Toy Corp.; walker, saran braids,
20in (51cm) **165-195**

Hollywood Doll Mfg. Co., 1947 on. Storybook and fashion dolls in various costumes; marked on back,
4-1/2-5-1/2in (12-14cm), boxed **20-30**

Lucy, 1950s. Virga. Ginny-type walker,
8in (20cm) **40-50**
boxed **65-75**

LuAnn Simms, 1953. Roberta, Horsman & Valentine; **Mark:** "Made in U.S.A." or "180," walker, 14in (36cm) **250-300**

Marion, 1949. Monica Studios; rooted hair, sleep eyes, 18in (46cm) **400****

Mary Jane, 1955. G.H. & E. Freydberg, Inc. Terri Lee-type doll, 17in (43cm) **275-300**

Miss Gadabout, 1950s. Artisan Doll Co.,
Mark: "Heady Turny" label; walker,
20in (51 cm) **165-195**

Pam, 1950s. Fortune Doll Co. Ginny-type walker, molded strap shoes,
8in (20cm) $ **40-50**
boxed **65-75**

Raving Beauty, 1953. Artisan Doll Co. Tag on some clothing: "Original Michelle// California." Separate clothing was available. Open mouth, walker, 20in (51cm) **325-350**

Susan Stroller, 1953. Goldberger Doll Mfg Co.
Mark: "Eegee." Walker, saran hair,
23in (58cm) **165-195**

Wanda the Walking Wonder, 1950s. Advance Doll Co.,
17-19in (43-48cm) **150-200**

**Very few price samples available for comparison.

18in (46cm) *Haleloke,* all original.
H & J Foulke, Inc.

HARD PLASTIC *continued*

HASBRO

25in (64cm) Ottolini fashion doll, all original. *H & J Foulke, Inc.*

Italian Hard Plastic: Ca. 1950 on. Bonomi, Ottolini, Ratti, Furga and others. **Mark:** usually on head. Heavy, fine quality hard plastic, human hair wig, sleep eyes, sometimes flirty; original clothes; all in excellent condition.

12in (31cm)	$	125
15-17in (38-43cm)		150-200
19-21in (48-53cm)		225-250
25in (64cm) fashion		275

English Black Hard Plastic Characters: 1950s. Pedigree and others. Curly black wig sometimes over molded hair.

16in (41cm)	150-175
21in (53cm)	225-275

Little Miss No Name, 1965. Large round eyes, molded tear, forlorn expression, original ragged clothes; all in excellent condition.

15in (38cm)	$	90-110
boxed		200-250

Aimee, 1972. All vinyl; original clothing; all in excellent condition   45-55

Jem Series, 1986-1987. All-vinyl fashion dolls; original clothing; all in excellent condition, in original box. Deduct one-third for an out-of-box doll. 12-1/2in (32cm)

Jem	$	25-35
Kimber		35-45
Aja		45-50
Roxy		45
Pizazz		55-60
Stormer		35-45
Rio		25-30
Boxed outfits		25-30

G.I. Joe: See page 270.

Little Miss No Name, all original and boxed; white streaks on box front are raindrops. *Rosemary Kanizer.*

HIMSTEDT, ANNETTE

Barefoot Children, 1986. 26in (66cm)

Ellen	$	700 - 800
Kathe		700 - 800
Paula		650 - 700
Fatou		900 - 1000
Lisa		700 - 800

American Heartland Dolls, 1987. 19-20in (48-51cm)

Timi and Toni	400 - 450 each

The World Children Collection, 1988. 31in (79cm)

Kasimir	1600 - 1900
Malin	1400 - 1500
Michiko	1000 - 1200
Frederike	1400 - 1500
Makimura	900 - 1000

Reflections of Youth, 1989. 26in (66cm)

Adrienne	750 - 850
Janka	750 - 850
Ayoka	900 - 1000
Kai	750 - 850

1990:

Fiene	750 - 850
Taki (baby)	650 - 750
Annchen (baby)	650 - 750

1993:

Kima	500 - 550
Lona	500 - 550
Tara	550 - 600

1994:

Panchita, Pancho, Melvin, Elke	425

FACTS

1986 on. Hard vinyl and cloth.
Designer: Annette Himstedt
Distributor: Mattel, Inc., Hawthorne, CA., U.S.A. Dolls made in Spain.
Mark: Wrist tag with doll's name; cloth signature label on clothes; signature on lower back plate and on back of doll's head under wig.

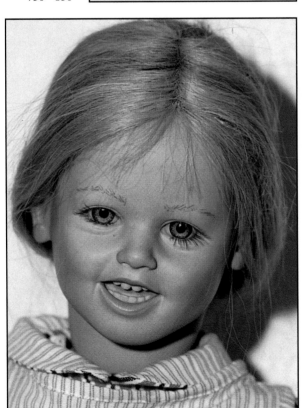

Lisa by Annette Himstedt. *Mary Barnes Kelley Collection.*

HORSMAN

Early Composition Dolls: Original or appropriate old clothes; all in good condition.

Billiken: 1909. Composition head, velvet or plush body. **Mark:** cloth label.

12in (31cm)	$	**350 - 400**

"Can't Break 'Em" Characters: Ca. 1911. Character head, hard stuffed cloth body. **Mark:** "E.I.H. 1911".

11-31in (28-33cm)	$	**200 up**
Polly Pru, 13in (33cm)		**325****
Cotton Joe, black, 13in (33cm)		**400 - 475**
Baby Bumps		**225 - 250**
Black		**250 - 300**

Puppy & Pussy Pippin: 1911. Grace G. Drayton. Plush body, composition head, cloth label.

8in (20cm) sitting.

Puppy Pippin	$	**400 - 450****
Pussy Pippin		**500 - 600****

Peek-a-Boo: 1913-1915. Grace G. Drayton. Composition head, arms, legs and lower torso, cloth upper torso. **Mark:** cloth label on outfit.

7-1/2in (19cm)	**150 - 175**

Baby Butterfly: 1911-1913. Oriental doll, composition head, cloth body, original costume.

13in (33cm)	$	**350****

Peterkin: 1914-1930. All-composition, various boy and girl clothing or simply a large bow.

11in (28cm)	**300 - 350**

Gene Carr Characters: 1916. Composition/cloth. Snowball (black boy); Mike and Jane (eyes open); Blink and Skinney (eyes closed). Designed by Bernard Lipfert from Gene Carr's cartoon characters.

13-14in (33-36cm)	$	**300 - 350**
Black Snowball		**450 - 550**

Jackie Coogan: 1921. Composition/cloth; appropriate old clothes. (For photograph see page 12.)

14in (36cm)	**500 - 550**

HEbee-SHEbee: 1925. All-composition; blue shoes indicate a HEbee; and pink ones a SHEbee.

11in (28cm)	**600 - 650**
Fair condition, some peeling	**325 - 375**
Mint, all original	**800 - 900**

FACTS
E.I. Horsman Co., New York, NY. Manufacturer; also distributor of French and German dolls. 1878-on.

Ella Cinders: 1925. Composition/cloth. From the comic strip by Bill Conselman and Charlie Plumb for Metropolitan Newspaper Service. **Mark:** "1925©MNS."

18in (46cm)	$	**550 - 650**

Baby Dimples: 1928. Composition/cloth; appropriate old clothes. **Mark:** ©

E.I.H. CO. INC.

16-18in (41-46cm)	$	**250 - 300**
22-24in (56-61cm)		**350 - 400**

Mama Dolls: late 1920s on. Composition/cloth. **Mark:** HORSMAN or E.I.H. CO. INC.

Babies, including **Brother** and **Sister**

12-14in (31-36cm)	$	**150 - 185**
18-20in (46-51cm)		**250 - 275**

Girls, including Rosebud and Peggy Ann

14-16in (36-41cm)	**250 - 275**
22-24in (56-61cm)	**325 - 375**

Marked Tynie Baby: 1924. Slightly frowning face; cloth/composition; appropriate clothes. Designed by Bernard Lipfert. **Mark:** © 1924

E.I. Horsman Inc.
Made in
Germany

Bisque head,

8-1/2–9-1/2in (22-24cm) h.c.	$	**550 - 650**
11-12in (28-31cm) h.c.		**750 - 850**

Composition head,

15in (38cm) long	**275 - 300**

All-bisque, swivel neck, glass eyes, wigged or molded hair.

8-10in (20-25cm)	**1900 - 2300**

Vinyl, 1950. 15in (38cm), boxed **90 - 110**

All Composition Child Dolls: 1930s and 1940s. Original clothes; all in very good condition; may have "Gold Metal Doll" tag. **Mark:** "HORSMAN"

13-14in (33-36cm)	$	**225 - 250**
16-18in (41-46cm)		**275 - 325**

Chubby toddler,

16-18in (41-46cm)	**300 - 350**

Jo-Jo, 1937. (See photograph on page 278.)
  12in (31cm)   **225 - 250**
Jeanne, 1937. 14in (36cm)   **300**
Naughty Sue, 1937. 16in (41cm) **400 - 450**
Roberta, 1937. 16in (41cm)   **400 - 450**
Bright Star, 1940. (See photograph on page 278.) 17-20in (43-51cm)   **450 - 500**

All-Hard Plastic Dolls: 1950s. Original clothing; perfect hair; good coloring; all in excellent condition.
Cindy: 1950-1955. Open mouth with teeth and tongue, synthetic wig, walker body. **Mark:** "160, 170 or 180 Made in U.S.A."
16-18in (41-46cm)   **$**   **250 - 300**
LuAnn Simms: Ca. 1953. Long brunette wig with front and side hair pulled to back, blue eyes. Mold number **180** or **170**.
  18in (46cm)   **350 - 400**

Vinyl Dolls: Original clothing; all in excellent condition with perfect hair and excellent color.
Rene Ballerina, 1957. Fully jointed with high-heeled feet, rooted hair.
Mark: "82//HORSMAN"
  19in (48cm)   **150 - 165**

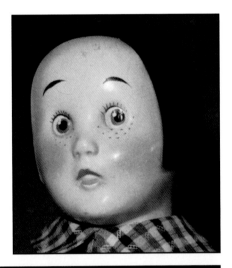

18in (46cm) *Ella Cinders*,
all original. *Rhoda
Shoemaker Collection*.

11in (28cm) *Poor
Pitiful Pearl*,
boxed. *Miriam
Blankman
Collection*. (For
further informa-
tion see page
278.)

HORSMAN
continued

20in (51cm) *Bright Star*, all original. *H & J Foulke, Inc.* (For further information see page 277.)

9in (23cm) *Angie Dickinson, Police Woman*, boxed. *Miriam Blankman Collection.*

Tweedie, 1958. Slender limbs, short hair.
Mark: "38 Horsman."
   14-1/2in (37cm)   **50-100***

*Depending upon designer costume.

Jackie Kennedy, 1961. Rooted black hair, blue sleep eyes, pearl jewelry.
Mark: "HORSMAN//19 © 61//JK25."
   25in (64cm)   **165 - 185**
Poor Pitiful Pearl, 1963. Cartoon character. (See photograph on page 277.)
Mark: "1963//Wm Steig//Horsman"
   11-12in (28-31cm)   **95 - 100**
   boxed   **195**
   16in (41cm)   **150**
   boxed   **250**
Hansel & Gretel, 1963. Character faces.
Mark: Michael Meyerberg, Inc.
   15in (38cm)   **200 - 225**
Walt Disney's Cinderella Set. 1965. Extra head and costume for "poor" doll.
Mark: "H"
   11-1/2in (29cm), boxed   **150 - 165**
Mary Poppins: 1964. Several different costumes.
   12in (31cm)   **30 - 40**
   boxed set with 7in (18cm) **Jane** and
     Michael   **150 - 165**
Flying Nun: 1965. 12in (31cm)   **85**
   boxed   **150 - 175**
Patty Duke: 1965. Gray flannel pants, red
   sweater, 12in (31cm)   **85**
   boxed   **150 - 175**
Elizabeth Taylor: 1976.
   11-1/2in (29cm)   **55**
Angie Dickinson, Police Woman: 1970s.
   9in (23cm) boxed $ **38**

13in (33cm) *Jo-Jo*, all original. *H & J Foulke, Inc.* (For further information see page 277.)

MARY HOYER

Marked Mary Hoyer: Original tagged factory clothes or garments made at home from Mary Hoyer patterns; all in excellent condition.

Composition, 14in (36cm) $	350 - 450

Hard plastic:

14in (36cm)	
In knit outfit	400 - 425
In tagged Hoyer outfit	425 - 525
In tagged gown	500 - 600
14in (36cm) boy with	
caracul wig	500 - 550
18in (46cm), **Gigi**	
In tagged dresses	600 - 700

In tagged gowns	**700 - 800**

---FACTS---
The Mary Hoyer Doll Mfg. Co., Reading Pa., U.S.A. Ca. 1925-on.
Mark: Embossed on torso:
"The
Mary Hoyer
Doll"
or in a circle:
"ORIGINAL
Mary Hoyer
Doll"

14in (36cm) hard plastic Mary Hoyer, all original. *H & J Foulke, Inc.*

IDEAL

Early Composition Dolls: 1910-1929. Composition heads, cloth bodies, composition lower arms, some with molded composition shoes; original or appropriate old clothes; all in good condition, some wear acceptable. **Head Mark:**

Happy Hooligan: 1910. Comic character, 21in (53cm) $ **500****
Ty Cobb: 1911. Baseball outfit   **500****
Naughty Marietta (Coquette): 1912.
Molded hair with ribbon band **300 - 350**
Captain Jenks: 1912.
Khaki uniform   **275 - 325**
Uneeda Kid: 1914-1919. Molded black boots; original bloomer suit, yellow slicker and rain hat, carrying a box of Uneeda Biscuits, showing some wear.
16in (41cm)   **450 - 475**
24in (61cm)   **650 - 700****
Bronco Bill: 1915. Cowboy outfit with gun and holster   **275 - 325**
ZuZu Kid: 1916-1917. Original clown suit. National Biscuit Co.
16in (41cm)   **400 - 450**
Liberty Boy: 1917. Molded clothes, cloth hat; some wear. 12in (31cm)   **250 - 275**
Soozie Smiles: 1923. Two faces, crying and smiling   **350 - 400**
Flossie Flirt: 1924-1931. Eyes move side to side.
14in (36cm)   **225 - 250**
20in (51cm)   **300 - 350**
Buster Brown: 1929. Red suit with hat, 17in (43cm)   **325 - 375**
Peter Pan: 1929. Original felt suit and hat, 18in (46cm).
Excellent with label   **550 - 600**
Good, some wear   **300 - 400**
Early Children:
12-15in (31-38cm)   **225 - 250**
Early Babies: Baby Mine, **Prize Baby**, etc. 15-16in (38-41cm)   **175 - 225**

Composition Babies: 1930s and 1940s. Composition heads and lower limbs, cloth bodies; original or appropriate clothes; all in good condition with nice coloring; light crazing acceptable.
Tickletoes: 1930-1947. Soft rubber arms and legs, flirty eyes.
14in (36cm)   **225 - 250**
Baby Smiles: 1931. Toddler with rubber arms. 17in (43cm)   **250 - 275**
Snoozie: 1933. Designed by Bernard Lipfert; yawning mouth, may have rubber arms.
Mark: ©
          By B. LIPFERT
16-20in (41-51cm)   **275 - 350**
Cuddles: 1933. Rubber limbs.
22in (56cm)   **325 - 350**
Bathrobe Baby: 1933. Rubber body.
12in (31cm)   **100 - 125**
Princess Beatrix: 1938. Magic eyes.
16in (41cm)   **225 - 250**
22in (56cm)   **325 - 350**

Betsy Wetsy: 1937-on. Drink and wet baby.
Head Mark: IDEAL
Composition head/rubber body,
14-16in (36-41cm)   **125 - 165**
Hard plastic head/rubber body,
12-14in (31-36cm)   **95 - 135**
All vinyl, 12in (31cm)   **55 - 65**

Composition Children: 1935-1947. All composition in excellent condition with perfect hair and good cheek color; original clothes.
Shirley Temple: 1935. See page 299.
Snow White: 1937. Black wig, gown with rayon skirt showing figures of 7 dwarfs.
Torso Mark: SHIRLEY TEMPLE
Dress tag: An Ideal Doll
11-13in (28-33cm) $ **500 - 550**
18in (46cm)   **600 - 700**
Molded black hair, painted blue bow, painted eyes,
13-14in (33-36cm)   **200 - 225**
All cloth, 16in (41cm)   **500 - 550**
Mint-in-box   **750**

```
┌──────── FACTS ────────┐
│ Ideal Novelty & Toy Co., Brooklyn, NY. │
│ 1907-on. │
└─────────────────────────┘
```

Deanna Durbin: 1938. Smiling mouth with teeth. Metal button with picture. (See photograph on page 282.)
Head Mark: Deanna Durbin
Ideal Doll, USA

14in (36cm)	$	**600 - 650**
20-21in (51-53cm)		**900 - 1000**
24in (61cm)		**1200**

Judy Garland as Dorothy from *The Wizard of Oz:* 1939.
Head Mark: IDEAL DOLL
MADE IN USA

16in (41cm)	$	**1500 - 1650**
Replaced clothes		**1000 - 1100**

Betty Jane, Little Princess (See photograph on page 282.), **Ginger, Cinderella:** 1935-1947.

14in (36cm)	$	**300 - 325**
18in (46cm)		**375 - 425**

Soldier: Ca. 1942. Character face; army uniform with jacket and hat.

13in (33cm)	$	**325 - 375**

Miss Curity: Ca. 1945. Nurse uniform.

18in (46cm)	$	**450 - 500**

Flexy Dolls: 1938 on. Wire mesh torso, flexible metal cable arms and legs. (See photograph on page 282.) 12in (31cm).

Baby Snooks		
(Fanny Brice)	$	**250 - 275**
Mortimer Snerd		**250 - 275**
Soldier		**200 - 225**
Children		**200 - 225**

Composition and Wood Segmented Characters: 1940. Label on front torso.

Pinocchio, 10-1/2in (27cm)	$	**350 - 450**
King Little, 14in (36cm)		**275 - 325**
Jiminy Cricket (See photograph on page 282.), 9in (23cm)		**400 - 450**
Gabby, 11in (28cm)		**375 - 425**

Magic Skin Dolls: 1940-on. Stuffed latex rubber body in very good condition (subject to easy deterioration). Original clothes; all in excellent condition. **Head Mark:** IDEAL
Magic Skin Baby: 1940.

14-15in (36-38cm)	$	**95 - 110**
Plassie: 1940. 16in (41cm)		**95 - 110**
Toddler, all-hard plastic, 14in (36cm)		**150 - 175**
Sparkle Plenty, 1947.		
15in (38cm) Baby		**160 - 185**
Toddler		**150 - 175**
Joan Palooka, 1953.		
14in (36cm)		**125 - 135**
Baby Coos: 1948-1952. Sounds like a baby when squeezed.		
14-16in (36-41cm)		**110 - 135**
Brother or Sister Coos:		
25-30in (64-76cm), dressed like toddlers		**200 - 300**

18in (46cm) *Judy Garland. H & J Foulke, Inc.*

11in (28cm) **Princess**, all original. *H & J Foulke, Inc.* (For further information see page 281.)

Jiminy Cricket, all original. *H & J Foulke, Inc.* (For further information see page 281.)

15in (38cm) **Deanna Durbin**, all original. *H & J Foulke, Inc.* (For further information see page 281.)

12in (31cm) flexy child, all original. *H & J Foulke, Inc.* (For further information see page 281.)

Top Left: 15in (38cm) *Miss Curity*.
H & J Foulke, Inc. (For further information see page 284.) *Right:* 16in
(41cm) *Toni Walker*, all original.
H & J Foulke, Inc. (For further information see page 284.)

18in (46cm) *Miss Revlon*.
Miriam Blankman Collection.
(For further information
see page 285.)

Toni Family: 1948-on. Hard plastic "Toni" home permanent doll and derivatives, nylon wig, original clothes, perfect hair, pretty cheek color; all in excellent condition. (See also photographs on page 283.)

Head Mark: IDEAL DOLL
Body Mark IDEAL DOLL
P-90
Made in USA

Toni:

14-16in (36-41cm)		
P-90 & P-91	$	**325 - 375**
Naked, untidy hair		**70 - 80**
Mint-in-box		**550 - 650**
19-21in (48-53cm) P-92 & P-93		**500 - 600**
22-1/2in(57cm) P-94		**850****

Mary Hartline:

14in (36cm)	**350 - 400**
22-1/2in (57cm)	**850****
Mint-in-box with accessories,	
16in (41cm)	**700**

Harriet Hubbard Ayer: vinyl head make-up doll.

14in (36cm)	**200 - 225**
Mint-in box with accessories	**400**

Miss Curity: Nurse. (See photograph on page 283.)14in (36cm) **350 - 400**

Mint-in-box with accessories	**650**

Sara Ann: Saran hair,

14in (36cm)	**350 - 400**

18in (46cm) *Saralee*, all original. *H & J Foulke, Inc.*
(For further information see page 285.)

IDEAL *continued*

Saucy Walker: 1951-1955. All-hard plastic with walking mechanism; original clothes, excellent hair and cheek color.
Mark: IDEAL DOLL

16-17in (41-43cm)	$	**125 - 150**
20-22in (51-56cm)		**175 - 200**
Mint-in-box		**350 - 400**

Saralee: 1950. Black vinyl/cloth body. Designed by Sarah Lee Creech; modeled by Sheila Burlingame. Original clothes; excellent condition. (See photograph on page 284.)

17-18in (43-46cm)	$	**300 - 350**
Undressed		**125**

Bonny Braids: 1951. Vinyl character head; hard plastic body; original clothes; excellent condition.

13in (33cm)	**150 - 200**
Mint in comic strip box	**325 - 350**

Revlon Dolls: 1955-1959. Vinyl head, rooted hair; hard plastic body with jointed waist, high-heeled feet; perfect hair, bright cheek color; original clothing, excellent condition. (See photographs on pages 283 and 286.)

Miss Revlon,		
18-20in (46-51cm)	$	**200 - 250**
Mint-in-box, lovely gown		**450 up**
Little Miss Revlon,		
10-1/2in (27cm)		**125 - 150**
boxed		**200 - 225**

Patti Playpal Family: 1959-1962. (See photograph on page 286.)

Patti, 35in (89cm)	$	**425 - 475**
Peter (See photograph on page 12.),		
38in (97cm)		**550 - 650**
Daddy's Girl, 42in (107cm)		**850 - 950**
Miss Ideal, 29in (74cm)		**400 - 450**
25in (64cm)		**375 - 400**
Patti, 18in (46cm)		**200 - 250**
Bonnie & Johnny,		
24in (61cm) babies		**225 - 250**
Penny, 32in (81cm)		**275 - 300**
Saucy Walker, 28in (71cm)		**285**
30in (76cm)		**325**
1982 **Patti,** mint-in-box		**100 - 110**
Black, mint-in-box		**200**

Tammy Family: 1962-1966. Mint-in-box; deduct 50% for an out-of-box doll. (See photograph on page 286.)

Tammy, 12in (31cm)	$	**75 - 85**
Pos'n Tammy, 12in (31cm)		**95-100**
Glamour Misty (Miss Clairol)		**75 - 95**

Ted (big brother), 12-1/2in (32cm)	**55 - 60**
Mom, 12-1/2in (32cm)	**60 - 65**
Dad, 13in (33cm)	**60 - 65**
Pepper (sister), 9in (23cm)	**55 - 60**
Pete (little brother), 7-3/4in (20cm)	**125**
Patti (Pepper's friend) 9in (23cm)	**55 - 60**
Dodi (Pepper's friend) 9in (23cm)	**55 - 60**
Salty (Pepper's friend)	
7-3/4in (20cm)	**125**∗∗
Bud (Tammy's boyfriend)	
12-1/2in (32cm)	**150**∗∗

Miscellaneous Vinyl Dolls. All original, excellent coloring, perfect condition.

Lori Martin (National Velvet),		
38in (97cm), 1961.	$	**750 - 800**
Magic Lips, 1955. 24in (61cm)		**125 - 150**
Thumbelina, 1961. Vinyl and cloth; wriggles like a real baby. 19in (48cm)		**125 - 150**
Mint-in-box, at auction		**350**
Kissy, 1961-1964. Toddler,		
22in (56cm)		**135**
Bam Bam, 1963. 12in (31cm)		**45 - 50**
16in (41cm)		**60 - 75**
Pebbles, 1963. 8in (20cm)		**25 - 30**
12in (31cm)		**45 - 50**
Betty Big Girl, 1968. 32in (81cm),		
boxed		**350**
Little Lost Baby, 1968. Three faces.		
22in (56cm)		**95 - 110**
Flatsy, 1968-1970. Each with		
accessory		**15 - 20**
boxed		**35**
Joey Stivic, 1976. Archie Bunker's		
grandson, 15in (38cm)		**65**
Dorothy Hammil, 1977.		
11-1/2in (29cm)		**25**
Diana Ross, 17-1/2in (45cm)		**150 - 175**
Giggles, 16in (41cm)		**65 - 75**

Crissy and Family: 1968-1974. Growing hair dolls. All original and excellent.

Crissy, Beautiful Crissy	**25 - 35**
Velvet	**20 - 25**
Cinnamon	**20 - 25**
Mia	**40 - 45**
Kerry	**40 - 45**
Tressy	**50 - 60**
Brandi	**45 - 50**
Dina	**45 - 50**
Cricket	**20 - 25**
Baby Crissy	**50 - 55**

35in (89cm) **Patti Playpal**, all original.
Doodlebug Dolls. (For further information
see page 285.)

12in (31cm) **Tammy**, all original. *Rosemary
Kinizer*. (For further information see page
285.)

10-1/2in (27cm) **Little Miss Revlon**. *Terri
& Kathy's Dolls*. (For further information
see page 285.)

KENNER

Dusty, 1974. Smiling face, freckles.
12in (31cm), boxed $ **50 - 60**
Outfits **25**
Skye, 1974. Black skin. 12in (31cm),
boxed $ **50 - 60**
Outfits **25**
Cover Girls, 1978-1980. Fashion doll with
bendable elbows and knees, jointed wrists.
12in (31cm) **Darci** $ **45 - 55**
Erica (auburn) **125 - 150**
Dana (black skin) **55**
Outfits **30 - 40**
Hardy Boys, 1978. Mint-in-box dolls.
Shaun Cassidy, Parker Stevenson $ **28**
Star Wars, 1974-1978. Mint-in-box dolls.
For excellent out-of-box dolls, deduct 50%.
Darth Vader, 15in (38cm) $ **150 - 175**
Han Solo, 12in (31cm) **450 - 475**

Luke Skywalker,
12in (31cm) **250 - 275**
Princess Leia,
11-1/2in (29cm) **160 - 180**
Stormtrooper, 12in (31cm) **200 - 225**
Obi Wan Kenobi,
12in (31cm) **125 - 135**
R2D2, 7-1/2in (19cm) **165 - 185**
C3PO, 12in (31cm) **125 - 135**
Boba Fett, 13in (33cm) **250 - 275**
Jawa, 8-1/2in (22cm) **90 - 100**
IG88, 15in (38cm) **550 - 650**
Chewbacca, 15in (38cm) **150 - 160**
Yoda, 9in (23cm) **85 - 95**

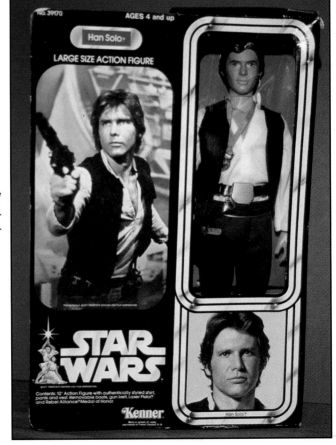

Star Wars, 1977
Han Solo, boxed.
George Humphrey.

KNICKERBOCKER

Composition Snow White: All-composition; black mohair wig with hair ribbon; original clothing; all in very good condition.

15in (38cm)	$	400 - 450
20in (51cm)		550 - 650

With molded black hair and blue ribbon,

13-15in (33-38cm)		300 - 400

Set: 15in (38cm) **Snow White** and seven 9in (23cm) **Dwarfs**   2200

Composition Seven Dwarfs: All-composition; individual character faces; original velvet costumes and caps with identifying names: **Sneezy, Dopey, Grumpy, Doc, Happy, Sleepy** and **Bashful.** Very good condition.

9in (23cm) $ 250 - 300 each

Additional composition dolls:

Jiminy Cricket, 10in (25cm)	**$450 - 550**
Pinocchio, 14in (36cm)	**550 - 650**
Mint-in-box, at auction	**1500**

Additional cloth dolls:

Seven Dwarfs,

14in (36cm)	$ 250 - 275 each
Snow White, 16in (41cm)	375 - 425

Donald Duck	**500 up**
Mickey Mouse, 1935.	**500 up**
Minnie Mouse	**500 up**
Two-Gun Mickey,	
12in (31cm), 1935.	**1300**

Raggedy Ann & Andy. See page 169.

Little Lulu,

18in (46cm)	**300 - 400****

Child Doll, 1935. Mask face (washable), original clothes,

12-14in (31-36cm)	**125 - 150**

Little Orphan Annie and Sandy, 1977.

16in (41cm)	**40 - 50**

**Not enough price samples to compute a reliable average.

FACTS

Knickerbocker Doll & Toy Co., New York, N.Y., U.S.A. 1937.
Head Mark:
"WALT DISNEY
KNICKERBOCKER TOY CO."

14in (36cm) *Pinocchio*, all original. *Kay & Wayne Jensen Collection.*

18in (46cm) *Little Lulu*.
H & J Foulke, Inc.

RICHARD G. KRUEGER, INC.

All-Cloth Doll: Ca. 1930. Mask face; oil cloth body with hinged shoulders and hips; original clothes; in excellent condition.

7in (18cm)	$ **50 - 60**
16in (41cm)	**125 - 140**
20in (51cm)	**175 - 195**

Pinocchio: Ca. 1940. Mask character face; cloth torso, wood jointed arms and legs; original clothes, all in good condition.

15in (38cm)	$ **400 - 450****

Kewpie: See page 129.
Dwarfs: Ca. 1937. All cloth, mask face.

12in (30cm)	**175 - 200**

Scootles:1935. Rose O'Neill. All cloth, mask face, yarn hair.

10in (25cm)	**450****
18in (46cm)	**850****

**Not enough price samples to compute a
reliable average.

FACTS

Richard G. Krueger, Inc., New York,
N.Y., U.S.A. 1917-on.
Mark: Cloth tag or label.

18in (46cm)
cloth girl of
the type
made by
Krueger.
*H & J
Foulke, Inc.*

MATTEL, INC.

Condition: Unless otherwise indicated, all dolls should be in excellent, unplayed with condition, in original clothes with all accessories, perfect hair, excellent coloring. (See photographs on page 290.)

Chatty Cathy Family: 1960-1965.
  Chatty Cathy,

20in (51cm)	$	**125 - 150**
boxed		**250 - 300**
Black		**600 - 800**
Charmin' Chatty, 25in (64cm)		**95 - 110**
Chatty Baby, 18in (46cm)		**95 - 115**
Tiny Chatty Baby, 15in (38cm)		**60 - 65**
Tiny Chatty Brother, 15in (38cm)		**60 - 65**
Singing Chatty, 17in (43cm)		**100 - 125**

Buffy & Mrs. Beasley: 1967. All vinyl Buffy, vinyl/cloth Mrs. Beasley.

6in (15cm) boxed	**200**

Mrs. Beasley: Vinyl and cloth, with glasses,

16in (40cm)	**125**
boxed	**250**

Skediddles: 1966. Mint-in-package **65 - 85**
Star-Spangled Dolls: 1976.
  New England Girl, Pioneer Daughter,
  Southern Belle **40 - 45**
Guardian Goddesses: 1979.

11-1/2in (29cm)	**150 - 175**

Toddlers and Babies. All original and excellent, unplayed with, in working condition.

Baby Secret, 1966. 18in (46cm)	**$45 - 50**
Baby First Step, 1966.	
18in (46cm)	**45 - 50**
Baby Pataburp, 1964.	
16in (41cm)	**25 - 30**
Baby Tenderlove, 1970-1972.	
Newborn, 13in (33cm)	**15 - 18**
Living, 20in (51cm)	**30 - 35**
Brother (sexed), 12in (31cm)	**35 - 40**
Cheerful, Tearful, 1966.	
13in (33cm)	**25 - 30**
Dancerina, 1970.	
12in (31cm)	**25 - 30**
16in (41cm)	**40 - 50**
24in (61cm)	**60 - 70**
Hi Dottie, 1969. 17in (43cm)	**25**
Sister Belle, 1961. 17in (43cm)	**65 - 75**
Mattie Mattel, 1961. 17in (43cm)	**65 - 75**

Above and Right: Chatty Cathy, 1960 first issue #681 in Party Dress, all original and boxed with booklet and warranty card, missing shoe horn. *H & J Foulke, Inc.* (For further information see page 289.)

Tiny Chatty Baby and ***Tiny Chatty Brother,*** all original. *Courtesy of McMasters Auctions.* (For further information see page 289.)

MATTEL, INC. *continued*

Timey Tell, 1964. 17in (43cm)
with watch $ **25 - 30**
Tippy Toes, 1967. 17in (43cm) with
tricycle or horse, good face **22**

Dolls from Television Shows: All prices are
for mint-in-box or package dolls.
Charlies's Angels, 1978.
11-1/2in (29cm) $ **50**
Debbie Boone, 1978.
11-1/2in (29cm) **65**
Dick Van Dyke, 1969.
25in (64cm), talks **125**
Donny Osmond, 1978. 12in (31cm) **35**
Marie Osmond, 1978. 12in (31cm) **35**
Jimmy Osmond, 1979. 10in (25cm) **45**
Grizzly Adams, 1971. 10in (25cm) **40**
Herman Munster, 1965.
Hand puppet **125**
Full body **225**
How the West Was Won, 1971.
10in (25cm) **30 each**
Welcome Back Kotter, 1973.
9in (23cm) **50 - 60 each**

Little Kiddles: 1966. Mint-in-box or package; deduct 50% for an out-of-package doll with all accessories in excellent condition.
Body Mark: 1965//Mattel, Inc.//Japan.
Sleeping Biddle $ **125**
Liddle Biddle Peep **165**
Peter Pandiddle **225**
Liddle Middle Muffet **185**
Liddle Red Riding Hiddle **185**
Sizzly Friddle **145**
Freezy Sliddle **135**
Howard Biff Boodle **135**
Orange Ice Cone Kiddle **60 - 65**
Violet Kiddle Kologne **40 - 45**
Loo Locket Kiddle **35 - 40**
Heart Pin Kiddle **30 - 35**
Lorelie Bracelet Kiddle **40 - 45**

MEGO CORPORATION

Television, Movie and Entertainment Dolls: All prices are for mint-in-box or package dolls.
Batman, 1974. 8in (20cm) $ **50 - 60**
Penguin, 1974. 8in (20cm) **60 - 70**
Captain & Tenille, 1977.
12-1/2in (32cm) **50 - 60 each**
Sonny & Cher, 1976.
12in (31cm) **60 - 65 each**
CHiPs, 1977. 8in (20cm) **35 - 40 each**
Diana Ross, 1977.
12-1/2in (32cm) **100 - 125**
Charlie's Angels, 1975.
12-1/2in (32cm) **40 - 50 each**
Happy Days, 1976. 8in (20cm) **50 - 55 each**
KISS, 1978. 12-1/2in (32cm) **125 - 135 each**
Kojack, 1977. 9in (23cm) **65 - 70**
Laverne & Shirley, 1977.
11-1/2in (29cm) **65 - 70 each**
Lenny & Squiggy, 1977.
11-1/2in (29cm) **75 - 85**
Joe Namath, 1971. 12in (31cm) **40 - 45**
Our Gang, 1975. 5in (13cm) **50 - 60 each**
Planet of the Apes, 1974.
8in (20cm) **60 - 70 each**
Pirates, 1971. 8in (20cm) **45 - 50 each**
Robin Hood Set, 1971.
8in (20cm) **50 - 55 each**

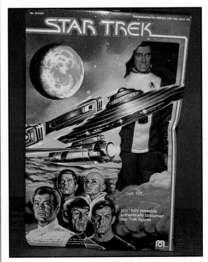

Star Trek 1979 *Captain Kirk,* boxed.
George Humphrey. (For further information see page 292.)

MEGO CORPORATION
continued

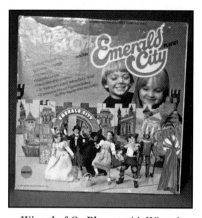

Wizard of Oz Playset with Wizard.
Miriam Blankman.

Starsky & Hutch, 1976.

8in (20cm)	$ 35 - 40 each

Suzanne Somers, 1978.

12-1/2 in (32cm)	50 - 60

The Waltons, 1975. 8in (20cm), two dolls in
each box   50 - 60
Wild West, 1974. **Buffalo Bill, Cochise,
Davy Crockett, Sitting Bull, Wild Bill
Hickok, Wyatt Earp**   35 - 40 each
Wonder Woman, 1976.

12-1/2in (32cm)	100 - 115

Wizard of Oz, 1974.

Dorothy	$	30 - 35
Munchkins		60 - 65
Tin Man, Cowardly Lion		30 - 35
Wizard with Playset		135

Star Trek, 1975. Fully jointed plastic.
Packaged on blister card. For unpackaged
dolls, deduct 50%, (See photograph on page
291.) 8in (20cm).

Captain Kirk	$	45 - 50
Mr. Spock		45 - 50
Dr. McCoy		100 - 115
Mr. Scott		100 - 115
Klingon		45 - 50
Lt. Uhura		100 - 115
Andorian		400 - 450
The Keeper		175 - 200
Romulan		625 - 700

Star Trek, 1979. Mint-in-box. 12-1/2in
(32cm)

Captain Kirk	$	85
Mr. Spock		85
Ilia		85

MOLLY-'ES

─────── **FACTS** ───────
International Doll Co., Philadelphia, Pa.
Made clothing only. Purchased undressed
dolls from various manufacturers. 1920s on.
Clothes Designer: Mollye Goldman.
Mark: A cardboard tag.

Molly-'es Composition Dolls: Beautiful
original outfits; all in good condition.

Babies, 15-18in (38-46cm)	$	**225 - 250**
Girls, 12-13in (31-33cm)		**160 - 175**
Toddlers, 14-16in (36-41cm)		**275 - 300**
Ladies, 18-21in (46-53cm)		**500 - 550**

Internationals: All-cloth with mask faces;
all original clothes; in excellent condition
with wrist tag.

13in (33cm)	$	**75 - 95**
Mint-in-box		**100 - 125**

Raggedy Ann & Andy: See page 169.
Thief of Baghdad Series, 1939. Orange
hang tag.
  Sabu, composition.

15in (38cm)	$	**550 - 600**

Sultan, 19in (48cm) cloth   **650 - 750**
Princess, 15in (38cm) composition or

18in (46cm) cloth	**600 - 650**

Prince, 23in (58cm) cloth   **750**
Vinyl Dolls: All original and excellent.
Darling Little Women,

8in (20cm)	**50 - 60****
12in (31cm)	**85 - 95****

Internationals,

8in (20cm)	**40 - 50**

Perky, 8in (20cm)   **50 - 60**

**Not enough price samples to compute a
  reliable range.

11in (28cm) Molly-'es all-cloth Dutch pair,
all original. *H & J Foulke, Inc.*

NANCY ANN STORYBOOK DOLLS CO.

Painted Bisque Marked Storybook Doll: Mohair wig, painted eyes; one-piece body and head, jointed legs and arms; original clothes; excellent condition with sticker or wrist tag and box. 5-1/2–7in (13-19cm).

1936: Babies only. Gold sticker on dress; sunburst box. **Mark:** "88 Made in Japan" or "87 Made in Japan" **$ 400 up**

1937-1938: Gold sticker on dress; sunburst box, gold label. **Mark:** "Made in Japan 1146," "Made in Japan 1148," "Japan," "Made in Japan" or "AMERICA" **500 - 600**

1938-1939: Gold sticker on dress; sunburst transition to silver dot box. **Mark:** "JUDY ANN USA" (crude mark), "STORYBOOK USA" (crude mark). Molded socks/molded bangs. **Mark:** "StoryBook Doll USA" **400 - 600**

Judy Ann in storybook box with extra outfits, sticker on dress **600 up**

Oriental	**1200**
Gypsy	**1100**
Pirate	**1100**

1940: Gold sticker on dress; colored box with white polka dots. Molded socks. **Mark:** "StoryBook Doll USA" **250 up**

Margie Ann **325 up**

1941-1942: Gold wrist tag; white box with colored polka dots; jointed legs. **Mark:** "StoryBook Doll USA" **85 up**

1943-1947: Gold wrist tag; white box with colored polka dots; frozen legs. **Mark:** "StoryBook Doll USA" (some later dolls with plastic arms) **60 - 80**
Socket head **85**

Hard Plastic Marked Storybook Doll: Swivel head, mohair wig, painted eyes, jointed legs; original clothes, gold wrist tag; white box with colored polka dots, excellent condition.
Mark: "Story Book Doll USA"
5-1/2-7in (13-19cm) **$ 40 up**

Bent-limb Baby:

Star hand baby	**$**	**140 - 160**
Bisque with closed fist, open mouth		**150 - 170**
Painted bisque, hard plastic arms		**100 - 125**
Hard Plastic		**95**
Boxed furniture		**300 up**

<hr>

FACTS

Nancy Ann Storybook Dolls Co., South San Francisco, CA. 1936-on.

Painted bisque *Florie*
Storybook Doll.
H & J Foulke, Inc.

NANCY ANN STORYBOOK DOLLS CO. *continued*

8in (20cm) *Muffie*, all original.
Terri & Kathy's Dolls.

10in (25cm) *Debbie*, all original.
Victoria's Dolls.

Debbie's labelled box.

NANCY ANN STORYBOOK DOLLS CO. *continued*

Special Dolls:

Painted bisque with white painted socks	$	**150 up**
Glow-in-Dark		**125 - 150**

Series Dolls:

Flower Girl	$	**200**
Masquerade, bisque jointed legs		**300**
Around the World, bisque		**200 up**
Sports, skiing, boxed with sticker		**600 up**
Powder & Crinoline, bisque		**150 up**
Operetta, bisque		**150 - 175**
All Time Hit Parade, bisque		**150 - 175**
Topsy and Eva, bisque pair		**600 - 650**

Special Holiday inserts:

Bisque	**100 up**
Hard plastic	**75 up**

Muffie, all-hard plastic, wig, sleeping eyes, 8in (12cm) tall:

Mark: "StoryBook Dolls USA" some with "Muffie."

1953: straight leg nonwalker, painted lashes, no brows, dynel wig (side part with flip); 54 complete costumes. Original clothes, excellent condition. **$200 - 250***

1954: walker, molded eyelashes, eyebrows after 1955, side part flip or braided wig; 30 additional costumes. Original clothes, excellent condition. **165 - 185***

1955-1956: hard plastic walker or bent-knee walker, rooted Saran wig (ponytail, braids or side part flip); vinyl head and hard plastic body; molded or painted upper lashes. **140 up**

1968: reissued, unmarked, **Muffie Around the World,** straight leg walker, molded eyelashes, glued on wig. 12 dolls in cellophane see-through boxes. **100 up**

Nancy Ann Style Show, hard plastic, 17in (43cm)	$	**425 - 600**
Miss Nancy Ann, 10-1/2in (27cm), teenage body, high-heeled feet		**95 - 115**
Debbie, hard plastic toddler. 10in (25cm)		**125 - 135**
Mint-in-box		**350**

*Allow extra for red hair.

OLD COTTAGE DOLLS

FACTS

Old Cottage Toys, Allargate, Rustington, Littlehampton, Sussex, Great Britain. 1948.
Designers: Greta Fleischmann and her daughter Susi.
Mark: Paper label - "Old Cottage Toys" - handmade in Great Britain.

Old Cottage Doll: Composition or hard plastic head with hand painted features, wig, stuffed cloth body; original clothing; excellent condition.

8-9in (20-23cm)	$	**135 - 165**
12-13in (31-33cm), mint-in-box		**300 - 350****

Tweedledee & **Tweedledum,**

9in (23cm), at auction	$	**625 pair**

**Not enough price samples to compute a reliable average.

9in (23cm) *Old Cottage Doll* with box.
H & J Foulke, Inc.

RALEIGH

RAVCA

Raleigh Doll: All heavy composition; appropriate clothes; all in good condition.
Child:
11in (28cm) wigged	$	450 - 500
13in (33cm) molded hair		600 - 650
18in (46cm) molded hair		900 - 950

Baby:
12in (30cm)	400

FACTS
Jessie McCutcheon Raleigh, Chicago, Ill. 1916-1920.
Designer: Jessie McCutcheon Raleigh.
Mark: None.

Bernard Ravca Doll: Paris, France, 1924-1939; New York, 1939 on. Stockinette face individually needle sculpted; cloth body and limbs; original clothes; all in excellent condition.
Mark: Paper label: "Original Ravca Fabrication Française"

10in (25cm) French peasants	**$100 - 125**

Ravca-type fine quality peasant man or lady 17in (43cm) **225 - 265 each**

Frances Diecks Ravca Doll: New York, 1935 on.
36in (91cm) 1952. Queen Elizabeth II and others $ **650 - 850**
12in (30cm) "Easter Sunday" 1973, Black child **250**

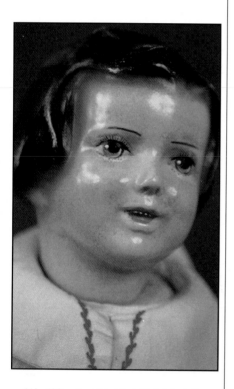

11in (28cm) molded hair Raleigh doll.
H & J Foulke, Inc.

10in (25cm) Ravca man, all original.
H & J Foulke, Inc.

RELIABLE TOY CO.

Marked Reliable Doll: All-composition or composition shoulder head and lower arms, cloth torso and legs, sometimes composition legs; painted features; original clothes; all in good condition, some light crazing acceptable.

Scots Girl or **Boy,**
14in (36cm) $ **85 - 110**
Military Man, 14in (36cm) **225 - 275**
Canadian Mountie, 17in (43cm) **300 - 350**
Hiawatha or **Indian Maiden,**
13in (33cm) **85 - 110**
Barbara Ann Scott (Ice Skater),
15in (38cm) **400 - 500**
Clicquot Club Soda Eskimo,
14in (36cm) **250 - 275**

FACTS
Toronto, Canada. 1920 on.
Mark:
RELIABLE//MADE IN//CANADA

14in (36cm) *Clicquot Club Soda Eskimo,* original clothes. *H & J Foulke, Inc.*

REMCO INDUSTRIES

Littlechap Family, 1963. Basic doll, unplayed with, in original box. Deduct 50% for out-of-box dolls.
Dr. John, 14-1/2in (37cm) $ **75 - 85**
Lisa, 13-1/2in (34cm) **75 - 85**
Judy, 12in (31cm) **75 - 85**
Libby, 10-1/2in (27cm) **75 - 85**
Rooms **200**
Office **200**
Tagged clothes (packaged outfits) **20 - 75**

Television Programs & Personalities: All prices are for dolls that are mint, in original box.
Addams Family,
5-1/2in (14cm) $ **100 - 125**
I Dream of Jeannie, 6in (15cm) **50 - 60**
Laurie Partridge (Susan Dey), 1973.
19in (48cm) **85 - 95**
Orphan Annie, 1967. 15in (38cm) **35 - 45**

Libby Littlechap, boxed.
Rosemary Kanizer.

SANDRA SUE

SASHA

Sandra Sue: 1952 on. All hard plastic, slender, Saran wig, molded eyelashes, unmarked.

8in (20cm) basic doll (camisole, panties, half slip, shoes and socks) $	**125**
Boxed	**200 - 225**
In street dresses	**125 - 150**
In gowns	**175 - 225**
Little Women	**200 - 225**
Outfits, packaged	**25 - 75**
Bridal gown	**125**
Communion dress	**110**

Cindy Lou: 1951. All-hard plastic walker, saran wig. Many outfits matched **Sandra Sue's.**

14in (36cm) basic doll (camisole, panties, half slip, shoes and socks) $	**200**
In street dresses	**250**

FACTS
Richwood Toys, Inc., Annapolis, MD.
1952 on.
Designer: Ida H. Wood

Sandra Sue twins, original boxed set.
Rosemary Kanizer.

Sasha: All-vinyl of exceptionally high quality, long synthetic hair; original clothing, tiny circular wrist tag; excellent condition.

16in (41cm) $	**210 - 225**
Boxed	**250**
In cylinder package	**350 - 400**

FACTS
Trendon Toys, Ltd., Reddish, Stockport, England. 1965-1986.
Designer: Sasha Morgenthaler.

Sasha cylinder. *H & J Foulke, Inc.*

SASHA *continued*

Gregor (boy)	$	210 - 225
Boxed		250
Cora (black girl)		275 - 300
Caleb (black boy)		275 - 300
Black baby		200 - 225
White baby		165 - 185
Sexed baby, pre 1979		250 - 275
Packaged clothes		85

Limited Edition Dolls:

1980 Velvet Dress	$	350 - 375
1982 Pintucks Dress		350 - 375
1983 Kiltie		350 - 375
1984 Harlequin		350 - 375
1985 Prince Gregor		350 - 375
1986 Princess		1000 - 1500

"Serie Sasha": (For photograph see *12th Blue Book*, page 316.) Götz model, 1965 - 69. With wrist tag.

	1500 - 1800

Early model 1950s:

21in (53cm) child	6000 - 8000
13in (33cm) baby, at auction	3800
1995 Sasha and Gregor, issue price	300
1996 Baby, issue price	150

Gregor Fair #302, all original.
H & J Foulke, Inc.

SHIRLEY TEMPLE

FACTS

Ideal Novelty Toy Corp., New York,
N.Y. 1934 to present.
Designer: Bernard Lipfert.

All-Composition Child: 1934 through late 1930s. Marked head and body, jointed composition body; all original including wig and clothes; entire doll in very good condition. Sizes 11-27in (28-69cm).

Mark: On body:

SHIRLEY TEMPLE
13

On head

13
SHIRLEY TEMPLE

On cloth label:

Genuine
SHIRLEY TEMPLE
DOLL
REGISTERED U.S. PAT OFF
IDEAL NOVELTY & TOY CO
MADE IN USA

25in (64cm) composition *Shirley Temple*,
all original. *H & J Foulke, Inc.*

13in (33cm) composition *Shirley Temple*, rare dress, all original. *H & J Foulke, Inc.*

18in (46cm) composition *Shirley Temple*, all original in unusual "music" dress from *Our Little Girl*. *H & J Foulke, Inc.*

11in (28cm)	$	850 - 950*
13in (33cm)		850 - 900*
15-16in (38-41cm)		850 - 900*
18in (46cm)		1000 - 1100*
20-22in (51-56cm)		1200*
25in (64cm)		1400*
27in (69cm)		1800 - 2000*
Button		135
Dress, tagged		150 up
Trunk		175 - 200
Carriage		600 - 650

Hawaiian Shirley,
18in (46cm)	900 - 100

Baby Shirley: Composition/cloth; original clothing; good condition. (For photograph see page 9.)
16-18in (41-46cm)	1200 - 1300

Other Composition Shirley Temples:
Made in Japan,
7-1/2in (19cm)	$	275 - 325

Reliable (Canada), all original and boxed,
18-22in (46-56cm)	1200

Vinyl and Plastic: Excellent condition, original clothes.
1957, 12in (30cm)	$	200 - 225
15in (38cm)		275 - 300
17in (43cm)		350 - 375
19in (48cm)		400 - 425
36in (91cm)		1500 - 1800
Script name pin		40
Name purse		25
Tagged or Boxed dress		65 up
1973, 16in (41cm) size only		100 - 110
Boxed		150
Boxed dress		35

1972, Montgomery Ward	
14in (36cm)	225 - 250
1982, 1983.	
8in (20cm)	40 - 50
12in (30cm)	70 - 80

*Allow 50-100% more for mint-in-box doll. Also allow extra for a doll with unsual outift, such as *Texas Ranger*, *Little Colonel*, and *Captain January*.

SHIRLEY TEMPLE *continued*

SKOOKUM INDIANS

17in (43cm) 1957 *Shirley Temple*, all original. *H & J Foulke, Inc.*

Skookum Indian Doll: Composition character face, dark eyes painted to the side, black mohair wig; clad in an Indian blanket (fold in the blanket represents arms), cotton print dress or cotton shirt and felt trousers, headband with one or more feathers, beads, suede boots; all very colorful. Excellent, unplayed with condition.

6in (15cm)	$	**45 - 55**
10-12in (25-31cm)		**175 - 225**
16in (41cm)		**300**
36in (91cm)		**1000 - 1200****

**Not enough price samples to compute a reliable average.

FACTS
Created and designed by Mary McAboy, Missoula, Montana and Denver, Colorado. Dolls made by various companies including Arrow Novelty Co., New York and H.H. Tammen Co., New York, Denver and Los Angeles. 1913 on.
Mark: Sometimes a paper label on the sole of the foot.
Trademark: Skookum (Bully Good)

11in (28cm) *Skookum*, all original. *H & J Foulke, Inc.*

SUN RUBBER CO.

Silly and **Popo**. 1937. Comic characters with molded clothes. 10in (25cm) $ **55 - 65** **

Minnie Mouse. 1937.
10-1/2in (27cm) in red-and-white polka dot sundress. $ **125 - 150** **

Bonnie Bear, Wiggy Wags, Happy Kappy, Rompy. 1940s. One-piece squeeze dolls with molded clothes and hats. Designed by Ruth E. Newton.
6-8in (15-20cm) $ **15 - 25** **
So-Wee. 1941. Designed by Ruth E. Newton with painted or sleeping eyes, molded hair. Excellent.
10-12in (25-31cm) **65 - 75**

Sunbabe. 1950. Drink and wet baby with painted eyes and molded hair. Excellent.
11-13in (28-33cm) **45 - 55**
in original box **110 - 125**

Baby Bannister. 1954. All vinyl drink-and-wet doll based on the famous baby photographs by Constance Bannister. Excellent
12 in (31 cm) in original box **95 - 110**

Gerber Baby. 1955. All rubber with inset eyes and molded hair, open/closed mouth. Excellent.
11-13in (28-33cm) $ **90 - 100**
in original box **275 - 325**

**Not enough price samples to compute a reliable range.

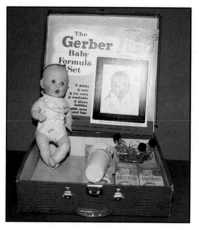

+------------------ FACTS ------------------+
Barberton, Ohio. 1930s on.
Marks: Sun Rubber Co. with various numbers, names and dates

Gerber Baby,
boxed with accessories. *Terri & Kathy's Dolls.*

12in (31cm) all-vinyl *Baby Bannister* in original box. *H & J Foulke, Inc.*

TERRI LEE

Terri Lee Child Doll: Original wig, painted eyes; jointed at neck, shoulders and hips; all original tagged clothing and accessories; very good condition.

16in (41cm)

Pat. Pending	$	325 - 350*
Terri Lee only		275 - 325*
Mint-in-box		500*
Patty-Jo (black)		500 - 600**
Jerri Lee, 16in (41cm)		300 - 400
Benjie (black).		500 - 600**
Tiny Terri Lee, inset eyes.		
10in (25cm)		165 - 185
Tiny Jerri Lee, inset eyes,		
10in (25cm)		185 - 210
Connie Lynn		350 - 400

Gene Autry	1500 - 1800**
Linda Baby, 10in (25cm)	185 - 195
Ginger Girl Scout,	
8in (20cm)	150

*Allow extra for special outfits or gowns.
**Not enough price samples to compute a reliable range.

— FACTS —

TERRI LEE Sales Corp., V. Gradwohl, Pres. 1946- Lincoln, Neb.; then Apple Valley, Calif., from 1952-Ca. 1962.
Mark: First dolls:
"TERRI LEE
PAT. PENDING"
raised letters
Later dolls: "TERRI LEE"

16in (41cm) *Terri Lee*, all original. *Courtesy of Susan Babkowski.*

16in (41cm) Pat. Pending *Terri Lee*, all original except umbrella. *Courtesy of Susan Babkowski.*

TINY TOWN DOLLS

Tiny Town Dolls: Molded felt faces with painted eyes and mouths, mohair wigs of various styles and colors; wrapped cloth bodies over wire armatures, felt hands, weighted white metal shoes; original clothes; excellent condition.

4in (10cm)*	$	**48 - 52**
Boxed		**62 - 68**

—FACTS—
Alma LeBlane dba Lenna Lee's Tiny Town Dolls, San Francisco, CA. Trademark registered January 11, 1949.
Mark: Some have a gold octagonal wrist tag with **Tiny Town Dolls** on one side and name of doll on the other.

*Other known sizes are 5in (13cm) and 7-1/4in (19cm) but no prices are available.

7-1/4in (19cm) *Tiny Town Doll. Courtesy of Eleanor Guderian.*

Tiny Town Dolls, all original. Left to right possible identification: *Chickie, Blondie, Jean, School Girl, Lucy Ann. Courtesy of Mary Elizabeth Poole.*

UNEEDA DOLL CO.

Composition Dolls:
Lucky Lindy (Charles Lindbergh): 1927. Composition/cloth; brown aviator suit, good condition.
14in (36cm) $ **300 - 400****

Rita Hayworth: 1939. All-composition, red mohair wig, all original clothes, excellent.
14in (36cm)   **400 - 500**

Toddler: Ca. 1940. All-composition, all original clothes, very good condition.
13in (33cm)   **225 - 250**

**Not enough price samples to compute a reliable average.

Hard Plastic and Vinyl Dolls: Excellent, unplayed with condition with original clothes, perfect hair, rosy cheeks.

Dollikin: 1957. Fully jointed hard plastic.
8in (20cm) mint-in-box $ **35**
11in (28cm) mint-in-box   **50 - 60**
19in (48cm)   **95 - 125**

Baby Dollikin: 1958. Jointed elbows and knees, 21in (53cm)   **150**

Saranade: 1962. With phonograph and record, 21in (53cm)   **150**

Pollyana: 1960. Haley Mills in pink-and-white checked outfit.
10-1/2in (27cm)   **35 - 40**
17in (43cm)   **50 - 60**
31in (79cm)   **295**

Wee Three: Mother, daughter and baby brother. Set   **125**
Boxed set   **200**

```
┌──────── FACTS ─────────┐
  New York. 1917 on.
└────────────────────────┘
```

13in (33cm) composition Uneeda toddler, all original. *H & J Foulke, Inc.*

17in (43cm) *Pollyana,* all original. *H & J Foulke, Inc.*

VOGUE

All-composition Girl: 1940s. Original clothes; all in good condition, with perfect hair.
Mark: None on doll; round silver sticker on front of outift. May have name stamped on sole of shoe.

13in (33cm)	$	**375 - 425**
19in (48cm)		**500 - 550**

All-composition Toddles: 1937-1948. Painted eyes looking to side; original clothes; all in good condition.
Mark: "VOGUE" on head
"DOLL CO." on back
"TODDLES" stamped on sole of shoe

7-8in (18-20cm)	$	**200 - 250***
Mint condition		**350***

*Allow extra for unusual outfits, such as cowboy.

Hard Plastic Ginny: Original wig and tagged clothes; all in excellent condition with perfect hair and pretty coloring.
Mark: On strung dolls: "VOGUE DOLLS"
On walking dolls: "GINNY//VOGUE DOLLS"
7-8in (18-20cm)

1948-1949:		
Painted eyes	$	**350 - 400***
1950-1953:		
Painted eyelashes, strung	$	**325 - 425***
Caracul wig		**350 - 450***
1954:		
Painted eyelashes, walks		**250 - 300***
1955-1957:		
Molded eyelashes, walks		**175 - 225***
Davy Crockett		**450 - 500**
Girl Scout or Brownie		**225 - 300**
1957-1962:		
Molded eyelashes, walks, jointed knees		**125 - 150***
1962 on.		
Vinyl head, hard plastic body with jointed knees		**90**

*Allow extra for mint-in-box dolls and desirable outfits, such as Tiny Miss Series

---FACTS---
Vogue Dolls, Inc., Medford, Mass.
Creator: Jennie Graves.
Clothes Designer:
Virginia Graves Carlson.
Clothes Label: "Vogue," "Vogue Dolls,"
or

VOGUE DOLLS, INC.
MEDFORD, MASS. USA
® REG U.S. PAT OFF

8in (20cm) composition *Toddles*, all original. *Jensen's Antique Dolls.*

10in (25cm) *Jill*, boxed. *Terri & Kathy's Dolls*. (For further information see page 308.)

13in (33cm) all-composition Vogue girl, all original. *H & J Foulke, Inc.* (For further information see page 306.)

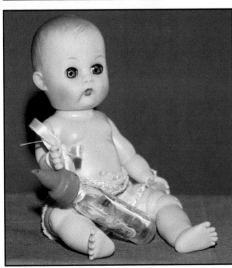

8in (20cm) *Ginnette*, all original with bottle. *Terri & Kathy's Dolls*. (For further information see page 308.)

8in (20cm) *Ginny*, painted lash walker, all original. *Terri & Kathy's Dolls*.

VOGUE *continued*

Black Ginny	$	900 up
Crib Crowd Baby, 1950		650*
Queen		700 up
Wee Imp, red hair		275 - 325

*Allow extra for mint-in-box dolls.

Accessories: All in excellent condition:

Ginny's Pup	$	225 - 275
Cardboard suitcase with contents		50
Parasol		15 - 18
Gym set		250 - 300
Dresser, bed, rocking chair, wardrobe		55 each
School bag		75 - 85
"Hi I'm Ginny" pin		75
Ginny's First Secret book		125
Swag bag, hat box, auto bag and garment bag		35 each
Roller skates in cylinder		25
Hats		10 - 15
Headband		8
Dress and panties, tagged		35 - 55
Glasses		4 - 5
Shoes, center snap		30 - 40
Shoes, plastic		9 - 10
Locket & chain		65
Purse (Ginny)		6

Vinyl Ginny: 1972.

Children and internationals	$	35 - 40
Gift Set		65 - 75

Vinyl Ginny: 1977 on.

8in (20cm) children	$	40 - 50
International costumes		35 - 40
Sasson		35
Black Ginette		15 - 20

Jill: 1957. All-hard plastic, adult body. All original and excellent. (See photograph on page 307.)
  10in (25cm) $ 175 - 225
Jeff: 1957. Vinyl head, all original and excellent.
  10in (25cm)   125 - 150
Jan: 1958. All vinyl   75 - 95
Ginnette: 1957. All vinyl baby. All original and excellent.(See photograph on page 307.)
  8in (20cm) boxed   150 - 175
Jimmy: 1958. 8in (20cm) painted eyes,
  boxed $ 150 - 175
Lil Imp: Vinyl head, hard plastic body with bent knees. Original clothing. Excellent condition.
  11in (28cm) boxed   200 - 225
Baby Dear: 1959. Designed by Eloise Wilken. Vinyl head and limbs, cloth body. All original and excellent.
  18in (46cm)   125 - 150
Miss Ginny, 1962. 16in (41cm)   40 - 50
Ginny, 1960. 36in (91cm)   300 - 500**
Brikette, 1961.
  16in (41cm)   85
  22in (56cm)   125

WRIGHT, R. JOHN

CLOTH DOLLS:

Adult Characters	$	1200 - 1500
Children		750 - 1500
Timothy, Rosemary		**2000 each**
Snow White & 7 Dwarfs		**2500**
Snow White Rags		**750**
Red Riding Hood		**1000**

Christopher Robin &
   Winnie the Pooh   **2400**
Winnie the Pooh
   18in (46cm)   **1300 - 1500**
   14in (36cm) with honeypot   **700**

Emma by R. John Wright. *H & J Foulke, Inc.*

GLOSSARY

Applied Ears: Ears molded independently and affixed to the head. (On most dolls the ear is included as part of the head mold.)

Bald Head: Head with no crown opening, could be covered by a wig or have painted hair.

Ball-jointed Body: Usually a body of composition or papier-mâché with wooden balls at knees, elbows, hips and shoulders to make swivel joints; some parts of the limbs may be wood.

Bébé: French child doll with "dolly face."

Belton-type: A bald head with one, two or three small holes for attaching wig.

Bent-limb Baby Body: Composition body of five pieces with chubby torso and curved arms and legs.

Biscaloid: Ceramic or composition substance for making dolls; also called imitation bisque.

Biskoline: Celluloid-type substance for making dolls.

Bisque: Unglazed porcelain, usually flesh tinted, used for dolls' heads or all-bisque dolls.

Breather: Doll with an actual opening in each nostril; also called open nostrils.

Breveté (or Bté): Used on French dolls to indicate that the patent is registered.

Character Doll: Dolls with bisque or composition heads, modeled to look lifelike, such as infants, young or older children, young ladies and so on.

China: Glazed porcelain used for dolls' heads and *Frozen Charlottes*.

Child Dolls: Dolls with a typical "dolly face," which represents a child.

Composition: A material used for dolls' heads and bodies, consisting of such items as wood pulp, glue, sawdust, flour, rags and sundry other substances.

Contemporary Clothes: Clothes not original to the doll, but dating from the same period when the doll would have been a plaything.

Crown Opening: The cut-away part of a doll head.

DEP: Abbreviation used on German and French dolls claiming registration.

D.R.G.M.: Abbreviation used on German dolls indicating a registered design or patent.

Dolly Face: Typical face used on bisque dolls before 1910 when the character face was developed; "dolly faces" were used also after 1910.

Embossed Mark: Raised letters, numbers or names on the backs of heads or bodies.

Feathered Eyebrows: Eyebrows composed of many tiny painted brush strokes to give a realistic look.

Fixed Eyes: Glass eyes that do not move or sleep.

Flange Neck: A doll's head with a ridge at the base of the neck which contains holes for sewing the head to a cloth body.

Flapper Dolls: Dolls of the 1920s period with bobbed wig or molded hair and slender arms and legs.

Flirting Eyes: Eyes which move from side to side as doll's head is tilted.

Frozen Charlotte: Doll molded all in one piece including arms and legs.

Ges.(Gesch.): Used on German dolls to indicate design is registered or patented.

Googly Eyes: Large, often round eyes looking to the side; also called roguish or goo goo eyes.

Hard Plastic: Hard material used for making dolls after 1948.

Incised Mark: Letters, numbers or names impressed into the bisque on the back of the head or on the shoulder plate.

Intaglio Eyes: Painted eyes with sunken pupil and iris.

JCB: Jointed composition body. See *ball-jointed body*.

Kid Body: Body of white or pink leather.

Lady Dolls: Dolls with an adult face and a body with adult proportions.

Mama Doll: American composition and cloth doll of the 1920s to 1940s with "mama" voice box.

Mohair: Goat's hair widely used in making doll wigs.

Molded Hair: Curls, waves and comb marks which are actually part of the mold and not merely painted onto the head.

Motschmann-type Body: Doll body with cloth midsection and upper limbs with floating joints; hard lower torso and lower limbs.

Open-Mouth: Lips parted with an actual opening in the bisque, usually has teeth either molded in the bisque or set in separately and sometimes a tongue.

Open/Closed Mouth: A mouth molded to appear open, but having no actual slit in the bisque.

Original Clothes: Clothes belonging to a doll during the childhood of the original owner, either commercially or homemade.

Painted Bisque: Bisque covered with a layer of flesh-colored paint which has not been baked in, so will easily rub or wash off.

Paperweight Eyes: Blown glass eyes which have depth and look real, usually found in French dolls.

Papier-mâché: A material used for dolls' heads and bodies, consisting of paper pulp, sizing, glue, clay or flour.

Pate: A shaped piece of plaster, cork, cardboard or other material which covers the crown opening.

Pierced Ears: Little holes through the doll's earlobes to accommodate earrings.

Pierced-in Ears: A hole at the doll's earlobe which goes into the head to accommodate earrings.

Pink Bisque: A later bisque of about 1920 which was pre-colored pink.

Pink-toned China: China which has been given a pink tint to look more like real flesh color; also call lustered china.

Poupée: French lady doll, Ca. 1860-on.

Poupée Bois: French lady doll, Ca. 1860-on, with wood body.

Poupée Peau: French lady doll, Ca. 1860-on, with kid body.

Rembrandt Hair: Hair style parted in center with bangs at front, straight down sides and back and curled at ends.

S.G.D.G.: Used on French dolls to indicate that the patent is registered "without guarantee of the government."

Shoulder Head: A doll's head and shoulders all in one piece.

Shoulder Plate: The actual shoulder portion sometimes molded in one with the head, sometimes a separate piece with a socket in which a head is inserted.

Socket Head: Head and neck which fit into an opening in the shoulder plate or the body.

Solid-dome Head: Head with no crown opening, could have painted hair or be covered by wig.

Stationary Eyes: Glass eyes which do not move or sleep.

Stone Bisque: Coarse white bisque of a lesser quality.

Toddler Body: Usually a chubby ball-jointed composition body with chunky, shorter thighs and a diagonal hip joint; sometimes has curved instead of jointed arms; sometimes is of five pieces with straight chubby legs.

Topsy-Turvy: Doll with two heads, one usually concealed beneath a skirt.

Turned Shoulder Head: Head and shoulders are one piece, but the head is molded at an angle so that the doll is not looking straight ahead.

Vinyl: Soft plastic material used for making dolls after 1950s.

Watermelon Mouth: Closed line-type mouth curved up at each side in an impish expression.

Wax Over: A doll with head and/or limbs of papier-mâché or composition covered with a layer of wax to give a natural, life-like finish.

Weighted Eyes: Eyes which can be made to sleep by means of a weight which is attached to the eyes.

Wire Eyes: Eyes that can be made to sleep by means of a wire which protrudes from doll's head.

BIBLIOGRAPHY

Anderton, Johana.
Twentieth Century Dolls. North Kansas City, Missouri: Trojan Press, 1971.
More Twentieth Century Dolls. North Kansas City, Missouri: Athena Publishing Co., 1974.

Angione, Genevieve. *All-Bisque & Half-Bisque Dolls.* Exton, Pennsylvania: Schiffer Publishing Ltd., 1969.

Borger, Mona. *Chinas, Dolls for Study and Admiration.* San Francisco: Borger Publications, 1983.

Cieslik, Jürgen and Marianne.
German Doll Encyclopedia 1800-1939. Cumberland, Maryland: Hobby House Press, Inc., 1985.

Coleman, Dorothy S., Elizabeth Ann and Evelyn Jane.
The Collector's Book of Dolls' Clothes. New York: Crown Publishers, Inc., 1975.
The Collector's Encyclopedia of Dolls, Vol. I & II. New York: Crown Publishers, Inc., 1968 & 1986.

Corson, Carol. *Schoenhut Dolls, A Collector's Encyclopedia.* Cumberland, Maryland: Hobby House Press, Inc., 1993.

Foulke, Jan.
Blue Books of Dolls & Values, Vol. I-XII. Cumberland, Maryland: Hobby House Press, Inc., 1974-1997.
Doll Classics. Cumberland, Maryland: Hobby House Press, Inc., 1987.
Focusing on Effanbee Composition Dolls. Riverdale, Maryland: Hobby House Press, 1978.
Focusing on Gebrüder Heubach Dolls. Cumberland, Maryland: Hobby House Press, Inc., 1980.
Kestner, King of Dollmakers. Cumberland, Maryland: Hobby House Press, Inc., 1982.
Simon & Halbig Dolls, The Artful Aspect. Cumberland, Maryland: Hobby House Press, Inc., 1984.
Treasury of Madame Alexander Dolls. Riverdale, Maryland: Hobby House Press, 1979.
China Doll Collecting. Grantsville, Maryland: Hobby House Press, Inc., 1995.
German 'Dolly' Collecting. Grantsville, Maryland: Hobby House Press, Inc., 1995.
Doll Buying & Selling. Grantsville, Maryland: Hobby House Press, Inc., 1995.

Gerken, Jo Elizabeth.
Wonderful Dolls of Papier-Mâché. Lincoln, Nebraska: Doll Research Associates, 1970.

Hillier, Mary.
Dolls and Dollmakers. New York: G. P. Putnam's Sons, 1968.
The History of Wax Dolls. Cumberland, Maryland: Hobby House Press, Inc.; London: Justin Knowles, 1985.

Judd, Polly and Pam.
Hard Plastic Dolls. Cumberland, Maryland: Hobby House Press, Inc., 1985.
Hard Plastic Dolls II. Cumberland, Maryland: Hobby House Press, Inc., 1989.
Glamour Dolls of the 1950s & 1960s. Cumberland, Maryland: Hobby House Press, Inc., 1988.
Compo Dolls 1928-1955. Cumberland, Maryland: Hobby House Press, Inc., 1991.
Compo Dolls, Volume II. Cumberland, Maryland: Hobby House Press, Inc., 1994.

Mandeville, A. Glenn.
5th Doll Fashion Anthology. Grantsville, Maryland: Hobby House Press, Inc., 1996.

Mathes, Ruth E. and Robert C.
Dolls, Toys and Childhood. Cumberland, Maryland: Hobby House Press, Inc., 1987.

McGonagle, Dorothy A. *The Dolls of Jules Nicolas Steiner.* Cumberland, Maryland: Hobby House Press, Inc., 1988.

Merrill, Madeline O. *The Art of Dolls, 1700-1940.* Cumberland, Maryland: Hobby House Press, Inc., 1985.

Pardella, Edward R. *Shirley Temple Dolls and Fashions.* West Chester, Pennsylvania: Schiffer Publishing, Ltd., 1992.

Richter, Lydia. *Heubach Character Dolls and Figurines.* Cumberland, Maryland: Hobby House Press, Inc., 1992.

Schoonmaker, Patricia N.
Effanbee Dolls: The Formative Years 1910-1929. Cumberland, Maryland: Hobby House Press, Inc., 1984.
Patsy Doll Family Encyclopedia. Cumberland, Maryland: Hobby House Press, Inc., 1992.

Tarnowska, Maree. *Fashion Dolls.* Cumberland, Maryland: Hobby House Press, Inc., 1986.

ABOUT THE AUTHOR

The name Jan Foulke is synonymous with accurate information. As the author of the *Blue Book of Dolls & Values*®, she is the most quoted source on doll information and the most respected and recognized authority on dolls and doll prices in the world.

Born in Burlington, New Jersey, Jan Foulke has always had a fondness for dolls. She recalls, "Many happy hours of my childhood were spent with dolls as companions, since we lived on a quiet county road, and until I was ten, I was an only child." Jan received a B.A. from Columbia Union College, where she was named to the *Who's Who in American Colleges & Universities* and was graduated with high honors. Jan taught for twelve years in the Montgomery County school system in Maryland and also supervised student teachers in English for the University of Maryland where she did graduate work.

Jan and her husband, Howard, who photographs the dolls presented in the *Blue Book*, were both fond of antiquing as a hobby, and in 1972 they decided to open a small antique shop of their own. The interest of their daughter, Beth, in dolls sparked their curiosity about the history of old dolls — an interest that quite naturally grew out of their love of heirlooms. The stock in their antique shop gradually changed and evolved into an antique doll shop.

Early in the development of their antique doll shop, Jan and Howard realized that there was a critical need for an accurate and reliable doll identification and price guide resource. In the early 1970s, the Foulkes teamed up with Hobby House Press to produce (along with Thelma Bateman) the first *Blue Book of Dolls & Values*, originally published in 1974. Since that time, the Foulkes have exclusively authored and illustrated the twelve successive editions, and today the *Blue Book* is regarded by collectors and dealers as the definitive source for doll prices and values.

Jan and Howard Foulke now dedicate all of their professional time to the world of dolls: writing and illustrating books and ar-

ticles, appraising collections, lecturing on antique dolls, acting as consultants to museums, auction houses and major collectors, and selling dolls both by mail order and through exhibits at major shows throughout the United States. Mrs. Foulke is a member of the United Federation of Doll Clubs, Doll Collectors of America, and the National Antique Doll Dealers Association. Her biography appears in *Who's Who in the East*.

Mrs. Foulke has appeared on numerous television talk shows and is often quoted in newspaper and magazine articles as the ultimate source for doll pricing and trends in collecting. Both *USA Today* and *The Washington Post* have stated that the *Blue Book of Dolls & Values* is "the bible of doll collecting."

In addition to her work on the twelve editions of the *Blue Book of Dolls & Values*, Jan Foulke has also authored: *Focusing on Effanbee Composition Dolls; A Treasury of Madame Alexander Dolls; Kestner, King of Dollmakers; Simon & Halbig, The Artful Aspect; Focusing on Gebrüder Heubach Dolls; Doll Classics; Focusing on Dolls; China Doll Collecting, German 'Dolly' Collecting,* and *Doll Buying and Selling.* She has been a regular contributor to *Doll Reader*® magazine for 25 years. Her current column is the popular *Antique Q & A*.

MOLD NUMBERS